CONCEIVING THE FUTURE

Conceiving the Future

PRONATALISM, REPRODUCTION, AND

THE FAMILY IN THE UNITED STATES,

1890–1938

LAURA L. LOVETT

The University of North Carolina Press Chapel Hill

© 2007 The University of North Carolina Press
All rights reserved
Manufactured in the United States of America
Set in Quadraat and Citizen types
by Keystone Typesetting, Inc.
The paper in this book meets the guidelines for
permanence and durability of the Committee on
Production Guidelines for Book Longevity of the
Council on Library Resources.

Frontispiece: From Theodore Roosevelt, *Autobiography* (1913), 365.

Library of Congress Cataloging-in-Publication Data
Lovett, Laura L.
Conceiving the future : pronatalism, reproduction, and the family
in the United States, 1890–1938 / Laura L. Lovett.
p. cm. — (Gender and American culture)
Includes bibliographical references and index.
ISBN-13: 978-0-8078-3107-6 (cloth: alk. paper)
ISBN-13: 978-0-8078-5803-5 (pbk.: alk. paper)
1. Family—United States—History—20th century. 2. Family size—
United States—History—20th century. 3. Family policy—United
States—History—20th century. 4. Eugenics—United States—
History—20th century. 5. Nostalgia—United States—
History—20th century. I. Title.
HQ535.L68 2007
306.850973'0904—dc22   2006033616

cloth   11 10 09 08 07   5 4 3 2 1
paper   11 10 09 08 07   5 4 3 2 1

CONTENTS

ILLUSTRATIONS

ACKNOWLEDGMENTS

I began this book in the History Department at the University of California, Berkeley. My advisor, Mary P. Ryan, allowed me to complete this project by being both a model of scholarship and a model of support. Mary's comments were always insightful and encouraging even as she tried to keep this far-ranging project focused and on track. Waldo Martin's wisdom and humor kept me questioning my sources and assumptions. Elisabeth Lloyd, whose seminar at UCSD on feminist philosophy of science allowed me to imagine working in this field, helped me see this project to its end. They were a wonderfully supportive committee, then and now.

Mary P. Ryan's dissertation-writing group shared comments, support, and camaraderie. I still think fondly of the discussions with Jessica Weiss, Jill Schlessinger, Laura Schwemm, Karen Leong, Valerie Mendoza, Linda Song, and Beatrix Hoffman.

The faculty at UC Berkeley provided inspiration and encouragement. Leon Litwack's commitment to undergraduate teaching and to centering questions of race and power were particularly important to me. Paula Fass, who helped introduce me to the Progressive Era and to the classic texts in U.S. history, never stopped pushing us to interrogate the unexamined assumptions in these materials. Her encouragement, both intellectual and personal, was profoundly important to my completing this project.

Funding for the interdisciplinary dissertation support group from the Dorothy Townsend Center allowed me to develop this project in conjunction with work from a range of fields and areas. Lynne Haney and Lisa Pollard helped to shape the Maternalism, Motherhood, and the Welfare State Group in a way that helped me to imagine how this subject might have ramifications beyond U.S. history. Sonya Michel's early encouragement of the group allowed for some important explorations of "familialist politics."

Lisa Rubens, Cita Cook, and Jane Morrison helped me to navigate the often-tough terrain of balancing graduate school and home. I am grateful for their support and friendship.

I was lucky enough to have the support of colleagues in the UC Davis History Department when writing part of this project. They were generous in making the campus a second graduate departmental home for me. I especially appreciated the encouragement and comments from Sarah Projansky, Lucy Barber, Jill Hough, Wendy Kline, Linda Payne, Jen Selwyn, and Margaret Jacobs. Roland Marchand was an especially encouraging critic, and I wish to acknowledge his influence on me.

Donald Pisani commented on unsolicited chapters on irrigation, providing important encouragement to someone trying to work improbably in the field of hydrology as a cultural historian. I truly appreciate his scholarship and generosity.

An array of scholars offered their comments on various parts of this project over the course of its development. I appreciate the insights and sources provided by Laura Briggs, Christina Cogdell, David Danbom, Rebecca Edwards, Kathleen Jones, Seth Koven, Tom Lacqueur, Kriste Lindenmeyer, Miliann Kang, Eric Miller, Diane Paul, Mary Renda, Jessica Riskin, Martha Sandweiss, Betty Smocovitis, Alex Stern, John Sweet, Molly Ladd Taylor, Tom Wellock, and Elliott West.

Portions of this book have been presented at various meetings. I am grateful for comments from conference participants at the American Historical Association, the American Society for Environmental History, the American Studies Association, the Asian Studies Association, the Berkshire Conference of Women Historians, the Feminist Research Seminar at Dartmouth College, the Five College History Seminar, the Five College Reproductive Politics Group, Monmouth University, the Organization of American Historians, the University of Kansas, the University of Massachusetts, the University of Southern Mississippi, the University of Tennessee, Chattanooga, the Western History Association, and Yale University.

I benefited greatly from the skill and knowledge of archivists at the American Philosophical Society, the Kansas State Historical Society, the Arizona State Archives, the Massachusetts Institute of Technology Archives, the National Archives, the Spencer Library, the Tuskegee Institute

Archives, and the Yale University Archives. I am especially grateful to Rob Cox for his help both at the American Philosophical Society and the University of Massachusetts.

The University of California, Berkeley, the University of Tennessee, Chattanooga, the University of Massachusetts, and the Agrarian Studies Program at Yale University generously supported research for this project. The American Philosophical Society and the Spencer Research Library at the University of Kansas provided research grants to use their collections.

An Institute for Agrarian Studies fellowship at Yale in 2004–5 both allowed me to finally complete needed research and gave me a chance to write. The incredibly democratic yet challenging discussions, integrating participants from the community as well as academics from a wide range of disciplines and backgrounds, were the special gift of that year. The touchstone for this rare space for interdisciplinary conversation was James C. Scott, who fed us, nurtured us, and pushed us with a vision for sustainable scholarship. M. Kay Mansfield made all things happen socially, intellectually, and practically—a true marvel. Fellow "agrarian agitators" insisted on clarity, rigor, and range, but all with a sense of adventure and fun: Steven Dorondel, Harriett Friedman, Lei Guang, Lauren Leve, Marilda Aparecida de Menezes, Wendy Wolford, and Karl Zimmerer. Other faculty at Yale were generous with their time and energy, including Glenda Gilmore, Daniel Kevles, Linda-Anne Rebhun, Cynthia Russett, and Steven Stoll.

The Pioneer Valley has offered me the kind of intellectual community that has made it possible to work in a myriad of ways. I am particularly grateful to my colleagues for their continual curiosity, willingness to share ideas and commitment to making UMass an affable place. David Glassberg delayed a much-deserved leave to cover classes for the year I was off and supplies me with a model for scholarly inquisitiveness. I am singularly lucky to have found a position teaching in a place where such commitment to constant learning sets the standard. My colleagues at UMass and the Five Colleges are an inspiration as well as a supportive network. While I am particularly delighted to be where I feel I can draw on anyone, some have given me direct comments on this project, and I wish especially to thank them for their support on this project: Audrey Altstadt, Joyce Berkman, Joye Bowman, Brian Bunk, John Higginson, Bruce Laurie, Alice Nash, and Larry Owens.

The extensive comments of Francoise Hamlin, Tom Hilbink, Rick Lopez, Dayo Gore, and Heather Cox Richardson remind me that it is good to have friends with sharp pencils and soft hearts for last-minute critiques.

The Reproductive Politics Group at the Five Colleges has provided a special forum for exploring the ramifications of this project. Banu Subramaniam, Elizabeth Hartmann, Marlene Fried, Leslie King, Joyce Berkman, Betsy Krause, and others associated with the center have inspired me to think hard and explore the consequences of these policies.

While at Dartmouth, the special support of colleagues such as Celia Naylor, Mary Kelley, Bruce Nelson, Margaret Darrow, M. Cecilia Gaposchkin, Susan Brison, Colleen Boggs, Jane Carroll, Rich Kremer, Colin Calloway, Donald Pease, and Lauren Clarke helped me to stay focused. Companionship, critical readings, and conversations with Annelise Orleck and Alexis Jetter made it possible to imagine completing the manuscript. Their generosity and hospitality were an extraordinary gift.

The comments of Eileen Boris and the other, anonymous readers of this manuscript for the University of North Carolina Press were invaluable. They pushed me toward greater clarity and understanding. This is certainly a better book as a result of their critical insight. Sian Hunter at UNC Press has been patient, kind, and encouraging, sticking with this project long beyond I expected anyone beside myself to be interested. I appreciate her doing so.

Scholarship demands more time alone than we often imagine, as well as space to read, make connections, and draw conclusions. The efforts of a number of people allowed me to have this time and space while raising my daughters. Lynne Haney took my older daughter on many Sundays in graduate school and shared with me how her mother had balanced graduate school and a child. Mary Ryan, Paula Fass, Tom Lacqueur, and Waldo Martin made it quite clear that motherhood and graduate school could and should be compatible endeavors. My colleagues at UMass have consistently acknowledged and supported personal and professional commitments, whether by covering when children were ill or, miraculously, hosting fourteenth birthday parties. My parents, Bill Lovett and Sandra Lovett, have taken my daughters at key moments that have allowed me to complete drafts or papers and offered immeasurable support for this project in a myriad of ways. Lydia Lovett-Dietrich and Arlena Lovett-Dietrich have made me a better teacher, scholar, and critic by their very existence. My partner, Michael Dietrich, alone knows what I owe him. His support, encouragement, example, and companionship are immeasurable.

1

NOSTALGIA, MODERNISM, AND THE FAMILY IDEAL

To study the American family is to conduct a rescue mission into the dreamland of our national self-concept. No subject is more closely bound up with our sense of a difficult present—and our nostalgia for a happier past.

JOHN DEMOS,
"Myths and Realities in the History of the American Family," 1976

The United States invested heavily in the reproduction of its citizenry during the early twentieth century. However, these investments did not take the form of legislated child allowances or baby bonuses. Instead, national campaigns for reclamation, conservation, country life, and eugenics became prominent expressions of American pronatalism. Recognizing them as such is not a matter of understanding how they altered the birthrate but a matter of understanding how reproduction was associated in each campaign with nostalgic ideals of the family, motherhood, or the home. In the United States, reproduction was regulated as much by social pressure and created conventions as by actual legislation.

Feminist scholars grasped the importance of recognizing pronatalism in the early 1970s as they spoke out against the social pressure to bear children. Motivated by concerns regarding overpopulation and individual reproductive freedom, scholars such as Judith Blake argued that a new population policy could not be created until the existing pronatalist policy was recognized. Social and cultural messages regarding sex roles, family norms, and even feminism, Blake argued, carried implicit and explicit endorsements of women's purported responsibility to reproduce. The relentless and pervasive nature of these messages led Blake to argue that American pronatalism was coercive, not because women were forced to act against their will, but because the decision to not reproduce was not presented to them as a reasonable alternative. As such, she saw pronatalism as a "barrier to self-determination for women."[1]

Blake was reacting to cultural messages presented to women in the 1970s. Like Blake, I have found pronatalism in a set of cultural messages, but these messages were associated with an earlier array of Populist and Progressive efforts. In the early twentieth century, coercive means of reproductive regulation as social control were created, articulated, and woven into cultural constructions such as the "home on the land" or the "fitter family." These constructed ideals helped create social pressure by enrolling the cultural force of tradition and nostalgia to justify intrusions into what had been private deliberations concerning reproduction.

In contrast to the United States, pronatalism in countries such as France and Germany has been much more overt.[2] With state-sponsored programs, subsidies, and even medals for mothers, countries such as Nazi Germany articulated their interest in promoting the reproduction of its

The Family Ideal

citizenry explicitly and directly. Historians regard the United States as much more reserved in its policies, if indeed any such policies are recognized at all.[3] The U.S. government did not provide subsidies for large families; instead, reformers and politicians promoted pronatalism indirectly as part of public campaigns for land reclamation, playgrounds, or suburban development. These reformers knowingly promoted families, but their efforts were not always explicitly framed in terms of reproduction —they promoted reproduction indirectly.

The challenge for the historian of American pronatalism is to detect the often-indirect campaigns that promoted reproduction. Contemporary analysts of population policy recognize pronatalism in a range of efforts including loans to start families; child allowances; child tax exemptions; guaranteed income for care-givers; parental leave and flex time; subsidized housing, child care, and playgrounds; restricted access to birth control and abortion; and the creation family-friendly civic environments, as well as pronatalist educational and propaganda campaigns.[4] Within the United States, reformers embraced some of these policies, but their implications for reproduction were seldom given voice.

Rather than focus on individual decisions to have children on not, in this book, I focus on how ideological and cultural ideals influenced and shaped pronatalist policies and reform efforts in the United States. I claim that from 1890 to the 1930s nostalgic idealizations of motherhood, the family, and home were used to construct and legitimate political agendas and social policies concerning reproduction. Ideologically, motherhood and childbearing in general have been understood as bearing on issues of nationalism, individualism, and feminism.[5] In the United States, pronatalism continued these associations even as it drew on particularly American ideas of agrarianism and scientific racism.

By focusing on nostalgic idealizations of motherhood, the family, and the home, I have recovered American pronatalism in some unlikely places, such as George Maxwell's national irrigation campaign, as well as some more-expected places, such as Florence Sherbon's eugenics efforts. In this book, I consider the ideologies and practices of American pronatalism by contrasting five significant historical figures and their signature social agendas or policies. These five figures do not exhaust the range of American pronatalism nor the uses of nostalgia by reformers. Instead, they represent a sample of contrasting cases that address key differences concerning the indirect nature of American pronatalism, its implications for women's agency, and its exclusionary and racist presumptions. Beginning with Mary Elizabeth Lease's Populist agenda and ending with Florence Sherbon's eugenic campaign for fitter families, I examine how the ideology of the rural family facilitated women's public leadership in a popular political movement on the one hand and within governmental and educational bureaucracies on the other. In contrast, George Maxwell assumed women's subordination when he promoted land reclamation and irrigation as a means to reconstruct society through home building. Theodore Roosevelt's campaign for conservation and country life and Edward Ross's sociological theory of social control made race an explicit part of the ideal of the family and the rural home. For Ross and Roosevelt, controlling and directing a changing social order by employing an ideal of the family was a means of reasserting their perception of racial order.

MATERNALISM AND REPRODUCTIVE REGULATION

At the turn of the century, the place and status of women was undergoing tremendous change. Victorian doctrines of separate spheres had assigned women moral authority over the private sphere of familial life and assigned men to the competitive world of the public sphere. In the Populist and Progressive Eras, women challenged this division as more and more of them sought higher education, careers, and divorces. Many women who found a greater say in public politics argued that their responsibility as mothers extended well beyond the private sphere. For women in the Progressive Era, domesticity bound them to the home while paradoxically justifying their growing public agency.

Muckraking journalist and Heterodoxy Club member Rheta Childe Dorr exemplified this trend when in 1910 she wrote: "Woman's place is Home. . . . But Home is not contained within the four walls of an individual home. Home is the community. The city full of people is the Family. The public school is the real Nursery. And badly do the Home and the Family and the Nursery need their mother."[6] This declaration justified the efforts of female reformers engaged in "municipal housekeeping" both in terms of the reformers and the working-class, immigrant recipients of

4   *The Family Ideal*

this reform.[7] But Dorr's maternalist manifesto does not end with simply moving the mother into the city as home, it concludes with a biological and, at the time, scientific explanation of why reform must take place. As Dorr continues: "For woman's work is race preservation, race improvement, and who opposes her, or interferes with her, simply fights nature, and nature never loses her battles."[8]

Dorr's manifesto suggests two interpretive strands within maternalist thought: one emphasizing the reformulation of women's roles in public policy in terms of the wider application of maternal values of care and nurture, and another emphasizing the reformulation of women's roles in public policy in terms of the biology of motherhood and a eugenic ideal of family and race betterment. Although this second strand cannot be completely divorced from the first, it is the second interpretative thread that makes the "maternalist moment" unique to the late nineteenth and early twentieth century.[9] Maternalism at the turn of the century addressed women's biological roles as mothers and the interest of elite reformers and the state in maintaining that role.

Many scholars interpret the reformulation of women's roles in public policy in terms of the wider application of maternal values of care and nurture as a form of maternalism.[10] In her analysis of the development of welfare in the United States, Linda Gordon identifies three tenets that characterized most expressions of maternalism. First, maternalists regarded domestic and family responsibilities and identities as essential to the vast majority of women and to the social order; they strongly associated women's interests with those of children. Second, maternalists imagined themselves in a motherly role toward the poor. Lastly, maternalists believed that it was their work, experience, and/or socialization as mothers that both made them uniquely able to lead certain kinds of reform campaigns and made others deserving of help.[11] Maternalist agendas were thus limited to those domains where women could claim that their role as mothers gave them special insight. The creation of the welfare system is perhaps the most widely recognized impact of maternalism's ideology of motherhood in the United States.

Welfare programs in the United States have typically assumed and reinforced an ideal of the family with a "father/breadwinner who works for a wage and a mother/wife who provides unpaid domestic work."[12]

Whether one emphasizes ideologies of the family wage or ideologies of motherhood, this ideal of the family or "family ethic" is understood to have structured the origins and development of welfare in the United States. This "industrial family ethic" became institutionalized and refined during the nineteenth century, with the result that women became increasing excluded from economically productive labor, while their reproductive and homemaking roles expanded.[13] The family ethic contributed to the image of men as "providers" and to the ideology of the family wage, which asserted that industry provided wages sufficient to support an entire family. Protective labor legislation, child labor laws, mother's pensions, and compulsory education further reinforced this ideal of the family and the family wage, as did tenement and housing reforms, insofar as they permitted "mothers to fulfill their duties in safe, clean domestic environments."[14] As the state gained greater authority to regulate aspects of public and private life, the industrial family ethic ensured that a set of hierarchical power relationships based on who did the wage earnings would be maintained within the family.

Regardless of the family ethic invoked, welfare policies that bear on women, children, and the family were either directly or indirectly pronatalist.[15] While histories of welfare and maternalism rightly have emphasized these policies as struggles for women's agency and authority, they were also sites where reforms with indirect effects on reproduction and population were articulated. Maternalism builds on and makes use of an essentializing image of women as reproducers and thereby limits their political activity to issues directly relevant to their status as reproducers.[16] As women, Mary Elizabeth Lease and Florence Sherbon had a responsibility toward their families and the maintenance of order in private life. If their political or scientific work in the public realm could be closely associated with the family or motherhood, their activity could be justified as extensions of their culturally sanctioned duties in private life. As we shall see in Lease's case, it was possible to make a wide variety of economic issues relevant to motherhood during the Populist movement.

Mary Lease and other Populist women justified their political involvement by arguing that political decisions had effects on the daily lives of women and children. In effect, Lease articulated the connection of the home to politics. As the nostalgic image of the home or the family continued to be used by reformers and politicians, the connections between family life and political issues invited increasing government management of private life. Theodore Roosevelt's concern over the possibility of race suicide, for instance, led him to see motherhood as women's duty to the state. Although he did not dictate that women reproduce, his concerns with regulating reproduction were embodied in the Children's Bureau and their campaign against infant mortality. In this context, nostalgic images of the family helped legitimate the increasing regulation of reproduction and family life by government experts.

In the decades surrounding the beginning of the twentieth century, the American family was widely perceived to be in a state of crisis. By 1889, the United States had the highest divorce rate in the world. Coupled with falling birthrates among "native-born" Americans, the divorce rate raised doubts about the survival of the family and the "American race."[17] By "the race" or "the American race," reformers, politicians, and social commentators meant the white population of the United States, usually of Northern European or Anglo-Saxon descent.[18] Anxieties concerning race and divorce were associated with the changing roles of women. In general, white women were working more outside the home, obtaining more higher education, and increasing their public activity in a variety of civic clubs ad organizations. Motherhood and family seemed to be endangered as women's morals, dress, and behavior changed in the early twentieth century.

Increasing immigration and urbanization compounded anxiety over shifting women's roles. New immigrants from Asia and Southern Europe fueled fears among many elite reformers that "American values" and traditions were slipping away as these new immigrants failed to adopt American traditions as their own. At the same time, the nation's population was becoming more concentrated in the cities. In 1900, two out of every five people in the United States farmed. Three out of every five lived in a rural community. In the first decades of the twentieth century, the numbers of farmers and rural inhabitants slowly declined, lowering the percentages of land ownership and increasing the amount of land tenancy.[19] Demographically, fewer rural families contributed to declining birthrates, since the rural family was on average larger than its urban counterpart. The confluence of these trends contributed to a growing sense of crisis that many modernist reformers believed they could resolve. They made their new and invasive proposals to regulate reproduction more palatable by presenting them behind a facade of motherhood, the farmer, the home, and the "traditional" family.

When Theodore Roosevelt or Edward Ross appealed to the "American family," they appealed to a nostalgic image of the rural, white family. In effect they recast Jeffersonian agrarianism in racial terms. Jefferson held that yeoman farmers were "the most vigorous, the most independent, the most virtuous citizens."[20] Roosevelt, Ross, and others naturalized the alleged characteristics of the farmer by arguing that they were produced in response to the farmer's struggle to survive in the frontier environment. These characteristics acquired through the frontier experience were passed on to succeeding generations or acquired anew as successive generations pushed the frontier west. This natural process produced what Ross called the "American racial character" or the "American type." The crucial point here is that the ideal of the rural family was a white racial ideal. When Roosevelt and others referred to the race or the rural family, they made specific racial associations.

With the closing of the frontier, increasing immigration, and urbanization, Roosevelt, Ross, and others began to forcefully advocate the rural family as an ideal social and reproductive unit. Roosevelt cast women's role in this unit as bearing and raising children for the benefit of the race and the state. This distinctively American form of pronatalism was widely debated during the controversy over race suicide but also informed Roosevelt's commissions on conservation and country life. Ross translated this racial ideal into economic terms as he used it to naturalize the standard of living for the "American type." Inherent in nostalgic ideologies of the home, motherhood, and family were assumptions about race. Pronatalism in the early twentieth century was not about reproduction per se but about racial reproduction and its regulation.

Ideological and cultural campaigns to promote reproduction have frequently been associated with nationalism and conservative politics as exemplified in Nazi Germany, for instance. In the United States, the eugenics movement in the early twentieth century is probably the most recognizable expression of pronatalist thought. Although American policies never reached the level of Nazi Germany's, American sterilization laws and the

The Family Ideal

American eugenics movement had a strong influence on the development of German policies and thought.[21] Charles Darwin's cousin, Francis Galton, coined the term "eugenics" and envisioned it as a science of human hereditary improvement. Rooted in breeding practices, eugenics renewed interest in reproduction as a means for Progressive reformers to address a wide range of perceived social ills. Where social Darwinians were willing to let natural selection take its course, eugenicists imagined that their knowledge of heredity allowed them to select the supposedly fit and unfit in human populations.[22] Both social Darwinists and eugenicists, therefore, embraced biological solutions to social problems.

Most of the history of eugenics has concerned the enactments characteristic of "negative" eugenics: voluntary and involuntary sterilization, segregation of the supposedly "unfit," immigration and marriage restriction, and euthanasia.[23] These efforts constitute forms of coercive pronatalism in so far as they eliminated reproductive choice.[24] While these pernicious efforts certainly warrant historical investigation, this book also considers what was called "positive" eugenics, which sought to promote reproduction among those considered to be "fit." The resulting form of pronatalism was not overtly coercive, but was profoundly influential.

In Building a Better Race, Wendy Kline argues that there was a "significant strategic shift in the eugenics movement" when in the 1930s its proponents incorporated the environment into their arguments and "focused on the importance of motherhood and family to the race." This emphasis became the center of eugenic campaigns in the 1930s, according to Kline, and marked a new concern with positive eugenics—the promotion of the "procreation of the eugenically fit."[25] Kline specifically locates the turn to the family and positive eugenics in the 1930s as a response to the Great Depression and the concern for families that it generated.[26] In a footnote, Kline acknowledges that "positive eugenics gained popularity in the 1920s as some eugenicists initiated 'Fitter Families for Future Firesides' contests," but, using a narrow definition of positive eugenics as marriage and family counseling, argues that it did not fully emerge until the 1930s. Kline further justifies her neglect of earlier pronatalist efforts with Elaine Tyler May's argument that positive eugenics "never took hold among the population at large." Quoting May on race suicide, Kline writes, "if the American people did not respond to the pronatalist moral suasion, little could be done to boost the birthrate of the "best" stock; . . . the crusade for positive eugenics failed" (92)."[27] Actual changes in birth-rates do not reflect the influence of positive eugenics within the eugenics movement and so are not evidence that a shift in the movement toward positive eugenics did not occur before the 1930s. The popularity of eu-genics education and contests during the 1920s demonstrates that the shift to positive eugenics occurred earlier than Kline suggests and was considered worthwhile. Indeed, the originator of the shift to positive eu-genics in Kline's account, Paul Popenoe, strongly endorsed a wide range of positive eugenic activities in his 1926 book, *The Conservation of the Fam-ily*.[28] Early efforts by Popenoe, Irving Fisher, the American Eugenics So-ciety, and especially the fitter family contests mark the shift to positive eugenics and family-oriented eugenics in the United States.

NOSTALGIA AND THE MODERNIST IMPULSE

When historians discuss the modernist impulse in the science, culture, and politics of the twentieth century, they emphasize a sense among Amer-ican artists and intellectuals of change, impermanence, subjectivity, and possibility.[29] While many artists and intellectuals embraced these features of modernism, some social reformers found them threatening. To many, the realization of impermanence exposed the groundlessness of tradi-tional sources of morality and order. Hence, modernist social reformers and politicians sought to restore a sense of order. Unlike their literary or artistic counterparts who created a modernist sense of order by "opening the self to new levels of experience" and then "fusing together disparate elements of that experience into new and original 'wholes,' "[30] modernist social reformers and politicians attempted to create a sense of order by directing the process of the continual construction of modern society. For Progressive reformers and politicians, the impermanence of social institu-tions created the possibility for their reconstruction and redirection. It created a mandate for increasing and consolidating the power of the state in order to manage and maintain social order.

Modernist reformers embraced the possibility of social change, but their future society was created in the image of an idealized past. In the words of historian Dorothy Ross, "the American love of the new turns out to carry within it the desire to recreate the old."[31] As modernism flourished in the United States during the late nineteenth and early twentieth centuries, reactions to the modern predicament were widespread and diverse.[32] However, despite the attention given to the varieties of modernism, most historians do not come to terms with the fact that in the United States early twentieth-century modernists were influenced by a profoundly nostalgic culture.[33] The result was a paradoxical mix of a yearning to recreate a stable past while maintaining their belief in the constancy of change and their own ability to create the future. This sense of nostalgia for a stable past, according to historian Michael Kammen, "helped [the American people] to legitimize new political orders, rationalize the adjustment and perpetuation of old social hierarchies and construct acceptable new systems of thought and values." The inextricable mixture of nostalgia and modernism helped mask the scale of modernizing changes and lessened their impact by clothing them in the familiarity of the past. Nostalgia acted as a bulwark against a rapidly changing and modernizing world by offering the promise of "identity, integrity, and perhaps even a sense of security—however false."[34] In short, nostalgia facilitated the sense of order that modernist social reformers tried to achieve.

Nostalgic modernists were not traditionalists or antimodernists.[35] They did not advocate a return to the past or the strict preservation of traditional order. The resistance to change of the traditionalist and the search for authentic experience characteristic of the antimodernist were both backward looking. What made nostalgic modernist attitude distinct from traditionalist and antimodernist attitudes was its embrace of the possibilities that modernism presented for the reconstruction of society. Nostalgic modernists did not resist change. Even though they looked to the past, they always moved forward. Moreover, unlike sentimentalized nostalgia, nostalgic modernism could be extremely critical of both the past and the present even as it projected an ideal of the past in service of contemporary ends.

This paradoxical fondness for both tradition and progress appears in the work of historical societies, artists, politicians, and reformers.[36] Richard Slotkin sees the tension between tradition and progress in narratives of western expansion.[37] Lawrence Levine identifies similar tensions in 1920s nostalgia as a desire to retain the "old order" as well as the "fruits of progress." Such a return to the past was symbolic but significant as in-.

creased urbanization and immigration forced changes in the presumed social order. Indeed, the anxiety produced by social and cultural change in this period was eased by reviving and reinforcing old cultural beliefs and values.[38] Colonial recreations and "Old English" furnishings were not simple expressions of nostalgic longing. Popular colonial revivals signified the privileges of ancestry and the centrality of an assumed American "racial heritage." Whether embodied in the Daughters of the American Revolution or the Colonial Dames of Virginia, colonial ancestry marked a division between "old" and "new" Americans.[39] In the hands of eugenicists and other would-be reformers, however, nostalgia did more than reinforce existing forms of elite white patriarchal privilege. Using nostalgia made significant social, institutional, and political reforms possible by wrapping them in a vision of a past social order. Nostalgic ideology thus became a powerful tool for early twentieth-century reformers, especially with regard to reforms involving the family and reproduction.[40]

In this book I use nostalgic modernism as an interpretative framework for exploring how idealizations of motherhood, the home, and the family were used to promote and justify a range of pronatalist efforts in the Populist and Progressive Eras. The reformers I consider were nostalgic in so far as they idealized the values and characteristics gained by early American families as a direct result of their experience on the frontier. Building on a Jeffersonian tradition of agrarianism, these reformers promoted similar variants of a highly idealized vision of the "hearty, pioneer family" made strong, physically and morally, by their efforts to settle on and make their living from the land.[41] By 1890, the frontier was closed, however, and the challenge for the modernist reformer was to determine how to continue to reproduce these ideal Americans socially and biologically.

CONCEIVING THE FUTURE

In the chapters that follow, I begin by exploring how an ideal of the farm family facilitated Mary Elizabeth Lease's rise to prominence in Populist politics during the 1880s and 1890s. American Populism was a major third-party, agrarian political movement advocating the end of the concentration of capital and power in the hands of bankers, railroad companies, and absentee landowners. The Populists offered an alternative conception of the organization of the state, which typically focused on the interests of "the people." Because Populists argued for a "producer ethic," claiming that wealth should belong to those who produced it, historians of American Populism have often understood the rhetoric of "the people" in terms of individual producers. I argue that "the people" appealed to in Populist political economy and in Populist reforms of education and state charities referred to an idealized rural family.

In Chapter 2, I argue that Populist arguments concerning overproduction, land ownership, temperance, and suffrage articulated a particular relationship between the family and the state. At these sites, the ideology of the rural family unit and its relation to the state was championed by such well-known orators as Mary Elizabeth Lease. Like many women reformers, Lease drew on her position as a mother to claim the authority to speak to issues that she thought bore on her family. Lease translated her advocacy of a maternalist agenda into her advocacy of a Populist Party agenda, because the political and economic issues of Populism were those that bore directly on the producer family. By connecting issues such as overproduction to the producer family, Lease could claim special privilege to speak to those issues as a mother and a woman. In doing so, however, Lease also contributed to the idealization of the farm family and to the essentializing of women as mothers.

In Chapter 3, I claim that visions of the American landscape advocated by national irrigation and land reclamation activists included who ought to inhabit that landscape. George Maxwell's National Irrigation Association was instrumental in efforts to gain support for the irrigation and reclamation of land in the West. A key part of the campaign for national irrigation was the argument that building dams would lead to more homes on the land. Maxwell's ideal of the home on the land, what he called a "homecroft," represented nostalgia for an agrarian past where the home and the family were sites of production. With his homecroft ideal, Maxwell literally sought to rebuild America, especially its cities, in order to bring Americans back into contact with the land. Rooting Americans in the soil was, according to Maxwell, a means to reclaim the perceived vitality of America's past.

By promoting "home-making" in the arid West, Maxwell was engaged in not only radically altering the landscape with dams and canals, but creating the conditions for the spread of homes on the land, which he thought would alter the degenerating effects of urbanization. Land reclamation, then, was as much an effort at social engineering as it was hydrological engineering. Images of the family or the home thus overcame the apparently paradoxical mixture of nostalgia and modernism by providing ideologies, institutions, and political policies with which to navigate change and modernity.[42]

Maxwell's national irrigation program had the support of Theodore Roosevelt, who shared similar sentiments for Americans who worked on the land. Part of Roosevelt's motivation for improving country life came from his fears of race suicide. Farm families were larger than urban families, and their racial identification as well as their nostalgic idealization allowed Roosevelt to cast them as the "nation's reserve." In Chapter 4, I examine how a nostalgic representation of the rural family was constructed as a racialized ideal in response to the perceived problem of race suicide. Instead of focusing exclusively on Roosevelt's heavy-handed public campaign concerning women's duty to reproduce on behalf of the state, I consider how the sociologist who coined the term "race suicide," Edward Ross, constructed a rural ideal as part of a plan of social control.

For Ross, race suicide was a matter of competition between "races" with different standards of living. According to Ross, part of the "American racial character" was a high standard of living. Immigrants, especially Japanese and Chinese immigrants, in his view, had lower standards of living, would not assimilate by adopting higher standards, and thus posed a threat because their lower standard allowed them to have more children earlier. According to Ross, this racial competition could be prevented by either restricting immigration or by better regulation of the birthrates of "native-born Americans." In either case a crucial part of Ross's agenda projected an ideal of social order as a means of social control. Ideals of a high standard of living or of the four-child family were based on a racialized reconstruction of the American farm family as the natural product of generations of experience on the frontier. As ideals of social order, the naturalized standard of living and rural family were promoted by Ross and others as a means of achieving social control of racial reproduction.

In Chapter 5, I return to Roosevelt's pronatalism. From its roots in his campaign against race suicide, I locate Roosevelt's campaign for population regulation in his administration's combined advocacy of the conservation and country life movements. For Roosevelt and his advisors, the effort to conserve the nation's natural resources was part of the movement to improve country life and keep families on the farm. The farm family thus became a natural resource to be managed. Invoking nostalgic ideals of the farmer and the rural family allowed Roosevelt to claim that both the conservation and country life movements were relevant to the future of the "American race."[43]

In Chapter 6, I consider the extension of nostalgia for the rural family to eugenics, a more-traditional arena for pronatalism and population politics. By documenting the development of the American Eugenics Society's "human livestock" competitions, known as the Fitter Families for Future Firesides contests, I recast how the family ideal was further racialized and deployed by experts as a part of the bureaucratic regulation of reproduction during the 1920s.

Dr. Florence Sherbon and her fellow organizers appropriated the moral authority of the mother by creating a science of motherhood. The key to such appropriation was a campaign of popular education that lent scientific credence to a nostalgic vision of rural motherhood and the family. Fitter family contests appealed to a deeply rooted sense of nostalgia for the rural family at a time when the nation was becoming increasingly urban, when rural children were choosing not to stay on the farm, and when the culture of the Roaring Twenties challenged "traditional values." In this context, the Fitter Families for Future Firesides contests allowed its participants to feel that they were actively creating a future by looking to the past.

These five individuals and their particular reform interests represent a range of pronatalist efforts as well as how these efforts were influenced by related, but not identical, ideologies of motherhood, home, family, and race. I am not concerned with the demographic success of any of these pronatalist efforts, but with how nostalgic ideals were deployed in early twentieth-century pronatalism. Together the figures I consider demonstrate that one of the features that made American pronatalism distinctive was its embrace of different forms of American agrarianism. The myth of a stable agrarian past had tremendous appeal given the vast social changes under way in the early twentieth century. While the agrarian ideal was certainly illusory in that it did not reflect the reality of the vast majority of farmers or rural residents, it did not impede progress, but rather served as an ideological instrument of perceived progress.[44] Idealized images of rural life and the rural family significantly shaped pronatalist efforts, and in doing so made the proposed changes and reforms seem conservative. Where issues concerning reproduction had previously been private, these pronatalist efforts allowed them to be thrown open to regulation by experts under the rubric of defending the "traditional" image of the home, family, and motherhood. This book considers the intellectual foundations for why and how this was possible in the first half of the twentieth century.

2

NEW OCCASIONS TEACH
NEW DUTIES

MARY ELIZABETH LEASE'S
MATERNALIST AGENDA

There are no conditions in life, no questions,
moral or political, no present or future, no ties,
foreign or domestic, no issues, local or national,
in which the mother is not equally interested
with the father.

Wichita Independent, 1888

In one of his few discussions of women and the political reforms of the Populist and Progressive Eras, historian Richard Hofstadter contrasted ideals of feminine beauty from 1860 and 1935. Where an 1860 farm journal satirized the refinement and affected beauty of the city girl, the 1935 *Idaho Farmer* advocated such beauty tips for farmer's wives as manicured nails. Hofstadter thought that most farm women probably found such advice ludicrously out of place in a farm magazine, but he thought that the presence of such an ideal was significant. To mark that significance Hofstadter invoked Mary Elizabeth Lease, the most famous orator of the Populist Party—a woman who had had tremendous political influence. Hofstadter asked: "Would Mary Lease, who was accustomed to addressing weary audiences of farm women in faded calico dresses, turn over in her grave at the suggestion of rosy-tinted fingertips? I am not sure. What she wanted to win for the farmers and their families was more of the good things of life." Indeed Hofstadter suggested that if Lease's farmer's rebellion had continued, farmer's wives might become their opposite—embodiments of urban beauty.[1]

Mary Lease did want to win things for farm families; economic reforms in particular topped her list. Suggesting that Lease would have embraced an ideal of urban beauty does not do justice to the Populist agenda that she advocated so forcefully. To the extent that she sought to transform women's lives, it was with arguments for political equality and economic security. Like many women reformers, Lease was a maternalist and drew on her position as a mother to claim the moral authority to speak to issues that she thought bore on her family. Indeed, Lease's success as a public figure depended not only on her incredible oratory skills, but also on her ability to connect the political and economic issues of Populism with issues that bore directly on women and the family.

Emphasizing the farm family was a familiar tactic among the Farmer's Alliances that preceded the Populist Party.[2] Within the Farmer's Alliances of the 1880s, women were treated as political equals—once political issues impinged on the private sphere of the home, women were allowed and expected to speak to them.[3] At the same time, the Farmer's Alliance supported a patriarchal model of the farm family where men were figured as economic and political decision makers. This tension between "the egalitarian political family" and "the patriarchal farm family" became more significant as it became an important aspect of the Populist campaigns of the 1890s. As a political party, the Populists had to concentrate their efforts on votes, and only men could vote.[4] While Populist efforts in general emphasized male political agency and the patriarchal model of the farm family, Lease and other women populists continued to argue for the relevance of politics to women and the entire farm family. Lease did not reject the patriarchal model but did forcefully advocate women's political agency and suffrage as part of her Populist agenda. From her position as a woman, Lease foregrounded the family and framed her advocacy of various issues in terms of their impact on women and children. Lease made the entire producer family relevant to Populists' economic and political considerations at the same time that she legitimated her own role as a public figure.

Both revered and reviled as the "Queen of the Populists," the "Wichita Cyclone," and the "Kansas Pythoness," Mary "Yellin'" Lease is one of the most controversial figures in Populist historiography. Walter Nugent and O. Gene Clayton actually assign Lease the lion's share of the blame for the Populist defeat in the election of 1896.[5] Mary Jo Wagner praises her ability to reach the people but questions the consistency of her political views.[6] Michael Goldberg's contrast of Lease with another leading woman in Populism, Annie Diggs, portrays Lease as more masculine, more aggressive, and more mercurial.[7] While she may not have been typical of many women in the People's Party, Lease was without question one of the best-known advocates of Populism regardless of sex. Although she would leave Populist politics by the late 1890s, Lease did not abandon her maternalist perspective or her political advocacy during the Progressive Era. As a Populist and Progressive reformer, Lease embraced change and the possibility of remaking society. Her vision of reform for women, however, was rooted in a naturalized and divinely mandated conception of motherhood that informed her advocacy of economic and political rights for women as well as their reproductive duties.

MARY LEASE AND THE DEVELOPMENT OF WOMEN'S POLITICS IN KANSAS

Mary Lease was born Mary Elizabeth Clyens in Ridgeway, Pennsylvania, in 1853 to an Irish father who, according to one story, had been a modest

Catholic landowner in County Monaghan, Ireland, when he was declared a criminal by the English for collecting rifles, powder, and bullets to lead a rebellion. He fled Ireland for the United States, where he met and married his second wife, Elizabeth Moray, a woman of Scottish descent who was the niece of the Bishop of Dublin. Both Lease's father and two of her brothers were killed while serving as substitutes in the Union Army during the Civil War.[8]

Lease graduated in 1870 from St. Elizabeth's Academy, a boarding school in Allegheny, Pennsylvania. She taught locally for a while before accepting a post as a teacher in the West at St. Anne's Academy in Osage Mission, Kansas. While a teacher, Mary Clyens met and married Charles Lease, a thirty-year-old assistant in one of the town's two pharmacies. The couple moved one hundred miles west to Kingman, Kansas, in the midst of the prairie. The Leases homesteaded in a dirt-walled dugout from 1873 to 1874 but were driven out of Kingman by the Panic of '73. That year had been a particularly productive farm year with enough rain for good crops. However, the effect of the depression in the East meant that crops could not command high enough prices to allow farmers in the West to pay off their debt. The Leases squeezed through the year, banking on a good crop in 1874, but they were wiped out by a plague of grasshoppers that swept through the West from Oregon to the Mississippi River, from Canada to Texas. The devastation was so vast that Kansas governor Thomas Osborn issued a nationwide appeal for relief and authorized some state relief to help farmers get through the winter.[9]

Like many other farmers in the western part of Kansas, who were especially fearful that the eggs laid by the grasshoppers of the previous year would bring even more devastation, Mary Lease and her husband left their homestead to the loan agency who had financed their (devastated) spring wheat crop and moved to a new town at the end of the new Missouri, Kansas and Texas Railroad named Denison. Denison, Texas, was just across the Red River from "Indian Territory." Denison was besieged by hard-drinking outlaws who could flee into Indian Territory at the first sign of legal trouble. In 1874 the town of four thousand had twenty saloons, five liquor stores, and only two churches. While Charles Lease supported the family as a pharmacy clerk, Mary joined the local branch of the newly formed Women's Christian Temperance Union, which met at the house of Charles's employer's wife, Sarah Acheson.[10]

The Leases stayed in Denison from 1874 to 1884, during which time they had four children: Charles, Evelyn Louise, Ben Hur, and Grace. Willing to try farming again, Mary persuaded Charles in 1884 to return to Kingman as tenant farmers. The Lease family's second stint as farmers lasted two years. In 1886, unable to pay their rent, they decided to move to Wichita, where Mary could contribute an income to the family. Charles began working for a wholesale druggist, Aldrich and Brown, and Mary took in washing and read law.[11] According to a tale she frequently told on her political campaigns and lecture tours, she taped legal papers to the wall of her kitchen and memorized them while she scrubbed the laundry, which she took in for fifty cents a load. With tutoring from Tom Mac-Meechan and Charles Ebey at a local law office, Lease learned enough law to be admitted to the state bar in 1889.[12]

In the mid-1880s, Mary Lease, like many other women in the late nineteenth century, organized a club for women interested in education. She advertised the meetings for the "Hypatia Club" in the *Wichita Eagle*. Her local renown in the Women's Club led to a request that she address the Caldwell, Kansas, St. Patrick's Day celebration on Irish history and struggles. She gave the money she earned for this particular address in Caldwell, and later for similar addresses all over the state, to the Irish National League.

Lease's speech, "Ireland: Her Poets, Warriors and Statesmen," valorized Ireland, castigated English oppression, and used both to address the plight of the American farmer. Locating the ignorance of Irish history in British colonial policy, Lease proclaimed it a "treason and crime for those born on her [Ireland's] shores . . . to be ignorant of the very names of those who stood in the forefront of the hottest battles of these long centuries of struggle and daring valor." Throughout her speech, Ireland was personified as a subjugated female, "abused and scorned alternately, and if her beautiful voice broke forth in song she was forthwith gagged, and the iron heel of despotism placed more firmly upon her prostrate neck." For Lease, the key to understanding English oppression was the "withering, blighting curse of Landlordism." Blaming English landlords for the

Irish potato famine of 1848, she claimed that, "the great hearted American people sent shiploads of corn meal to greet the starving lips of the Irish race, and as they sailed up the Irish harbor they were met on their way coming out by English vessels carrying away the products of a dying, hungry people." For farmers struggling with debts, the analogy with Ireland was apt regardless of their nationality.[13]

Lease's great skill as an orator earned her quick notoriety, and she was soon in demand for her speech on Ireland and for speeches on other topics. While Lease used her family's Irish ancestry to legitimate her role as a public speaker on St. Patrick's Day, in her later speeches she shed her Irish persona in favor of that of a maternalist reformer. Throughout the 1880s and 1890s, Lease would frequently invoke her position as a woman and mother as she sought moral authority to address a wide range of economic and political problems.

On the evening of December 9, 1886, the men and women gathered for the first State Sanitary Convention in Wichita, Kansas, heard Mary Elizabeth Lease begin to read a paper on the topic of "School Hygiene." Both the title of the talk and Lease's humble introduction to her topic were soon cast aside. Lease began by claiming that she was qualified to speak only as a mother interested in the hygiene of home and school, but she quickly became less circumscribed. In the vibrant oratory that political opponents during the next ten years would claim was typical of her, Lease apologized that she found it "almost impossible to confine myself to the subject allotted me." Instead, she warned that the issue she needed to address was much grander. Her topic concerned the potential for scientific advancement of "the race"; such advancement, she claimed, depended upon assuring that all children would be "well-born" to parents trained in the laws of heredity. Beginning with the question of ventilation and pure water, Lease immediately connected these questions of hygiene with ideas that could best be called eugenic: "The two great objects of the best men and women of this life should be first to improve the race morally and physically; secondly, to make this earth a fit abode for the superior people who will then occupy it." Decrying the tendency of the Gilded Age toward self-indulgence with its resultant drift into "physical degeneracy and mental imbecility," Lease advocated that proper ventilation and purified water for the schools be established by the Kansas State Board of Health. Such improvements, she argued, would allow schoolrooms to create "the perfectly physical race of a new era."[14] While Lease celebrated the influence of her scientific audience in the body of her speech, in her conclusion she enshrined mothers as divinely appointed guardians of "the race." Indeed, Lease gave the impression that with God's imprimatur and science's knowledge, women would be unrivaled in their ability to better humanity.

Lease's faith in the potential to produce scientific answers to present and future problems coincided with the platform and strategies of one of the first organizations that she joined in Kansas, the Women's Christian Temperance Union. The same year that Lease first spoke in public, the president of the WCTU, Frances Willard, called for a congress of the major reform parties that led, some historians argue, to the formation of the Populist Party. With her advocacy of "Do Everything" reform, Willard's efforts formed an important precedent for Lease's political causes.[15]

Like Lease's address to the Sanitary Convention, Willard's Tenth Annual Address to the WCTU in Chicago in 1889 displayed an obsession with scientifically gathered statistics and the purported significance of those statistics. Beginning with the daunting statistic that of 7 million young American men, 5 million "never darken a church door," Willard went on to calculate that sixty-seven of one hundred criminals were young men. Pointing out that 5 percent of the population was under arrest each year, she further noted that while the population of the United States as a whole doubled every twenty-five years, the number of criminals doubled every ten, with twice as many foreign-born as native-born criminals. Decrying that "America has become the dumping ground of European cities," she concluded, "these are the figures of our degradation."[16]

Like Lease, Willard saw the solution to this problem in terms of motherhood: "Some are born mothers, some achieve motherhood, some have it thrust upon them." Willard further advocated a motherly role in reform that was not strictly of biological proportions: "Blessed beyond all is she who has carried a motherly heart in her breast since ever that heart began to beat, and in these gospel days her holiest work will be to play the part of mother to the thousands worse than motherless to whom she goes with Bible in hand and Christ enshrined in body and soul." Indeed, Willard drew the specter of motherhood on a national level, saying, "I have always looked upon America as the Majestic Mother whom her grateful daughters should gladly serve or die to save."[17]

Willard's call to action had a clear agenda, part of which served to reinforce an articulated division between an ideal of home and what ought to be excluded from such a place. In making a case for the institutionalization of alcoholics, Willard advocated "the peace, order and quiet that pertain to a normal idea of home"; she asserted however that "the kleptomaniac, the libertine, gambler and drunkard" were "morally insane and totally unfit to be harbored within home's sacred walls."[18] In drawing her domestic fortress, Willard included in her speech a biology lesson,

> There are thousands of these . . . embodied penalties of the violation of natural law in some ancestral or pre-natal state, and they are the curse of the homes in which their youth is spent. Those homes deserve protection from society, those victims of an abnormal make-up, as visible to the spirit's eyes as a humped back or goitered neck are to the physical, deserve protection from themselves. The drunkard in Chicago who pounded his sick wife to death with the body of their newborn child, was an illustration, *carried to the supreme degree, of the cruelty to which the state is not yet awakened on behalf of the home.* When women statesmen come to their own, let us hopefully believe, the home will not be left so shelterless as it is now.[19]

With the brutality of her example Willard underscored the danger those with biologically "abnormal makeup" posed to themselves. For her, the "ill-endowed" joined the "ill-conditioned" as threats to the sanctity of the home. Her solution lay in the hands of women statesmen whom she assumed would act in a maternalist fashion. Both Willard's maternalist framework and her message concerning health and hygiene influenced Lease's speech to the Sanitary Commission. As Lease's political involvement continued, she expanded this maternalist framework to encompass a much wider range of economic and social issues.

"NEW OCCASIONS TEACH NEW DUTIES"

The November election in 1888 saw Mary Lease expand both her public and political roles in significant ways. She joined the emergent Union

Labor Party, which, along with other third parties throughout the United States, rose to challenge the two parties in control. In the late 1880s, public debt almost tripled (from $15 million to $41 million), and private debt in Kansas was at nearly four times that of the nation.[20] This increase in per capita debt in Kansas thrust debt onto the political stage. Indeed with nearly 60 percent of taxed acres in Kansas mortgaged, the Union Labor Party made the state's indebtedness the major focus of its campaign in an effort to break old party lines.

In the campaign for the election of 1888, the Union Labor Party presented a platform that stressed crop failures, low crop prices, and mortgage pressure as political issues. This platform, given the situation in Kansas, was well supported by reform Republicans such as William Alfred Peffer, editor of the *Kansas Farmer*, but was not strong enough to pull the election.[21] The Republicans responded that the Union Labor Party's "senseless howls" about poverty and mortgage did more to destroy Kansas's credit and economic growth than the notorious droughts, grasshopper infestations, and tornadoes. Nevertheless, the Republican platform included a number of planks inspired by the Union Labor Party's critique of government, including promises to reduce legal interest rates, to increase penalties for usury, remedial labor legislation, destruction of the dressed beef trust, and protection for farmers from excessive railroad charges. The GOP won 39 of 40 seats in the Kansas State Senate and 121 of 125 seats in the House. Kansas in 1888 was called the "Banner State" for Republicanism.

These political victories came with a price, however. The adopted reform platform of the Republican Party in Kansas raised expectations of change. The presence of the Union Labor Party meant there was also an expectation of accountability. When the Republican legislature responded to reform legislation by sending reform proposals to the conservative Senate Judiciary Committee (where they died), some Kansans objected; most notably, William A. Peffer. A reform Republican, Peffer had called for farmers to organize themselves to defeat the manipulating party machinery; indeed his aim to "purify politics" reached back to 1881, before the drought, poor crops, and low crop prices turned everyone into a reform advocate. Peffer launched a series of editorials objecting to the business-as-usual atmosphere in state political circles and suggested that where support for a third party had seemed hasty in the 1888 election, it would actually be advisable in the 1890 election.[22]

Mary Lease's involvement in these debates went beyond participating in the union party; she also became editor of a newspaper, the *Wichita Independent*, in 1888. The inaugural issue of the *Wichita Independent* had on its masthead a verse from James Russell Lowell's ode to progress: "New Occasions Teach New Duties." The newspaper, like the poem and hymn it inspired, was devoted to "reform, truth and justice." Once again, Lease returned to her position as a mother in defending her entrance into this particular public realm:

> We have always believed in the truth and appropriateness of the candid statement, "The hand that rocks the cradle is the hand that rules the world" and as we have spent the brightest, best and happiest years of our life rocking the cradle, and finished up in that department to the entire satisfaction of all concerned, we feel it incumbent upon us to pay due regard to the remainder of the adage, and in no way can we do this as effectually as to bring the great guns of influence to the level of public opinion through the medium of a newspaper, and point them as occasion requires it straight into the faces of our foe.

Having established that her role as mother justified her role as political agitator, Lease clarified that since her biological offspring were well raised, her print offspring would be as well. The journal would be "strong and human, helpful and sympathetic, with whatever is truest and best in life and life's work." The parallels between Lease's personal situation and her position as a political commentator would end, she promised in the first issue, with her role as a mother: "Although edited by a woman, we do not intend to make it distinctively a 'Woman's Paper.'" The editorial went on to promise that the paper would not be "devoting a moments' time to the advocacy of woman's rights," though it would promote the "full and free discussion of this and other reform movements."[23]

Lease's caution with regard to women's rights was both telling and short lived. Just two years before, the American Woman Suffrage association had held its national convention in Topeka.[24] The following year, the Kansas State Convention met while the state legislature was in session and managed to secure the passage of a bill granting Kansas women municipal suffrage. The significance of this feat was noted by the national association's adoption of the yellow ribbon as the badge of suffrage in honor of the Sunflower State's accomplishment (or in honor of the Kansas state flower, the sunflower). In fact, Kansas was considered in the rhetoric of suffrage leaders at the time to be the "most progressive State in regard to women."[25]

Lease's editorials in the *Wichita Independent* acknowledged the importance of the issue of women's suffrage in Kansas, but suggested that the significance of the issue would not force the paper to compromise its independent political format: "We intend to make our paper thoroughly independent, scientific and informational." This neutral and scientific orientation would lead to a discussion of women's suffrage along with other pressing issues: "As such the question of universal franchise will be treated as one of the inevitable issues of the near future, which we must meet fairly and squarely on the broad plane of Justice."[26]

The seeming neutrality of this position was in line with the wishes of the State Suffrage Convention. Indeed, at the November 1888 meeting in Emporia, overseen by Susan B. Anthony, Laura Johns declared that the state association, in response to the rising political tensions in Kansas, would not be affiliated with political parties." Keeping women's suffrage as a single-issue, nonaffiliated political problem assured the eventual passage of the women's vote in Kansas. In a state dominated by Republicans but divided within the political ranks, Lease's paper proposed a similar, nominally neutral coarse: both parties stood in need of reform.

Though Lease declared that women's issues would not serve as the focus of the paper, her introduction of her role as mother began and ended the statement of purpose. Indeed the issue of motherhood returned in later editions of the paper often in a series of "Select Morsels" or editorial positions that included such aphorisms as: "Let us have the mother-thought on all questions"; "Woman, as well as man, should have an equal voice in wielding the destiny of the nation"; and "wctu means a nation of mothers roused in defense of their children."[28] Women's political participation was further justified by presenting mothers and children as those who bore the brunt of economic hardship. For instance, Lease saw the spread of Iowa evictions as a clear omen that English-style landlordism was establishing itself in the United States. As she noted, "the cheek of every true woman blanches as she looks in imagination upon the home-less mothers with little babes in their arms and little weeping children clinging to her skirts, turned sick and well indiscriminately from the shelter of the homes they toiled for years to build, and at the beginning of the frigid winter left homeless on the blizzard swept prairies of the North-west." Of course, the culprit of these abuses was "monopoly [which] steps in under the very folds of the stars and stripes [and] enacts scenes of robbery and brutality that puts to shame the twelfth century methods and brutal rule of blood-dyed England." As Lease noted, the Iowa evictions coincided with the government giveaway of 300,000 square miles of public domain land to railroad corporations. Her evaluation of this procedure was crystalline: "Congress was robbing the people, spoilating the public domain and instituting a stupendous system of landlordism which is to-day giving the cruel evictions and robbery of Iowa settlers to the world as its legitimate fruit."[29] By the end of November 1888 the *Wichita Independent* declared itself to have a circulation approaching a metropolitan paper and attracting letters not only from all over Kansas but from other states as well.[30] It joined 848 other publications in the state, including 18 edited by women.[31] Increasingly, however, Lease was less of an editor and more an orator for the Populist cause.

Although the Union Labor Party had been defeated in the 1888 election, Lease and others had seen the value of a third party. In response to the col-lapse of crops and crop prices in 1888, 700 local chapters of the Farmers' Alliance opened in Kansas as farmers sought both support and an organi-zation to represent their grievances. Although it mobilized thousands of farmers and, notably, their wives and families, the Alliance was politically neutral. In 1889, Alliance representatives from different states met in St. Louis to articulate a reform agenda. The St. Louis Platform included calls for the elimination of national banks, direct election of senators and the federal judiciary, a graduated income tax, postal savings banks, free and unlimited coinage of silver, and a prohibition on foreign land owner-ship.[32] The Alliance platform was politicized in 1890 when the newly formed Kansas Populist Party, who then fielded their own slate of candi-dates for the 1890 election, adopted it with only slight modification.[33] Lease addressed the Populist Party convention and was enlisted to cam-paign for the Populist ticket. As part of the 1890 campaign, Lease gave 160 stump speeches, including her now famous injunction to farmers to raise less corn and more hell.[34] The 1890 election was a decisive victory of the Populists. With 40 percent of the vote in Kansas, they sent five representatives to Congress and one to the Senate.

The election of 1890 made clear that the third-party movement needed national support to be effective, and Populists began what newspaper editors called the "Southern crusade" of "Kansas missionaries."[35] Mary Lease, along with Annie Diggs and Jerry Simpson, went to Alabama and Georgia on this campaign. Indeed, these three traveled very widely throughout the South, the Plains, and the Mountain West advocating Populist politics. It was on these various campaign trips that Lease demonstrated the extent to which Populist economic and political reforms bore directly on the home and so justified her and other women's political involvement.[36]

WOMEN AND ECONOMICS

Throughout the early 1890s, Lease worked hard to maintain her status as a mother and to demonstrate the relevance of Populist politics for the family. As she had in the case of the Iowa evictions in 1888, Lease continued to argue that politics and economics had direct impact on the home by appealing to the hardships faced by women and children.

The subject of the care of children was an especially powerful weapon in the rhetorical arsenal of the Populists. For instance, as the price of staple crops such as cotton, corn, and wheat fell from post–Civil War highs to two-thirds and even one-half their former worth in the 1880s, farmers sought explanations. The answer they were given did not make them happy, however, based as it was on something the farmers perceived as a paradox: overproduction—farmers had grown too much and so lowered prices. This was not an explanation that made sense to rural listeners. As one critic put it: "We were told two years ago to go to work and raise a big crop that was all we needed. We went to work and plowed and planted; the rains fell, the sun shone, nature smiled, and we raised the big crop that they told us to; and what came of it? Eight-cent corn, ten-cent oats, two-cent beef and no price at all for butter and eggs—that's what came of it. Then the politicians said that we suffered from over-production."[37] As this quotation makes clear, the critique of overproduction as an explanatory factor in the farmers' plight was taken to its logical, and as posited here, ridiculous extreme. How could more productivity create more want? As W. Scott Morgan put it, "To say that over-production is the cause of 'hard times' is to say that the people are too industrious; that they could make a better living if they did not work so hard."[38] This could roughly be translated into a clear indictment: "Over-production in the general and the aggregate is impossible."[39]

To answer the argument of overproduction, Populists posited an alternative scenario. To their understanding, overproduction could not provide an explanation for dropped prices as long as there existed consumers for their goods. The problem with fluctuating markets was produced by two "artificial" mechanisms: transportation or distribution and the monetary system. These two mechanisms were always in motion, changing with the whims of politicians.

Mary Lease's rhetoric replaced indignation at the absurdity of over-production arguments with indignation at systems of distribution that allowed children to starve. As she put it in an 1891 Kansas City speech: "The politicians said we suffered from over production, when 10,000 little children . . . starve to death every year in the United States and over 100,000 shop girls in New York City are forced to sell their virtue for the bread their niggard wages deny them."[40] Lease's use of this image of the shop girl argues that once the shop girl has left for the ravages of the city, she has lost the shelter of the family. This choice of depictive element is significant. It fixed the farm family in the listener's mind as one in which young women were not forced to labor outside of the family. Advocating economic and political reforms in support of a producer ethic supported the safety of the farm family and thereby supported a rural family ideal.[41]

While appeals about starving children and abused shop girls certainly made a case for the relevance of economic issues to the home and farm family, women were drawn more directly into the political and economic arena by a different type of argument forcefully presented by Lease in the 1890s. In her arguments for women's suffrage, Mary Lease made one of her strongest cases for women's full political involvement based upon the relevance of politics to the home. For instance, asked in 1893 to comment on the question, "Do Kansas Women Want the Right to Vote?", Lease responded that women have "seen the moral and spiritual eliminated

New Occasions Teach New Duties

from government, the mother-voice silenced, the mother-influence excluded, and the boy she prayed over in childhood go out from the home-
floor, from her wise counsel (for she must not follow him), and sell his
soul, prostitute his manhood, and barter his God for an image in gold on
the altar of partisan masculine politics." This lack of maternal influence in
politics, according to Lease, has effects which "enter into every detail of
the home life. When the cupboard is empty, [women] know it first."
Rather than become the "victims of men," Lease urged that if women had
the vote, they would set things right. In her words, the Kansas woman
"sees the cancer of usury eating the industries of the people—a pall of
indebtedness darkening the nation, and woman-like, she says: 'I can't
make a more complete failure than the men have made; I believe I can do
better; I want to help the laws that govern me!' "[42] The implication of
Lease's argument is that if women were allowed to vote, their maternal
influence would reform politics and restore the nation.

Lease's maternalist call for women's equality was spelled out in much
more detail the following year. On February 7, 1894, Lease delivered an
address entitled "The Legal Disabilities of Women" to a Topeka audience.
Her speech was a call to right the legal limitations imposed upon women.
Calling upon constitutional principles, Lease argued that women "are a
governed class, and governed without consent," contrary to the Fourteenth Amendment. More specifically, Lease claimed, "We have fettered
[women] with man-made laws, enslaved her and her children to debts she
had no part in incurring, made her amenable to laws she had no voice in
making, denied her representation, while imposing upon her taxation and
penal legislation, denied her that right, guaranteed by the constitution to
the citizens of the United States, 'the right to trial by a jury of her peers,'
obeying, in dumb silence the laws of man." These limitations created by
"masculine politics" not only oppressed and enslaved women, according
to Lease, they undermined the foundations of government. Lease's attack
on these injustices, however, did not proceed solely on grounds of fairness
or in defense of the constitution.

Lease's response to the "legal disabilities" imposed upon women was
to detail the consequences for the home and women's roles as mothers
before proceeding to detail how women would transform masculine politics. Echoing her 1893 speech on the women's vote, Lease claimed, "It has

been said that woman has a higher and holier sphere within the home, but the government, whose laws we must obey, whose laws we had no hand in making, comes unbidden into every home and broods at every fireside." Not only had the sacred sphere of the home been degraded, the maternal care extended to Kansas's sons was belittled, according to Lease, by teaching young men who had reached the age of majority that those women who had raised them were politically and legally "inferior." Despite their reluctant welcome and rare recognition, Lease presented women as equal to men in "every domain," and in politics possibly even superior. Women, according to Lease, were the solution to the "muddle" that men had made of politics. In her words, "Our entry as wives and mothers into the political and legislative fields is not the result of individual tastes or morbid sympathies, but as a prime necessity, for the purification of politics and the elevation of the race—a factor to remove political and legal disabilities, weed out corrupt political tricksters and bestow a blessing upon posterity." The form of that blessing from women's politics was spelled out further as "the solemn protest against mentally and physically dwarfed children, the despairing cry of crushed and starving prolitarianism, destined, despite the religious prejudice of the day, to become a mighty factor in the up building of that true republic where souls shall not know sex, where millionaires and paupers shall be unknown, and 'injury to one shall be the concern of all.' "[43] Invoking women's maternal nature for Lease held the promise of political and legal equality, but more importantly promised the transformation of society by the extension of maternal values more broadly into public life.

Lease's maternalist strategy of invoking the sanctity of women's roles as mothers was also used against her. In July of 1891, the *Topeka Capital* reported that Lease's time away from her family on the campaign trail had resulted in her son's arrest for stealing a watch.[44] Lease and her friends were quick to respond that the charge was a fabrication. In fact on a number of trips, one or more of her children had accompanied Lease. At the Omaha convention of the People's Party in 1892 and at Kansas Day at the 1893 World's Fair, Mary Lease's daughter Louise was herself a speaker. Although this attack on Lease as a mother was isolated, attacks on her femininity were common.

Hostile accounts of Lease's mannish appearance and behavior sought to undercut her ability to speak as a woman and a mother. Consider William Allen White's description of Lease's appearance: "She stood nearly six feet tall, with no figure, a thick torso and long legs. To me, she often looked like a kangaroo pyramided up from the hips to a comparatively small head. . . . She wore her hair in a Psyche knot, always neatly combed and topped by the most ungodly hats I ever saw a woman wear. She had no sex appeal—none!"[45] The preoccupation with Lease's masculinity spoke to her position as a public speaker and echoed many of the descriptions of suffragists at the time. In the eyes of her critics, the attempt to upset the "natural" position of the sexes could only be accomplished by an "unnatural" woman.

Even more vitriolic attacks on Lease extended assaults on her lack of femininity by questioning her morality. One especially vehement editorial described Lease as follows:

> At the opera house last Monday night, a miserable caricature upon womanhood, hideously ugly in feature and foul of tongue, made an ostensible political speech, but which consisted mainly of the rankest kind of personal abuse of people in this city, among which the editor of this paper understands that he came in for the principle share. . . . All we know about her is that she is hired to travel around the country by this great reform People's party, which seems to find a female blackguard a necessity in its business, spouting foul-mouthed vulgarity at $10 a night. . . . The petticoated smut-mill earns her money, but few women want to make their living that way. . . . Her venomous tongue is the only thing marketable about the old harpy, and we suppose she is justified in selling it where it commands the highest price. . . . In about a month the lantern-jawed, goggle eyed nightmare will be put out of a job, and nobody will be the worse for the mud she has tried to bespatter them.[46]

Not only was Lease's appearance unwomanly, her speech was certainly a way in which "few women would want to make a living." This allusion to illicit and immoral professions unbecoming a "reputable" woman and mother was further reinforced by describing Lease as a "petticoated smut-mill" selling herself and her "foul-mouthed vulgarity at $10 a night." Instead of taking Lease to task on economic or political issues, critics like these attacked Lease's self-professed maternalist motivations. Attacking Lease's femininity and propriety undercut her ability to speak as a reputable woman and to invoke the moral sanctity of motherhood on behalf of her political agenda.

CHARITY AND POLITICS

With the election of 1892, the Populists further strengthened their position in Kansas. The Populist candidate for governor, Lorenzo D. Lewelling, and a host of Populist legislators were voted into office. Lease herself was proposed as a Populist candidate for the U.S. Senate in 1893. With strong support from suffragists and populists, Lease contemplated a Senate campaign if only to prevent the Populist Party from fusing with the Democrats against the Republicans. A severe illness and subsequent hospitalization prevented Lease from running but not from opposing fusion. Under Lewelling's administration, Lease did hold her one and only public office, but this Populist administration was not trouble free, especially for Lease.[47]

On December 28, 1893, Governor Lewelling sent Mary Lease notice that she was being removed as chair of the State Board of Charities after only nine months of service. Newspapers and historians attribute Lewelling's maneuver to Lease's unwillingness to aid Democrat-Populist fusion by rewarding Democrats with patronage positions. Indeed Lease seems to have ignored Lewelling's specific suggestions for appointments made shortly after she took office in March 1893. As a result Lewelling was forced to approach Moses Householder, a Populist senator and board member, with suggestions for appointments, though without success. One historian has gone so far as to claim that Mary Lease "was in fact psychologically incapable of cooperating with Democrats . . . [as] an inheritance from the Civil War."[48] Lease not only refused to enact the governor's agenda, she enacted her own.

Kansas had followed the lead of legislators in Massachusetts who had formed a State Board of Charities in 1863 to oversee the various institutions that made up what was called "the pauper system." This was the first attempt to centralize state welfare activities, and Kansas was fairly innovative in its attempt to do so. As of 1886, only twelve states had such coordi-

New Occasions Teach New Duties

nating boards. The goal of these boards was not only to scientize the dispensing of charity; it was to bring efficiency, rationality, and middle-class values to philanthropy. The effect of this organization of charity was, as historian William Trattner puts it, "similar to the monopolization and trustification of big business."[49]

The Board of Charities oversaw two state insane asylums, a soldiers and orphans home, an industrial school, a reform school, a school for the blind and for the deaf and dumb, as well as an institution called the "Idiotic and Imbecile Asylum." The board met once a month, usually on the site of one of the institutions for an inspection. As her notes reveal, Lease sometimes took her children with her on these site visits. The meetings appeared without event until the December 11–13, 1893, visit to the Topeka Insane Asylum.

It was at this meeting that Mary Lease, as the only female to ever serve on the board and as its chair, spoke out. She expressed a desire to initiate a "complete sweep of republican officials from cellar to garret" by January 1st.[50] In place of these officeholders, Lease hoped to install some interesting people. First, in the role of matron of the State Insane Asylum, Householder proposed the former publisher of the Farmer's Wife, Emma D. Pack.[51] In addition, Lease proposed Dr. Anna M. Kniberg, a homeopathist, for assistant superintendent of the insane asylum. Both of these appointments speak to a reform agenda. The Farmer's Wife had served as a forum for Lease and other women's reformers for many years as well as a place to create a political agenda for women. For example, Fannie McCormick organized her campaign as the Populist nominee in 1890 for the Kansas state superintendent of public instruction and also her tenure as the first president of the National Women's Alliance in its pages.[52]

Following these proposals and a number of resignations, the state board removed to the reform school and continued its "stormy meeting" until the 16th. The stormy atmosphere seemed to be precipitated by the board's makeup. Two board members remained from the previous (Republican) administration, while Lease and Householder were Populist members.

For whatever reason, the governor removed Lease from the board in January. She responded by filing a suit with the Supreme Court contesting Lewelling's capacity to remove her without cause. The Republican court sided with Lease, who continued to make appointments in a radical way. On February 13, 1894, the board elected Fannie Vickery to be the matron of the Assawatomie Insane Asylum. By August 1894, Dr. Anna Kniberg's husband, V. R. Kniberg, would be appointed, as would Emma Pack's husband and former copublisher at the *Farmer's Wife*, J. W. Pack, who would serve as supervisor. In addition, Lease helped to secure the appointment of Mary Merrill, who would soon become the first woman to pass the bar in Lease's home county of Sedgwick.[53]

While Lease's appointments were politically informed, in other words, aimed at removing Republicans, they were also expressions of her maternalist agenda. Lease's appointments of women echoed Francis Willard's call for placing women physicians on state boards of health. (Willard reasoned that "as sanitarians [women physicians] are unexcelled if not unrivaled.")[54] Indeed, it was the WCTU's explicit policy to advocate for limited suffrage in municipal elections in order to make temperance women eligible for positions on school boards and as superintendents of education.[55] Lease used her position as head of the State Board of Charities to appoint women to posts overseeing institutions and asylums key to maintaining public health and hygiene.

Just as Willard had predicted, women statesmen (Lease and her appointees) acted to provide "expert care and treatment" for the "ill-endowed" and "ill-conditioned" in public institutions.[56] The *Topeka Advocate* noted that "the inmates of the different institutions are being fed better than ever before," at the same time the cost to taxpayers was being reduced. More far-reaching reforms were noted at the institution for "imbecile youth" at Winfield, where "attendants at lower wages, who take the inmates out and bring them in contact with fresh air and sunshine and natural objects which they have so long been denied," replaced "high priced teachers."[57] This decision was credited to the recognition by Lease's board of "the folly of attempting to educate beings absolutely destitute of mind."[58] This decision that certain wards were uneducable was a significant shift in state policy. In addition, the institutions for the blind were introducing the "Delsarte system of physical culture," which allowed the children to become more graceful and feel "less and less the difficulties of their misfortune."[59]

Lease also began to forcefully oppose Lewelling's bid for fusion. Join-

New Occasions Teach New Duties

ing forces with Cyrus Corning, editor of the *New Era*, Lease publicly attacked Lewelling in January 1894. Lease's fierce opposition to fusion and insistence on a suffrage plank fueled her criticism early in 1894. As the election neared her position softened, probably as a result of Lewelling's renewed support for workers in his Tramp Circular and the adoption of a suffrage plank by the Populists. By late 1894, Lease backed Lewelling for reelection, but Republicans capitalized on Lease's inconsistencies to belittle her and the Populist ticket. The Republicans swept the 1894 elections using suffrage to divide Populists and Democrats. The equal suffrage amendment was also defeated, further widening the split between Republicans and Populists within the Kansas Equal Suffrage Association. By March 1895, Lease had been replaced on the State Board of Charities by a Republican appointee.[60]

THE PROBLEM OF CIVILIZATION SOLVED

After the 1894 elections, still recovering from rheumatism, Lease took stock of her political future. She resisted calls to again run for office and instead decided to express her views in a book purporting a new solution to society's problems. Lease's *The Problem of Civilization Solved* (1895) drew from popular political tracts such as Edward Bellamy's *Looking Backward* (1888) and Sarah Emery's *Seven Financial Conspiracies* (1887), but added a new twist by advocating massive tropical colonization.

Unlike Bellamy, who claimed the Sphinx's Riddle for the nineteenth century was the question of labor, Lease articulated a problem she saw rooted in the redistribution of land and goods. Her opening chapter set the problem of civilization as one of "how to convert the bounty of Nature into wealth and how to divide that wealth so none may want?"[61] Lease did not offer a typical Populist solution. She did advocate strong national legislation, but not to regulate finance as much as the distribution of people and land. The problems of poverty, social unrest, and degradation of "inferior races" could be solved, according to Lease, by giving "every toiler access to the soil." With faith in the redemptive power of farming and home ownership, Lease embraced agrarian ideology completely as she argued that "a cabbage garden or potato patch with the incentive of proprietorship and compensation will keep drunkards from tippling, dead beats from mendacity, criminals from crime, and prove not only the source of health, happiness, and honesty as well as a source of revenue to the commonwealth, but a panacea also for tough sinners where soap and water, sunshine and air, work and play will take the place of the seven sacraments and the forty days fast on fish and eggs."[62] The poverty and overcrowding that made cities breeding grounds for "anarchists" would be resolved by redistributing people on the land. The problem, however, was that there was not enough available land in the Northern Hemisphere. As a result, Lease advocated colonization of the southern tropics by northern nations.

Lease's plan for tropical colonization had at its core a four-family model explicitly based on a supposed racial hierarchy. According to Lease, "fifty million white families" would be established as "planters on estates of 200 acres each."[63] These "enlightened Caucasians" would be joined by three families of tillers who would be "Negroes and Orientals." Slavery was deemed an unacceptable relationship between different races, but tenantry was considered a necessity since Lease believed that northern Caucasians were incapable of "hard manual labor under the equatorial sun."[64] Moreover, because Lease considered "negroes and Orientals" to be debased and degraded in their own societies, she argued that the tillers would be bettered by farming in contact with white families. Indeed, Lease argued that as a "superior race," it was the "duty and destiny" of whites "to become the guardian of the inferior races," and in doing so "improve his physical, moral, and spiritual being."[65] Unlike missionary work, tropical colonization would remove "Orientals" from their societies and traditions, making their conversion to Christianity more effective. In addition, the four-family approach to colonization would, according to Lease, significantly improve the lives of women. The condition of the "Oriental female" was described by Lease as one of "misery, degradation, and despair" as a result of their compulsory seclusion within the home or behind the veil, the custom of prearranged marriages, the denial of education and often medical care, and frequent female infanticide. Lease was confident that "Caucasian[s] would revolt at such barbarism."[66] Offering nonwhite families a life of "comfort and Christian influence" as farmers on tropical colonies was Lease's racial solution.

Lease admitted that her idea of governmental intervention was "paternalistic." However, she argued that unlike government support of railroads, her scheme did not give handouts to corporations but instead "aids the individual to help himself."[67] This paternalism was justified by analogy: "we acknowledge the wisdom of the state in providing asylums for the deaf, the dumb, and the blind," Lease argued, "then why should we forget and ignore the swarming millions of mankind who are afflicted with *inheritable incapacity*." The incapacity that Lease had in mind was an affliction of those "who are poor but industrious, generous to a fault . . . refined and sensitive, ardently wishing for wealth and with a deep appreciation of the comforts and luxuries of civilized life, yet hopelessly desponding and unsuccessful in the fierce battle for life within *our course and brutal civilization*." The urban poor typified this class of people that Lease depicted as "enslaved by the chain of hereditary failure and thriftlessness." Her scheme of tropical colonization would remove impoverished producers from the "pitiless, competitive system," "provide homes for the homeless," and so rescue "the victims of hereditary failure from the present state of despair."[68] This biological justification for governmental reforms distinguished Lease from typical Populist reformers who, though they also portrayed producers as victims in need of governmental support, usually pointed a finger at financial conspiracy, not hereditary failing.[69]

Lease's solution of tropical colonization was an answer to the brutal competition she saw in American cities. Farmers who had been shaped biologically and socially by their experience on the land were not able to compete in an urban environment with people bred for the competitive acquisition of wealth. Placing farmers or producers back on the land was a eugenic action in that it selected and created conditions that favored the reproduction of select groups of people with traits considered to be valuable. Lease's colonization scheme broke with the competitive ethos of social Darwinism in favor of the more-interventionist attitude typical later of eugenicists who sought to control and direct the course of human heredity.

Lease's confidence in colonization as a "vent for political danger" may have been grounded in Irish immigration. Access to land had been a major issue in Irish nationalism as it was popularized in the United States by Henry George beginning in 1882. Lease had supported George in the 1880s and would campaign again for him in 1897 when he ran for mayor of New York City.[70] But while George made known his anti-Chinese sentiments, Lease seems to have thought that the Chinese could assimilate to "American standards" and would in fact do so under her colony model.[71]

Other colonization schemes, such as Alfred K. Owen's effort to resettle midwestern farmers in Topolobampo, Mexico, may have also influenced Lease's thinking.[72] During the 1898 campaign, she wrote of "a Topolobampo schemer" who lent his support to William Jennings Bryan at the Democratic convention.[73] By this point, the Topolobampo Colony's finances had collapsed, but at the time of her writing *The Problem of Civilization Solved*, it may appeared as a viable colonization precedent.

These local colonization efforts probably were less influential than the national debates during 1893 concerning the annexation of Hawaii and widely read works on American expansion, such as Frederick Jackson Turner's speech on the American frontier or Josiah Strong's *Our Country*. Strong's celebration of the Anglo-Saxon "genius for colonization" certainly seems compatible with Lease's imperialism and racist hierarchy. Indeed, Strong's advocacy of colonization as a natural extension of Christianity would certainly have appealed to Lease.[74] Unfortunately, since *The Problem of Civilization Solved* makes no references to any other works, it is impossible to pinpoint the influences on Lease with certainty.

The response to *The Problem of Civilization Solved* was muted. It did not become the success that Sara Emery's *Seven Financial Conspiracies* or William Harvey's *Coin's Financial School* were among Populists. Nevertheless, it represented Lease's attempt to articulate a vision of political and social reform that went beyond the typical Populist agenda. Her confidence in the role that the United States should play in the world and her advocacy of the poor and exploited remained with her long after the Populist moment had faded.

A POPULIST IN NEW YORK CITY

In 1895, Populists made a strategic decision to concentrate on financial issues, most notably that of Free Silver, instead of the "more-radical" planks of the party platform, including women's suffrage. Free Silver had wide appeal as it would greatly benefit most individuals holding debt by making more money available and eliminating the gold standard for currency. For Lease and others committed to the entire party platform, this was an unacceptable compromise. Lease's disaffection with Populism did not lead her away from politics, however. As the Populists concentrated on Free Silver and fusion, Lease warily lent her support to the Democratic presidential candidate, William Jennings Bryan. Lease spent less time on the campaign trail than she had in past elections, although she did second Bryan's convention nomination. Following a miserable showing in the election, Lease found herself in financial trouble. The woman who had railed against banks' unfair mortgage practices found her own house subject to foreclosure. Her legal fight was unsuccessful, and she left for New York City by early 1897.[75] Lease took her four children with her but separated from her husband, whom she would divorce in 1901.[76]

Lease's renown as an orator followed her to New York. On October 17, 1896, her lecture at New York's Cooper's Union left her with the title "the foremost woman politician of the times" in the New York City monthly, Metropolitan magazine. As the reporter noted, Lease was "an orator whose flow of language held for three hours one of the largest audiences ever gathered in Cooper Union."[77] One historian claimed her reputation and appeal in the East at the time could be compared to that of "Buffalo Bill" Cody a few decades earlier.[78] This popularity bolstered her position reporting for Joseph Pulitzer's New York World in 1896 and 1897. Later, she would practice law, though not for a fee, and lecture as a member of the New York Socialist Literary Guild, where her subjects ranged from Einstein's theory of relativity to political economy.[79]

Politically, after leaving Kansas, Lease changed from a committed anti-fusion Populist to a Socialist campaigning for Eugene Debs, a McKinley Republican, and, finally, a Roosevelt Progressive. While this trajectory has allowed some historians to consider Lease inconsistent and struck Lease herself as strange, each political affiliation spoke to specific issues to which she was committed. After the Populists narrowed their concerns to Free Silver, the Socialists seemed like a political party still working on behalf of producers oppressed by unfair labor and banking practices. While she deplored the killing in the Philippines, the Spanish-American War reinforced Lease's imperialist inclinations and drew her to the Republican Party. In her words, "I had not sacrificed my principles. I took the stump against Bryan because he had abandoned the cause for which we

Populists had fought."[80] She had met McKinley during the 1896 campaign and publicly supported his expansionist policies. She later avidly backed Theodore Roosevelt, although she would note, "his Progressive party stole the Populist Platform plank by plank, clause by clause, without casting even the faintest shadow of a word of credit."[81]

While Lease's political affiliations shifted, her commitment to women's political equality was unwavering. In New York City she continued to push for suffrage. As she had in Kansas, she retained her maternalist persona in order to champion causes from mother's pensions to birth control. In a 1905 speech to the Eastern Commercial Teacher's Association, for instance, she argued, "We say that woman is good enough and intelligent enough to care for the bodies of the little children in the home and in the school; we impose upon her the duties of motherhood—the highest that God has intrusted—but we forbid her to enter the arena of politics. We say that while she is good enough to be the mother to our children, to care for the bodies and souls of our little ones, that she isn't intelligent enough and hasn't wisdom enough to compete with the man who collects taxes on our dogs."[82] Lease was less sure about the values ascribed to "new women." She explained in 1901 that she believed women were shaped by "industrial conditions." They rejected domesticity in favor of work as they sought "to develop their individuality." Problematically, for Lease, motherhood seemed to be undervalued by New York women. In her words, "the dog is supplanting the child as a domestic feature" on Fifth Avenue. "The man who took a census of the children there and only found fifteen in one mile of the most aristocratic portion of the avenue ought to have carried his investigations a little further and taken a census of the dogs in the same district."[83] Later, as concerns about dropping birthrates made national news, Lease asserted that "woman's part in the economy of nature is first and distinctively most important, that of motherhood." Every married couple, Lease argued, had an obligation to have at least three children.[84] Of course, she believed that the reward for this patriotic duty lay with the ballot.

Drawing on a long tradition of Agrarianism, Lease and other Populists valorized the farmer and the producer, more generally. While Populists usually targeted their appeals to voting farmers, Lease and other women repeatedly demonstrated that the economic and political issues at hand bore directly on the entire producer family. Indeed, Lease's success as a political figure depended on her ability to articulate the relationship between Populist politics and the family. When she could make this connection, Lease could invoke an ideal of family that simultaneously championed the rural producer and granted her moral authority as a mother and a woman to speak to the conditions of that producer family. Populist arguments concerning overproduction, land ownership, and ideas of health and hygiene informing the actions of the Kansas State Board of Charities articulated a relationship between the family and the state. Lease's agrarianism championed families on the land, while her maternalism suggested that greater political equality for women would strengthen the farm family by allowing women to publicly advocate economic and political reforms.

Because agrarian ideology celebrated the farmer as the source of American virtue, when Populists depicted farmers as the victims of corporate robbers or villainous bankers, they did not aim to produce sympathy for a "duped hayseed." Rather, Populists intended the victimization of the virtuous producer to generate rage at their unfair exploitation. This sense of outrage was heightened when recast in terms of the producer family. In the hands of Mary Lease, the bankers not only robbed the farmer, they starved his wife and children. Lease's maternalist strategy thus reinforced the Populists' appeal to agrarian ideology. Moreover, Lease gave this form of agrarianism a biological underpinning. Using terms familiar to nineteenth-century hereditarian thought, Lease understood the virtuous farm family to be a product of both ancestry and environment. The farmer's contact with the soil thus had significant biological and social consequences, according to Lease, as evidenced in her justification for tropical colonization in *The Problem of Civilization Solved*. Indeed, from her later perspective as a New Yorker, Lease declared in 1931 that the Great Depression was having such dire consequences because the people's "feet are no longer firmly fixed on the soil." In her mind, "a great agricultural nation should stand rooted in the soil and flourishing in the sunshine of such favored regions."[85]

3

RECLAIMING THE HOME

GEORGE H. MAXWELL AND THE HOMECROFT MOVEMENT

But there were tales of long ago, when some
brave investigator had seen it—a Big Country,
Big Houses, Plenty People—All Women.
CHARLOTTE PERKINS GILMAN,
Herland, 1915

Charlotte Perkins Gilman's 1915 novel, *Herland*, begins as three male explorers discover a utopian country inhabited only by women and children. Drawing a connection between the Edenic landscape and the civilized nature of its inhabitants, Gilman's misogynist antihero first notes the ways in which the women of Herland have managed their forests: "Talk of civilization. . . . I never saw a forest so petted, even in Germany. Look, there's not a dead bough—the vines are trained—actually! And see here . . . the kinds of trees. . . . Food-bearing, practically all of them. . . . The rest, splendid hardwood. Call this a forest? It's a truck farm!"[1] With this image of a highly cultivated, scientific forest, Gilman sets the stage for imagining a new relationship between land management and the social world in which such management occurs. Indeed *Herland* extends a long tradition of American thinking that posited a direct connection between the land and civil society.[2] Within Gilman's lifetime, debates about how land should be managed were at the heart of conservation efforts and political debate at the national and local levels. Gilman's idealized conservationist aesthetic bound together the management of surroundings and society.

Environmental management was a recurring theme in Gilman's fiction. Her earlier novel, *What Diantha Did*, first serialized in 1909 and 1910, graphically represented how a hotel run for working women could turn a profit for its investors as well as rescue women from household drudgery. The heroine was described as carefully choosing the town, Orchardina, because of its climate and conditions. As in Herland, the constructed environment enabled greater autonomy for women: "The young captain of industry had deliberately chosen Orchardina as her starting point on account of the special conditions. The even climate was favorable to 'going out by the day,' or the delivery of meals."[3] The setting for Orchardina strongly resembles the Pasadena orchards near the home of Gilman's close companion Grace Ellery Channing, which became a sort of retreat for Gilman during this time. The even climate of Orchardina and the assumption that aridity and sun were best for health echo the most idyllic pro-irrigation propaganda, since these arid climates demanded artificial means to make them flourish.[4]

In both *Herland* and *What Diantha Did*, remaking the physical structure of the setting were important parts of social change. Where the earlier novel advocated architectural methods of altering gender roles, the latter posited the relationship between the cultivation of forests and the cultivation of a culture in which gender equality was possible.[5] In both cases, the remade landscape coincided with a reconceptualization of the social world that Gilman and other women inhabited.[6] The same type of connection between the environment and social order grounded claims that land reclamation and irrigation were forms of social engineering.[7] Advocates of nationalized irrigation and land reclamation at the turn of the century shared Gilman's modernist sense of possibility and transformation with regard to the landscape. However, where Gilman imagined a new sexual order, irrigation advocates championed a nostalgic ideal of the home on the land. Indeed, the very ideal of the home that Gilman rejected in her remade landscape was the ideal of the home used to promote the reclamation of the western United States.

National reclamation and irrigation legislation passed in 1902 in part because George H. Maxwell publicly associated reclamation and homemaking. For Maxwell, "homes on the land" were as much a product of national irrigation and reclamation as the dams and canals that we now associate with efforts to bring water to the arid West. Like Gilman, Maxwell saw in the opportunity of reclaimed land the promise of social engineering, but Maxwell's vision of the society to be built on reclaimed land was profoundly nostalgic and conservative. Where Gilman envisioned greater female equality and autonomy, Maxwell envisioned women as members of male-headed families. Because "homes on the land" were promoted as a means to populate the West, Maxwell's reclamation and resettlement policies assumed women's reproductive role within the home and the family. Moreover, Maxwell's ideal of the home on the land, or what he called a "homecroft," represented a nostalgic return to an agrarian past where the home was a site of production. Emphases in Maxwell's homecroft ideal on the garden and arts and crafts were intended to shift the home from a place of consumption to a place that produced some of its own food and furnishings. Like the Populists' celebration of the farmer and producer family as both social and economic entities, Maxwell saw in reclamation and the homecroft an opportunity to refashion both production and consumption within the home.

Convinced that the city was a site of "degeneracy and decay," George Maxwell believed the salvation of the cities lay in the frontier.[8] Unlike Frederick Jackson Turner, who had just declared the frontier closed, Maxwell spent much of his time arguing that the frontier was not gone; it was merely underwatered. Nationally subsidized water valves would restore social and political order by allowing the frontier to continue as the nation's "safety valve."[9] Convinced that frontier expansion had acted as a check to the effects of industrialization and urbanization, Maxwell sought to create new "frontiers" by resettling urban families in "homes on the land" created by national irrigation and land reclamation efforts.

Born in Sonoma, California, in 1860, Maxwell invented his own system of shorthand and at an early age became the official stenographer for the U.S. Circuit Court and Superior Courts of California. This was quite an accomplishment for someone educated in the public schools in Sonoma and San Francisco. Courtroom stenography introduced Maxwell to both the law and to legal disputes over water rights, which filled the California courts in the 1880s. As a lawyer practicing in San Francisco, Maxwell defended the water rights of local farmers. With funding from the Atcheson, Topeka, and Santa Fe Railroad, Maxwell founded the National Irrigation Association in 1897 and his career as a lobbyist was born.[10] In this new career, Maxwell made a case for national rather than state control of irrigation. Fashioning himself as irrigation's "militant evangelist," Maxwell sought to publicize as widely as possible what redirecting rivers and digging ditches would produce. The consequences of irrigation were often represented in the press as schemes to increase land values for large landowners or as a source of new competition for midwestern farmers. As a result, Maxwell was challenged to explain the benefits of irrigation to the American public in a palatable form. The image of homes filled with families offered a salable vision. Under Maxwell's direction, irrigation was constructed as more than an issue of land use; it was a means to put homes on the land and populate the West. Adopting the image of the rural home as the goal of nationalized land reclamation justified spending millions of dollars for land, equipment, and loans. More important, the ideology of the home, which Maxwell made the centerpiece for his reclamation campaign, gave the idealized and essentialized "American" rural family an equally idealized place.[11]

There were good reasons for Maxwell to adopt homemaking as the motive for the campaign for the national reclamation act. Fears of profiteering by large landowners were well founded. Land owned by one of Maxwell's early sponsors, J. J. Hill of the Northern Pacific Railroad, increased from $7.81 an acre in 1900 to $126.56 an acre in 1910 because of irrigation resulting from the national Reclamation Act.[12] Public lands allocated to Hill's predecessor at the Northern Pacific Railroad in 1864 stipulated that sections of land near tracks be sold to the public at the price of $2.50 or less per acre for five years after the grant.[13] The remaining lands held by the railroad represent one of the most extensive packets of land given by the government to encourage improvement. As early as 1883, the Northern Pacific distributed over 2.5 million pieces of literature and placed ads in 200 newspapers extolling the value of the lands it served (and owned). Promoting national subsidization of irrigation for these lands would make them easier to sell and naturally increase the profits for Hill.[14]

In addition to increasing the profits of railroad owners, nationalized irrigation was seen as extending far too much sectional favor to the West as well as stepping on the individualistic toes of Western pioneers. Indeed, historians have pointed to western opposition to the bill as evidence that the ideology of individualism was too strong to allow for federal subsidies to be considered.

Until the mid-1890s, irrigation had been undertaken by private canal and land companies, with some exceptions; most notably, the Mormon settlements in Utah. The emergence of irrigation districts as a plan for watering the arid lands was in part imitative of cooperative irrigation by the Mormons. In 1887, California passed the Wright Act, which used the New England township ideal as a model for districts that would share the costs of irrigating and elect directors to oversee the projects. Local mismanagement (only 23 of 47 districts had begun construction by 1891, and of the districts with systems built, only one-tenth of the acreage was reclaimed) and problems, despite hundreds of legislative attempts to amend the act, led to the failure of the wealthiest western state to irrigate much of the proposed 2 million acres.[15]

Other western states attempted to learn by California's problems. Colorado, another wealthy state, granted oversight power to public authorities in the matter of irrigation but neglected to give such experts the jurisdiction to determine water rights. This kind of oversight led to problems similar to the kind of obstacles that had thwarted even private attempts to irrigate large swathes of land, since the first claimants to the water would use it all. This had been the kind of situation that Nevada's Francis G. Newlands had experienced in 1889 when he had tried to irrigate the Truckee River Valley. As a private developer, he had not been able to secure imminent domain and was thus subject to private speculators' claims on the water. Newlands's experience led him to back a state bill repealing common-law riparian rights and giving power to the state to appropriate water for irrigation. This, combined with other lessons from California and Colorado's attempts to irrigate, led Nevada to authorize bonds for reclamation, establish a state board of commissioners, and authorize a state engineer to allocate water rights. Despite these remedies, the state legislators would not release enough money from the School Fund to support irrigation.[16]

These state and local efforts, along with interstate conflicts over water rights, the U.S. Geological Survey's of the water supply in the arid West (funded by Congress in 1888 after years of lobbying by John Wesley Powell), and the addition of five new states and territories in 1889 set the stage for a push on the national level for irrigation. Efforts were slowed by the 1893–97 depression but resumed shortly thereafter. Elected to Congress in 1893 and to the Senate in 1903, Newlands turned to state and federal legislation to address the challenges of western irrigation. He was ultimately responsible for the passing of the Reclamation Act of 1902. With Theodore Roosevelt's support, Newlands crafted a national bill rather than an explicitly western bill. Maxwell provided the promise of homemaking, which, as historian Donald Pisani notes, united a range of political interests behind nationalized irrigation.[17] A pamphlet assessing the effect of the Reclamation Act on behalf of the Democratic Party noted that the act was "a long step forward toward the safeguarding of the welfare of the homeseekers of the Nation."[18] Roosevelt may have been more interested in winning over western republicans, however.[19] The Reclamation Act, or the Newlands Act, directed that the proceeds from the sale of public lands be expended for the "survey, examination, construction, and operation, and maintenance of irrigation works" in sixteen arid states.

IRRIGATION AND THE HOMEMAKER

The call for building great canals and reservoirs, for redirecting rivers and remaking the very lands through which they ran, was clearly a modernist call. The odes to building and the rate with which engineers rushed into the service of the irrigation districts and organizations spoke to the massive undertaking being proposed. The push to plant what had been called "the Great American Desert" was part of a call to expand: "Annex" the land, push the boundaries of "empire," and "Conquer Arid America."[20]

Indeed, "Annex Arid America!", the motto for the National Irrigation Association's magazine, National Irrigation, was more than a call for the manifest control that would someday be exerted over territories such as Arizona, Oklahoma, or New Mexico. It spoke of the vision of the West and the frontier as part of the American colonial enterprise that only a few years before had led to the annexation of Hawaii and had set its sights on Puerto Rico, Cuba, and the Philippines. William Smythe, a leading advocate for irrigation, extolled his vision of empire building in his aptly titled book of 1899, The Conquest of Arid America. The imperial promise of water pipes was laid bare in Smythe's frontispiece: "The nation reaches its hand into the Desert. The barred doors of the sleeping empire are flung wide open to the eager and the willing, that they may enter in and claim their heritage."[21] The call for the nation to reach its hand into the desert was actually set against imperial expansion into the Pacific. Smythe could not justify foreign expansion when so much of the continental United States had yet to be settled. Like Maxwell, Smythe urged the nation to construct a federal policy to assure the propagation of both its habitable territory and its citizenry.[22]

This earlier imperialist rhetoric yielded to a domestic paean when the case for nationalized irrigation was put before the public prior to 1902. Headlines introducing plans for irrigation proclaimed, "Homes for Millions." Looming class warfare and the problems of urbanization would be solved with homes on reclaimed land. As the national irrigation policy resolutions of 1901 phrased it, "rural homes are the safeguards of the nation, and the congestion of population in the great cities of the East is a growing menace to the stability of our Republican institutions, and there is no longer an outlet upon the public lands in their present condition for our surplus population."[23] Here was Turner's safety valve created by the national sponsorship of water valves. Indeed, "home-building in the West, under a broad and comprehensive national policy of irrigation, with the opening up to millions now homeless of an opportunity to secure a home on the land," became the keynote at the Trans-Mississippi Commercial Congress held in Colorado in 1901. Both Democrats and Republicans declared the same support of reclamation in the 1900 election, with the Republicans specifying that they advocated it "to provide free homes on the public domain."[24] Turner might have declared the frontier closed in 1893, but irrigation promised to extend its benefits. His wild and free lands were being reclaimed and domesticated.[25]

Maxwell often expressed his vision for reclamation in terms of filling the empty West with homes: "the creation of millions of prosperous and happy homes in places in the land which are now waste and desolate." In this way, the country could make better use of its space. The potentially troublesome masses would be removed from the eastern cities to become "a great population . . . planted where the coyote and the sage brush now hold undisputed sway."[26] While Maxwell's rhetoric emphasized the home, it often conflated homes, the people they contained, and the crops to be grown on reclaimed land. Filling the western lands with homes, for instance, was easily equated in Maxwell's rhetoric with filling the land with a crop of home builders.

Maxwell was not alone in his vision of linking reclamation and homes. As F. H. Newell, the first director of the reclamation service predicted, reclaimed lands would allow the United States to double its capacity to house its population. The object, Newell insisted, was to redistribute "the public domain into the hands of small land owners." As Donald Pisani points out, federal reclamation would visibly improve arid land, transforming deserts into watered, planted communities.[27]

The appeal of homemaking lay in more than shared domestic ideology, however. Maxwell and the National Irrigation Association emphasized the business benefits of homemaking in the West and portrayed the alternatives to homemaking in dire terms. Irrigation advocates repeatedly emphasized that homemaking on reclaimed land would create vast new markets for eastern businesses and that surplus goods produced in the West would be shipped to open new Asian markets rather than creating competition for markets on the East Coast. Without new homes on reclaimed land, these economic benefits would not be possible. Still worse, however, was the alternative—land speculation. Maxwell and his cohort sought to capitalize on the moral indignation generated by pitting the small farmer against the unscrupulous land speculator. Unless irrigation was nationalized, Maxwell argued, "the moment it was known that a reservoir or a canal was to be built to provide water for any government land, the last acre of land that could be irrigated from it would be gobbled up by speculators under scrip or desert-land locations." The result would be immense profits for a small number of speculators who were able to act quickly on the government's action.[28] To Maxwell it seemed the government should not make speculators richer; it should aid the homemaker and support the principle of the 160-acre homestead.

The power of the symbol of the home for a nationalized irrigation movement was confirmed in December 1901 when the organ for the National Irrigation Association changed its name from *National Irrigation* to the *National Homemaker*. The newly retitled journal featured a quote from Theodore Roosevelt on each issue: "Throughout our history the success of the homemaker has been but another name for the upbuilding of the nation." Roosevelt's support for reclamation was rooted in his vision of the rural home as well as the role of national government in reform. For Roosevelt, national irrigation and reclamation was an agrarian path toward national strength. "Upbuilding the nation" linked the rural home with nationalism.[29] When Roosevelt gave his first annual message in 1901, for instance, he advocated nationalized irrigation by asserting that reclaimed land "should be reserved for actual settlers." As Roosevelt put it: "The policy of National Government should be to aid irrigation . . . in such a manner as will enable people in local communities to help themselves."[30] Such statements allowed Roosevelt to justify strong national government in the name of aiding the settler or home builder. The resonance of Roosevelt's statement on irrigation with Maxwell's advocacy was not accidental; Maxwell had helped Roosevelt write this part of his annual address to the American people.[31]

Where Roosevelt and Maxwell allowed national government to impinge on Jefferson's ideal of the independent yeoman farmer, other contributors to the *National Homemaker* were also refiguring the Jeffersonian ideal as they interpreted the call to build homes on the land. The campaign for homemaking through irrigation included arguments about the "Anglo-Saxon-American desire to own a home," naturalized into "the Home-Getting Instinct." J. W. Heston, president of South Dakota Agricultural College, wrote that the farmer who owned his own home was "the chief corner-stone of our national life." Because the farm home lay "at the root of all true patriotism, and all social improvement and content," reasoned Heston, making it "easy for the average citizen to become a land owner" would "strengthen tenfold all his allegiance and devotion to his country and family." In the process the Anglo-Saxon race itself would also be strengthened.

Though Heston's article echoed Jeffersonian ideals, which tied the interests of the small farmer to those of the nation, it also naturalized the connection between farmer and nation in terms of race. By rooting the strength of the nation to the strength of a "home-getting instinct," Heston revealed that he viewed Anglo-Saxonism as something more than pride in an English heritage. Like many others at the time, Heston was part of a trend that understood Anglo-Saxonism in increasingly racial terms, although talk of racial instincts was far from the more-determinist views of race and racial traits that would come.[32] As such, satisfying "Anglo-Saxon-American home-getting instincts" by homemaking on reclaimed land strengthened the nation in agrarian terms by creating more farmers, but the same homemaking was perceived to strengthen the nation racially by encouraging the proliferation of Anglo-Saxon families. The emphasis on helping "Americans" own farm homes thus fed into a pronatalist effort: irrigation and home building signified an idealization of "our common people" whose "inherent yearning . . . to own in fee-simple some portion of the earth" would guarantee their spread.[33]

Maxwell's ideology of the home also shared this pronatalist aspect but was not explicitly racialized.[34] When he described the new homes to be built upon the land, they were filled with two things: in abstract form, an unimaged "population" and, in concrete form, "merry children." Maxwell contrasted what he characterized as the degeneracy insured by raising

Reclaiming the Home

children in city environments with an image of the home on the land as an ideal environment for raising children and shaping their character. Of course, the spread of such homes across reclaimed land also marked the spread of "merry children" necessary for the spread of the "race."[35]

Maxwell's depiction of western homes and families did not need to spell out an explicitly pronatalist vision. Much of his invocation of home included an image of the mother who would fill the site with both affection and children. The "angel in the household" resonating through Victorian culture included a western component. Art historian Corlann Gee Bush notes that women depicted in western genre paintings are almost always shown as either pregnant or with children.[36]

Compounding this essentialist understanding of women as reproducers are representations of their passivity. Historian Susan Armitage argues that where women inhabit the imagined western frontier, they exist as stereotypes primarily fulfilling the same kind of passive roles as the land and nature, in contrast to the dynamic, individualistic men "conquering" the country. The "refined lady" and the "steadfast helpmate" are the female counterparts to the Old Western myth. The former comes West as a schoolteacher, missionary, or Eastern-educated sophisticate companion who eventually demonstrates her genteel nature by somehow becoming a victim of the untamed environment. (This occurs through its "natural" agents—Native Americans, runaway horses, and unseen cliffs.)[37] Her victimization reinforces the image of her active, individualistic male rescuer counterpart. The other feminine stereotype is that of the strong, uncomplaining western wife who, unlike the "refined lady," fully adapts to the rough terrain, accepting its uncompromising hardships in silence. She becomes so unindividuated in this western saga that she can be seen as merely an extension of the farm or homestead itself. The efforts to modernize the West by reclamation fitted a new vision of technological frontier to the old frontier myth. The homes newly constructed on irrigated lands would be full of unindividuated female helpmates who could also be represented as dependent, helpless females when opponents raised cries of speculation or subsidization. Both female stereotypes could be utilized for the cause of reclamation under the rubric of "homes on the land." Woman, child, and home thus formed a holy trinity of settlement in the rhetoric of reclamation's self-described "militant evangelist" of irrigation.

By 1903, the National Irrigation Association had shortened the title of its magazine to simply, the *Homemaker*. Where issues of *National Irrigation* and the *National Homemaker* published before the passage of the 1902 Reclamation Act had naturally focused on the need for nationalized irrigation and its widespread support, issues of the *National Homemaker* and the *Homemaker* after the act passed celebrated the success and began to dwell on how national reclamation would be implemented. A new statement of the "plan of campaign" for the National Irrigation Association directed its membership to ensure that public lands be reclaimed by settlers, not speculators.

To help make the case, Maxwell's rhetoric about the home became even more sentimental. For example, in a speech before the American Hardware Manufacturers Association, to whom he promised that reclamation would create a considerable market for hardware implements because each new home would need equipment, he lauded "the man who has his home upon Mother Earth, the man who draws his living straight from Nature's granary." The recipient of the Newlands Act would be typified by "the man who is free from all the uncertainties of a wage-earners employment, the man who gathers his wife and children around his own hearthstone."[38] The ideology of the home employed by Maxwell in this instance and others drew on the sense of nostalgia associated with the home throughout the nineteenth century. The term "nostalgia" began its American usage as a medical diagnosis for an indefinable ailment appearing among soldiers during the Civil War. Similar to another medical condition of the time called "homesickness," it seemed to affect individuals who were fixated with images of home to the point that they were often unable to get up out of their cots. The early half of the nineteenth century had seen a profusion of images that linked the home with an ideal of protection, a haven that epitomized the source of affection and morality of Maxwell's "hearthstone." Popular literature, sermons, music, and paintings all equated the home with both love and beauty. Indeed, the "freshly minted cliché," "Home, Sweet Home" was penned in 1823 and quickly worked its way into the national consciousness.[39]

The furious pace with which domestic ideology proliferated in the nineteenth century attaches to its central tenant: the contrast between the home and the world. The eclipse of the home as the site of production with the introduction of industrialization and its attendant specialization and differentiation of tasks led to a separation of home and work. The resulting domestication of living space and the linking of home with both female dependency and nonmarketplace values created nostalgia for the past at the very moment of change. The emerging middle class defined its ideals by imaging its women and children as carrying on traditional practices in the shelter of the home.[40]

Prescriptive literature also began to appear that warned that homes helped to instill characteristics in malleable children. Catharine Beecher, writing the first treatise on home management without servants, noted in 1841 the impact of the home and its condition on the child. This perception about the relationship between the home and the characteristics of the individual who dwelled there changed, and the home itself came to be seen as possessing characteristics. Andrew Jackson Downing, an American popularizer of architectural reform, depicted homes "with feeling" (as revealed by their trellises and vines) and homes "without feeling" (identifiable by their barren facades and lack of landscaping). As homes themselves came to possess characteristics, they began to pictorially represent the feelings attached to them as ideals of family and affection.[41] The phrase "home feeling" was used to embody an indefinable, sentimental emotion that was registered by the evocation of home.

This image of the home and the homemaker presented in the later reclamation campaigns differed from earlier images. Before the depression of 1893, a similar attempt to nationalize irrigation had been waged by Newlands and John Wesley Powell. William Ellsworth Smythe, the primary publicist for reclamation before the mid-1890s, made the case as follows in an article titled, "The Republic of Irrigation": "Tens of thousands are menaced by real hardship, and thousands of desperate men are marching in the direction of the national capital to demand relief. . . . It almost seems as if there were more mouths to feed than food with which to satisfy them."[42] The reference to Jacob Coxey and his "Commonweal" Army, who had marched on Washington demanding federally funded jobs, was much more clearly sketched as a call to action than any of the later rhetoric about the millions who could now have homes. Nothing in the post-1902 rhetoric referred to the possibility that the small home-owners who would reclaim the land on behalf of the nation might have been "tramps." Smythe's suggestion that reclamation could solve the immediate problems of unemployed workers, such as those in Coxey's Army, would not be repeated. Instead of presenting reclamation as a stopgap effort, Maxwell was careful to emphasize its long-term rewards.

While the rhetoric of homes for the people had been used to promote the Homestead Act of 1862, the reintroduction of the ideology of the home in support of land reclamation and irrigation developed a life of its own in the hands of advocates such as Maxwell. By conducting the campaign for national water in terms of homes, irrigation and reclamation activists engaged themselves in a much more far-reaching effort to engineer homes and towns as well as dams and irrigation canals. As efforts on behalf of homemaking intensified after 1902, the social engineering associated with reclamation developed under Maxwell as a homecroft ideal and under William Smythe as a settlement ideal.

Like Maxwell, William Smythe worked as a publicist for irrigation, editing the *Irrigation Age* from 1891 to 1895. Motivated in part by the depression of 1893, Smythe articulated an ideal of the irrigation community whose self-sufficiency would insulate it from an erratic economy.[43] Smythe put this ideal into practice when he started the "Little Landers" colonies in Southern California. Named after Bolton Hall's concept of "Little Lands," these utopian communities were founded on the promise that with intensive cultivation a single acre would supply a living and food for a single family. Smythe sold the plots for between $350 and $550 an acre on land directly across from the Mexican border near San Diego in a place he called San Ysidro in 1908. Similar projects were undertaken by Smythe near Los Angeles (in a suburb now renamed Tujunga, from the Spanish for "little lands," "los terrenitos") and near San Francisco, where a third colony called "Hayward Heath" was established close to present-day Hayward.[44] Despite his high hopes, Smythe's Little Lands colonies revealed the problems with implementing the home-acre idea. Residents required outside employment to make ends meet, were unable to intensively cultivate if they were older or retired, and were too poorly trained in local growing practices to allow many of them to make a living from the Little Landers Market in San Diego where they sold their produce. In addition, fighting, which took place directly across the border in 1911 when the Industrial Workers of the World (IWW) encouraged socialist insurrection against the Mexican government, discouraged growth of the colony at a crucial stage in its development. Of those who stayed, a flood in 1916 left 150 Little Landers homeless, two dead, and land ruined for farming. Hopes of rebuilding were further undercut by the large number of younger men who joined the military to fight in Europe the next year. By 1918, Smythe's first colony was no longer viable, and he left Southern California.

George Maxwell's ambitious advocacy of home-building took the form of what he called the "homecroft movement." Like Smythe, Maxwell proposed settlements, but he also advocated the development of individual homecrofts in cities and towns all over America. Invoking a long tradition of agrarianism, Maxwell embraced a nostalgic ideology of the rural home as a place that fostered the development of valued traits through the productive relationship of its inhabitants and the land. Inspired by the rural housing built for workers by the Cadbury Company (made famous for its chocolates) outside of Birmingham, England, Maxwell borrowed the English term for small garden and offered it as the logical extension of reclamation efforts.[45] As he defined it, a homecroft was "an individual home on the land, however small, owned and intensively cultivated by the occupant and his family, which contributes to the family food supply, but is not large enough to be called a farm or to support them by its tillage, without other employment."[46]

He proposed a slogan for the homecroft movement that made crystalline the kinds of connections implied in the reclamation campaign. The assumed dependence of women suggested by the image of the home with its reproductive imperative for cultivating offspring as well as crops was made clear in the "Patriotic slogan" of the homecrofters: "Every Child in a Garden . . . Every Mother in a Homecroft . . . and Individual Industrial Independence for Every Worker in a Home of his Own on the Land."[47]

In 1902, Maxwell launched a magazine to publicize his vision of how irrigation could remake the entire country. Calling it *Maxwell's Talisman*, he offered it as an amulet for curing social ills. The magic of connecting people with land in a program calling for cooperative endeavors, home ownership for workers, and children's education reforms would reinforce civic and social interactions in country and suburban villages and towns "where Trade and Industry can be so firmly anchored that they cannot be drawn into the Commercial Maelstrom that is now steadily sucking Industry and Humanity into the Vortex of the Great Cities." Where Maxwell's reclamation efforts represent an attempt to rationally manipulate the country's land and population by redistributing both water and people, his homecroft efforts evince a determination to tie people to the land for the short and long terms. He would ease the population onto the land and instill in their children a love for it. Homecrofts, like the suburbs that would follow in the 1930s, would be built near factories or other places of employment and would contain special educational facilities for working with the children of laborers in public gardens.[48]

Maxwell was careful not to identify his efforts with the "back to the land" movement, which urged city workers to move to the country. A series of reforms after the Civil War had attempted to organize or implement efforts to cure the ills of urbanization by simply moving workers onto the land. These included Horace Greely's land colony in 1870, Archbishop John Ireland's attempt to have urban Catholics reproduce themselves at a higher rate by setting up five agricultural colonies near Minnesota in 1873, the Salvation Army's three settlements for the poor, and many others. Most of these colonies were a response to the depression of 1873 and its visible effects on displaced workers. Colonies had the appeal of housing and employing urbanites while developing the unimproved lands of the West. Theories about these lands included an argument that the Great American Desert could be fundamentally changed by cultivation, since abundant rainfall in the early 1870s produced the perception that plowing actually produced rain. The region's true aridity disproved this theory and provided an example of the need for irrigation that would be used by Maxwell and others.

Instead of entirely removing workers to the country, Maxwell urged giving the worker a home in the suburbs, "where he can have a garden and poultry yard, and where his children can have sunshine and fresh air without stint." The effects of this plan would become apparent since it would "have largely done away with the evils that are causing the denizens of the congested quarters of our great cities: physical degeneracy, tuberculosis, and social, moral and political dangers too numerous to be enumerated."[49] Maxwell argued for an organic connection between the physical surroundings and the physical welfare of the people inhabiting such places. As he described his ideal, having "each family in a home and each home on a garden" would produce "health and strength by the labor of cultivating food for the family."[50]

Maxwell's perception of a connection between social ills and the congested quarters of crowded city neighborhoods was widely shared. From 1865 to 1910, the parks and playgrounds movement used open space and trees as curative antidotes for urban life, with Boston initiating the first park movement under the guidance of Frederick Law Olmsted in 1893. This same year, the Columbian Exposition's "White City" demonstration of urban aesthetics launched a nationwide "city beautiful" movement with its increasingly rural-inspired aesthetics—sweeping vistas, tree-lined boulevards, parks, and civic centers constructed like monumental town halls.[51]

A shift in perceptions about ideal civic beauty also brought a shift in perceptions of civic problems. Notably, what for generations had been seen as the "housing problem," became, when localized in overcrowded tenements, a "slum problem," with the street and neighborhood along with the dwelling itself as the source of concern. Carol Christensen points out that Progressive Era focus on "family" as the primary group of influence meant that streets and neighborhoods had to be reformed for the sake of the children growing up in them. Tenements in the worst, most crowded quarters were torn down to build $5 million worth of small parks in New York in 1894, and large spaces were opened up near the most densely populated area in Boston in 1889. These actions addressed the characteristic darkness associated with slums, replacing it with open, grass-filled, natural spaces.[52]

Even as the city beautiful movement reworked the most crowded urban precincts, though, the problem was being redefined. It was not simply a need for light and nature that caused urban ills; it was congestion. Elgin Gould, a major proponent of the idea of philanthropic housing urged that reform-minded capitalists build worker housing on city peripheries. The newly emerging transportation technology—streetcars—would allow the better-paid workers to leave the tenement districts, reducing crowding in those neighborhoods.

As overcrowding came to be seen as the primary cause of urban problems, reformers turned to decentralization as the answer. The 1906 Committee on Congestion of Population in New York City urged that cities be allowed to restrict factories to suburban areas or to places where employers could assure urban officials that "due regard" for the "welfare" of workers, including "securing the proper transport facilities," had been paid. Concern about congestion inspired the first National Conference on City Planning and the Problems of Congestion in 1909, financed by Henry Morgathau. The "cure" for congestion embraced by the first decade of the twentieth century was redistributing the population from city centers to outlying areas.[53]

Maxwell's homecroft ideal sought to combine the connection to nature of the parks movement with the decentralization of the city planning movement. In 1905, Maxwell first attempted to establish a homecroft community in the Boston suburb of Watertown. He had left the Chicago headquarters of his publishing enterprise to accompany his children when they moved to Boston for college. Both Ruth Maxwell and her brother, Donald Hebard Maxwell, went to MIT from 1904 to 1908. They followed the trajectory of their father's ideas to some extent, with Ruth studying architecture and Donald learning sanitary engineering. It is not clear whether either child helped Maxwell plan his homecroft experiment.[54]

The central feature of the Watertown homecroft experiment was not the wholesale settlement of city dwellers but a series of gardens and guildhalls. In 1905, Maxwell bought the Wilson estate in Watertown. By 1906 he reported that the old Wilson residence was being used for a guildhall and shops. In addition, Miss Jenny Avis Turner had been selected to direct the guildhall's weaving department.[55] Maxwell's plan for Watertown was to "build a model demonstration and transform Watertown as it existed into what would have been, in reality, in a very practical way, an Educational Institute in the new Art and Science of living from the Land on the part of all people in an industrial Community."[56] As it came to be, the educational institute consisted of, on the one hand, a gardening program, which emphasized a connection to the land through nature study as well as the practical business of growing food, and, on the other hand, the guildhall, which emphasized the production of arts and crafts.

Maxwell's emphasis on guildhalls and gardens resonated with the sentiments of leaders of the flourishing Arts and Crafts movement who advocated a return to the land and a simpler life. Begun by artist William Morris in London when he built his Red House as a demonstration of the relationship between art, craft, and social reform, the Arts and Crafts movement sought to connect art and labor by encouraging the handmade over the machine-produced, particularly when it came to objects for the home.[57] Morris's aesthetic was antiurban and nostalgically projected a pastoral, anticapitalist image of the past as a guide to the future of England.[58]

In the United States, Gustav Stickley translated this craftsman ideal into the terms of American agrarianism. Echoing the Jeffersonian ideal of the self-reliant and independent farmer as the "backbone of the nation," Stickley argued that the combination of intensive agriculture and arts and crafts was "the best means of relieving the congestion in our cities, counteracting the evils of the factory system, and doing away with the menace of the unemployed."[59] Stickley even approached the U.S. Department of Agriculture with a plan for establishing handicraft training schools in farm communities. Stickley's alliance of agriculture and handicraft followed the philosophy developed by the anarchist leader Peter Kropotkin. As part of his effort to decentralize the economy, Kropotkin envisioned small-scale production combining intensive agriculture and small handicraft workshops.[60] Kropotkin's work on agricultural organization was serialized in Maxwell's Talisman and certainly influenced the construction of the homecroft ideal.

Maxwell's emphasis on the guildhall in Watertown, which was officially designated the Homecroft Guild of the Talisman, also borrowed from the earlier Roycroft movement founded by Elbert Hubbard. Aside from the obvious similarity in their names, the homecroft and Roycroft movements both advocated arts and crafts as part of a simpler way of life. Hubbard had created a Roycroft community in East Aurora, New York, which functioned as a set of workshops for men and women making and selling furniture and other decorative arts and crafts. The Roycroft community attracted a number of skilled artisans and employed a large number of local boys and girls in the production of different craft items, such as hand-tinted books. From the rustic English Tudor hotel built to house visitors to Hubbard's preferred form of address as Fra Elbertus, Hubbard manufactured an Old English style. This deliberately affected and romanticized connection to England allowed Hubbard to distance himself from the modern and industrialized American city and to promote the Roycroft

Advertisement for woven crafts produced in the Watertown guildhall.

(From Maxwell's Talisman, March 1907, 95)

community as an answer to urban ills.[61] Indeed in 1902, Hubbard claimed that "in one obscure village I have had something to do with stopping the mad desire on the part of young people to get out of the country and flock to the cities."[62] This kind of claim would have naturally attracted Maxwell's interest.

The fact that Maxwell would see the construction of guildhalls as part of social reform also speaks to his connection to Arts and Crafts ideas as they developed in Chicago, where the National Irrigation Association had its home office. The growth of "Nature's Metropolis" in the last half of the nineteenth century had been extraordinary. Chicago had used its emerging status as a center point of trade to fashion itself as the ascendant center of American progress. Indeed, the 1893 World's Colombian Exposition was as much a celebration of the "White City's" locale as the New World ideas presented for the country. The University of Chicago set itself as the central proliferator of newly fashioned scientific ideas about organizing society, following intellectually in the footsteps of social reformers such as Jane Addams and Ellen Gates Starr, who had set up the country's first settlement house in an attempt to refashion immigrants and neighborhoods from the streets where they lived.[63]

In fact, it was Addams and Starr who introduced the Arts and Crafts ideal to the Chicago public in 1897. The Chicago Society of Arts and Crafts was organized through the classes offered at Hull House, encouraging neighborhood residents to learn or practice such traditional crafts as lace making and bookbinding.[64] In the spring of 1898 this group's 128 members represented the most prominent figures in the city's business, philanthropy, academic, and reform circles. While they shared easterners' advocacy of a "just" aesthetic, the groups' members saw the role of Arts and Crafts as allowing the worker to resist the alienating processes of industrial labor and thereby aiding the processes of civic, social, and industrial reorganization.[65] While Maxwell viewed the social settlement tradition of Hull House as fundamentally flawed because he did not think that it addressed the urban environment as a cause of degeneration, he did value Arts and Crafts as a productive form of work and a valuable educational tool.[66]

Maxwell was not the only one blending "homecraft" and country life in Massachusetts. In 1902, Unitarian minister Edward Pearson Pressey had established New Clairvaux in Montague, Massachusetts. Luring college-educated men and women back to the land, Pressey's community mixed basic agriculture with arts and crafts such as woodworking, weaving, and printing. Inspired by Hubbard's Roycroft movement, New Clairvaux shared many of the same ideals as Maxwell's homecrofts. Closer to Boston, however, another Unitarian minister, George Emery Littlefield, established Fellowship Farms in Westwood in 1906. Designed as a cooperative, Fellowship Farms was influenced by Littlefield's socialism and was oriented toward workers. Workers would buy an interest in the farm's communal property and could buy additional land on installment. Because Littlefield was himself a craftsman, Fellowship Farms was intended to be organized around a Fellowship Workshop and the communal production of crafts. Most of Littlefield's "colonists" kept their jobs in Boston, but Littlefield went on to form six more Fellowship Farms around the country.[67]

It is hard to judge the success of the Watertown guildhall from the existing records, but *Maxwell's Talisman* was often filled with reports and photographs of the homecroft's garden programs. In addition to the grounds of the old Wilson estate in Watertown, Maxwell set up gardens on the outskirts of town for boys and also at his nearby Newton, Massachusetts, house—called "Homecroft-on-the-Charles"—where more than one hundred children were enrolled in yet another garden program. Elizabeth S. Hill was appointed the gardens director and supervised the program for children of all ages. Hill herself was an advocate for school gardens and promoted them as a means of nature study.[68] Both Maxwell and Hill were early leaders in the school garden movement, urging that each child spend some part of the day in direct contact with nature.[69]

Part of the attempt to connect an increasingly urban population with nature, school gardens granted children growing up in built environs a romanticized encounter with the outdoors, connecting them in the process with seasons, cycles, and a sense of order. As one advocate put it: "To allow a child to grow up without planting a seed or rearing a plant is a crime against civilized society," with "armies of tramps and hordes of hoodlums . . . the first fruits of an educational system that slights such a matter."[70]

Teaching children to plant small plots of land on school grounds disciplined children for work and taught them cooperation, patience, and responsibility. As an advocate of nationalized irrigation, Maxwell thought gardens would also train future reclamationists, promising them employment on the "under-utilized arid lands of the West." He actually made school gardens a platform issue for his reclamation campaign. He insisted that every citizen had a right to receive an education "which will train him to earn a living and get his living straight from Mother Earth."[71]

Maxwell's gardening scheme spoke to nostalgia for self-sufficiency as epitomized in gardens for growing the family's food. The vegetable garden or "kitchen garden" had long been considered a female domain. In all but the wealthiest homes before the turn of the century, tending the garden was an important part of household life. Even in town homes, any land behind the house was used for a kitchen garden and poultry yard along with other light agricultural pursuits, space permitting. In this way, even the urban or town home was a site of production.

With improved transportation and distribution networks as well as the rise of chain and self-service grocery stores, the home became a site of consumption. With a grocery store on the corner, there was a decreasing need for storing out-of-season fruits and vegetables in root cellars or in canning jars. The rise of suburban life and the emergence of domestic science further shifted the home and the woman in it from a domestic manager who oversaw the production of household goods into one of educated consumer, wisely selecting from the myriad of choices offered to her as "Mrs. Consumer."[72] As part of this shift, gardening books such as Mabel Osgood Wright's *The Garden of the Commuter's Wife* (1901) began to urge women to convert the kitchen garden into a showcase for flowers. The home as showcase was a symbol of upward mobility and modernization, where the backyard became a place to play rather than a "home factory."[73]

Maxwell's call for intensely gardened home plots was a nostalgic return to the home as site of production. Resisting the social changes that made the home a consumer showcase reinforced the family as a social unit and assumed that women would supplement their husband's wage income yet remain dependent. More important, keeping the family in contact with the land was a means for Maxwell of maintaining virtue and vitality associated with Jeffersonian agrarianism.

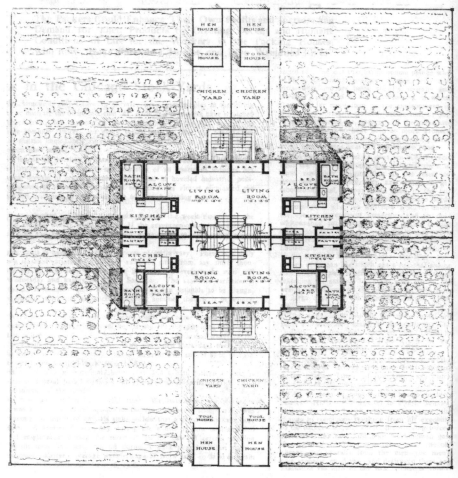

Ground plan for a four-in-one unit designed by Allen W. Jackson for
George H. Maxwell according to his homecroft ideas.
(From Maxwell's Talisman, August 1906, 9)

The garden was more than a means to remedy some of the harmful effects of the city, however; it was also an indicator of racial superiority. Maxwell was fond of holding up the Japanese as a model of a "nation of gardeners."[74] According to Maxwell, "the pygmy nation of Japan" was able to defeat Russia because of the physical and mental efficiency of the entire people. "The Japanese people," he continued, "are strong because they live as the human animal must live to be mentally and physically strong— next to nature. They breathe fresh air. They eat plain food. They neither starve nor gorge. They are an out-of-doors people. They understand the laws of health and obey them. Their children draw their strength from the bosom of Mother Earth. And above and beyond all, they are a nation of homes and home-owners."[75] If the guildhall celebrated Anglo-Saxon heritage, the garden in Maxwell's vision maintained the mental and physical strength of the nation.[76]

At roughly the same time Maxwell was establishing the Watertown homecroft, he established a second homecroft in Arizona as part of the Salt River Valley irrigation project. Where Watertown had emphasized gardens and guilds, the Salt River homecroft was a community of small truck farms. Maxwell had established ties in Arizona as early as 1901. Amid the turmoil surrounding the nationalization of irrigation, Maxwell pushed Arizonans to form the Salt River Valley Water Users Association in 1902 and used his familiarity with the Reclamation Act to help guide their federal appeal for funding of projects such as the Tonto Dam.[77] When Maxwell then moved to establish his Salt River Valley homecroft in 1906, he declared it to be "a logical enlargement of the central idea around which the National Irrigation Movement was organized."[78] Maxwell bought a 160-acre parcel of land, which he divided and sold as 5-acre plots. The land had been developed in that Maxwell had paid to have it leveled, to have trees planted, and to have irrigation ditches and wells dug. In order to buy a plot you had to have had some experience at truck farming or poultry raising.[79]

While Maxwell would eventually establish homecroft communities in Arizona, Minnesota, and Indiana as well as Massachusetts, he was always in need of funding to expand his efforts. Beginning in 1907, Maxwell promoted a National Homecroft Bill meant to support and spread the homecroft idea across the nation. This bill was, from Maxwell's perspective, "the only antidote for the mirage of political socialism and offers the only real solution of modern social problems and the only effective safe guard against the fast gathering dangers of social unrest and discontent." The key economic provision of the Homecroft Bill was the creation of a national postal savings bank. These banks were meant to offer an accessible form of banking for rural people, but the homecroft version was unique in that it would invest their savings in forestry and conservation projects. In addition to the bank, the Homecroft Bill called for the reclamation of swamp and arid land for use by homecrofters as well as the establishment of model homecroft villages.[80]

The National Homecroft Bill failed. Historian Donald Pisani suggests that perhaps Maxwell had lost his political clout in Washington by 1907.[81] But by 1907 Roosevelt's entire conservation agenda was meeting with congressional opposition. Maxwell's proposal asked for a substantial investment that would also create a source of funding for forestry outside of congressional control. The Homecroft Bill would have united forestry, irrigation, conservation, and the homecrofters, but Roosevelt had his own idea for how to unite conservation and country life.

Although this early effort was not successful, the return of U.S. servicemen from overseas after the Great War presented another opportunity to campaign for nationally subsidized homecrofts as an alternative to soldier's pensions. As a result, Maxwell's insistence on the economic independence to be gained through homecrofts reached its peak shortly after the Great War.

A tradition of granting bounty lands to veterans had begun after the American Revolution and continued through conflicts from the War of 1812 to the Mexican-American War. During the Civil War, the Homestead Act of 1862 superseded the tradition on the assumption that soldiers, like all Americans, would take the "free lands" in the West as they desired.[82] When the tradition was revived after the Great War, a series of a dozen national bills were proposed that changed the tradition of allocating land to soldiers. Each of the bills made some provision for associating the bounty lands with reclamation. One bill made land claims part of a provision that would employ returning soldiers in the reclamation service with a right to acquire the newly reclaimed land at a reasonable fee. Other bills suggested ways to put the soldiers directly onto the land. One called for the Treasury Department to establish a National Colonization Board to develop the colonization of agricultural lands, while another called for the Department of the Interior to finance the preparation of farmlands, including reclamation and clearing, and then supply the buildings, implements, and livestock needed by the returning veterans. Similar proposals were made in almost every state as well.[83]

On March 5, 1920, George Maxwell testified before the House Ways and Means Committee in support of the Fletcher-Smith Bill, which proposed settling returning soldiers on reclaimed land.[84] Maxwell favored the bill as an alternative to monetary bonuses or pensions for veterans. From his perspective, cash bonuses and pensions were not in the soldier's best interest because they did not stabilize present jobs or buffer against falling wages. With characteristic flair, Maxwell warned of the disastrous effects that vast numbers of unemployed men could have on wages and prices as they drove the economy into a depression. Pensions, he warned, would do little to prevent what he termed a "cycle of collapse." What was needed instead was a solution that would prevent complete unemployment and minimize competition for labor. Not surprisingly, Maxwell argued that his scheme of providing small farms and homecrofts on reclaimed land was exactly what was needed.

In this context, Maxwell presented homecrofts as an economic alternative first and a social alternative second. In his testimony before Congress, he explained that homecrofts provided a noncompetitive form of employment for the wage earner and unemployed alike. The food produced in homecroft gardens and the small income from the sale of household crafts would buffer against the effects of unemployment and prevent employers from lowering wages in a competitive job market. In his words, "Give the ex–service man the increased value of a quarter-acre lot near his place of employment, . . . and you have given him a larger bonus right there in the increased value of his property than it is proposed to give him in the form of a cash bonus, and you have in addition given him an anchorage on the land, which is of value to him beyond estimation in money. He has an anchorage against industrial vicissitudes that would enable him to ride out any storm." According to Maxwell, this small measure of self-sufficiency would also draw the homecrofter out of his dependency on wages and in the long run counter the social unrest inevitably produced with increasing class division.[85] The homecroft ideal thus entailed a revival of the family home on the land as a site of production instead of as a site of consumption. It was an economic plan designed to address the flaws of a wage-based economy and the type of society that it produces.

The idea of community-centered settlements was not always warmly received. Representatives of the National Grange argued that soldier settlements would increase competition with farmers. For them, the soldier settlement idea was "fundamentally un-American" and "paternalistic, socialistic, communistic, Bolshevistic, or anything of that kind" to boot.[86]

While Maxwell was not successful at creating homecroft-style soldier settlements, Elwood Mead was able to create two soldier settlement colonies in California's Central Valley. These communities were designed to use irrigated land to serve the dual purpose of providing farms for servicemen returning from World War I and providing white farm workers the opportunity to become landowners.[87] Mead's irrigation colonies at Delhi and Durham were state-subsidized communities modeled on settlements Mead had visited in Australia.[88] Unlike Smythe's Little Lands communities, Delhi and Durham were carefully planned and heavily overseen by agricultural experts and state authorities. Potential community members were screened for suitability, with special emphasis given to their interest and abilities to succeed in a rural farm setting. Mead's colony at Durham developed a cooperative economic strategy that entailed shared means of storage and distribution of their individual farm's produce. Like country life reformers, Mead also recognized the importance of the "Farmer's Wife."[89] The success of the farm depended on the training and support of farm women, according to Mead. If families were to stay on the land, they had to be incorporated into the economy of the household. By building communities, Mead also hoped to reduce the sense of isolation associated with rural farm life. Community centers in Delhi and Durham were crucial in Mead's vision as centers of an active social life necessary to keep families on the land. Despite Mead's careful planning, the community at Delhi did not flourish.

While Maxwell did not have the governmental support that Mead enjoyed, his ideas did take root in communities organized in Indiana and Minnesota. Before the First World War, Duluth, Minnesota, adopted Maxwell's homecroft plan. From vacant-lot gardens to backyard gardens, the homecroft idea inspired Duluth's developers to increase lot sizes and develop a neighborhood and school dedicated to homecrofting ideals.[90] A massive fire in 1918 destroyed the homecroft school and much of the neighborhood. The idea of a homecroft community was revived in Indianapolis in 1920. Touted by Maxwell as "the Indiana plan," the Indianapolis suburb designed by Maxwell and local developers featured long lots for vegetable gardens, chicken coops, rabbit hutches, and even a goat yard.[91] Homecroft, Indiana, was built and still stands today. The economic need for homecrofting was soon lost, however; "submerged," in Maxwell's words, "by a wave of riotous prosperity" in the 1920s.[92] The depression and New Deal could have led to a resurgence of homecroft ideals. Indeed, Maxwell saw homecrofting ideas revived in the form of the Subsistence Homestead Program. Maxwell has also been credited with inspiring the Civilian Conservation Corps.[93] Maxwell himself was involved in neither program. He spent his last years in Arizona, near his once-planned Salt River homecroft site. Incapacitated by a stroke in 1940, he died in 1946.[94]

RECLAMATION AS WELFARE

The Reclamation Act of 1902 has been interpreted as the first major national welfare act.[95] Like other policies usually considered under the rubric of welfare, reclamation policy, in Maxwell's hands, was a social policy; it was directed at creating and reinforcing social structures as much as structures of concrete and steel. Like other social welfare programs, it assumed an ideal of the family or family ethic, which had significantly different implications for men and women. Maxwell's family ideal, however, was not the family ideal assumed in other social welfare reforms. By returning production to the home, Maxwell articulated a producer family ethic.

Maxwell's image of the home and family on the land played on popular anxieties concerning the social ills created by urbanization and the economic and social turmoil caused by industrialization. The homecroft offered an ideal of the family whose self-sufficiency insulated it from industrial life and invoked a romanticized rural life at the heart of American agrarianism.[96] Maxwell tempered his nostalgia for the rural life by rejecting a complete return to the land, however. Over the course of his advocacy for homecrofts, Maxwell's ambitions for entire colonies on reclaimed land gave way to suburban communities, such as those in Duluth and Indianapolis, whose gardens and livestock yards could help insulate them from a fluctuating economy. Nevertheless, the ideal of the family that he advocated remained importantly different from the "industrial family ethic" usually associated with the U.S. welfare state.[97]

Institutionalized and refined during the nineteenth century, the industrial family ethic normalized a family structure in which a "father/breadwinner . . . works for a wage and a mother/wife . . . provides unpaid domestic work."[98] As this "industrial family ethic" became established women were increasingly excluded from economically productive labor, while their reproductive and homemaking roles expanded.[99] Protective labor legislation, child labor laws, mother's pensions, and compulsory education further reinforced this ideal of the family and dependence on a male-earned family wage.[100] The industrial family ethic ensured that a hierarchy based on wage earning would be maintained within the family. At the same time, stability in the face of economic change required some independence from wage earning.[101] This male breadwinner model cast women as subordinate and economically dependent.[102]

By refiguring the home as a site of production essential for economic stability, Maxwell sought to restore women's roles as producers as well as consumers. In doing so, Maxwell offered an alternative vision of how the state ought to intervene on behalf of the family. If the industrial family ideal allows most American welfare efforts to be characterized as a "strong male-breadwinner" ethic, Maxwell's producer family ideal allows his reclamation campaigns to be characterized as what Jane Lewis calls a "modified male-breadwinner" model.[103] Lewis takes France to be emblematic of a modified male-breadwinner state, because of a family-oriented policy of compensating parents for child-rearing costs. The French policy was historically motivated by pronatalist concerns and had the effect of making French policy sensitive to changing family roles and structures. Certainly Maxwell was sympathetic to American pronatalist concerns, and his family ideal acknowledged women's reproductive role. Where France paid direct family pensions, however, reclamation and resettlement provided more-indirect aid, which created further dependence on state supports.

Reclaiming the Home

Maxwell's focus on the producer family precluded support for the other types of policies being proposed, including veterans' and mothers' pensions, soldiers' bonuses, and various forms of insurance, which were meant to compensate for fluctuations in wages or employment. In Maxwell's opinion, because such policies were based on the principle of an exclusive male breadwinner earning a family wage, they provided little or no economic stability. Instead, the ideal of the producer family led Maxwell to emphasize social policies that established funds for the purchase of homesteads, the purchase of quarter-acre lots for homecrofts, or, in the case of returning soldiers, the direct transfer of reclaimed land. Maxwell touted these kinds of policies as individualistic, since they put families on the land, encouraged greater self-sufficiency, and did not require additional governmental support. Contrary to the rhetoric, however, every settlement project, including the homecroft settlements, required further intervention to provide agricultural training and sustain the community.[104]

Maxwell's ideal of the producer family certainly extended Populist concerns for the producer, yet the producer family was at odds with contemporary models of state intervention on behalf of urban families. Indeed, as agribusiness was modernized, it was even at odds with the model of the rural family being advocated by the government. National efforts to reform farm life under the rubric of the country life movement began with a similarly romanticized view of the value of the rural family, but by the 1920s the focus had shifted from rural life to farm business. Government programs for modernizing agribusiness had a direct impact on farm women. Government policies sought to separate women's labor from the farm's productive labor and the imposition of a separate-spheres ideology urged women to become consumers instead of producers. While many rural women resisted the suggestion that they take a less-active role as producers within the farm family, their views—and Maxwell's view—were in the minority.[105]

For Maxwell, reclamation was a social policy on behalf of working men, their wives, and their children—reclaiming the land was a means of reclaiming the family. Just as traditional U.S. welfare policies reinforced an "industrial family ethic," reclamation as homemaking argued for state support by appealing to an ideology of the home and family. Like the industrial family ethic, the ideal of the producer family featured women as mothers and homemakers, but it introduced a significant alteration to the ideology of the male breadwinner and family wage. The homecroft ideal maintained that women's responsibilities included productive labor in the garden, the orchard, and the livestock yard as well as the guildhall and community center. This labor by women was interpreted as freeing the family from total dependence on industrial wages. When considered from the perspective of pronatalism, the United States invested in reclamation for the same reason it invested in mothers' pensions; the reproduction of its citizenry. Maxwell's homecrofts represented more than a cure for urban ills and industrial woes. They were a means of producing "virtuous citizens." Women's contributions to the homecroft were therefore both productive and reproductive. Maxwell's advocacy of reclamation with home building may have revived an agrarian ideal of the yeoman farmer as a small, independent land-holder, but this ideal of the home and homemaking also assumed the unpaid labor of the women and children within those homes.

4

THE POLITICAL ECONOMY OF SEX

EDWARD A. ROSS AND RACE SUICIDE

In the days of cow-hide and grain-leather boots,
large families were the rule.
"Patent Leather and Babeless Marriage,"
Sacramento Bee, 1905

In the March 1911 edition of *Good Health* magazine, Ellen Swallow Richards claimed that she had discovered the "true cause of race suicide." As a founder of the field of home economics and an instructor of "sanitary chemistry" at MIT, Richards was a pioneer in the study of nutrition, and it was naturally in the field of nutrition that she found the real roots of what was seen as a pressing issue of the day, race suicide. Commenting as much on social habits as on nutrition, Richards argued that leisure and lack of "interesting occupations" allowed women the time to "sit in rocking chairs and read novels." Problems began, however, with "the habit of nibbling sweets with the novels," leading to "perverted taste in food as well as literature." More seriously, these women had too much food and not enough work, with "the logical biological result that grandchildren fail." In short, Richards declared, "it is not overeducation but overnutrition which threatens the race." Instead of the underfed failing to survive, it was the overfed who were failing. Richards's solution was an ideal of health based on complete nutrition.[1] There is no evidence that Richards's analysis of race suicide had an impact on the debates over declining birthrates in the United States, yet her assumption that birthrates were something that could be regulated and controlled was emblematic of the modern social sciences of which she was a part.

Historians have interpreted the debates over race suicide in the United States from the 1890s to the 1930s in a number of different ways. Most often, the public campaign to urge white, "native-born" women to reproduce has been seen as an antifeminist response to changing mores and opportunities for women after the Civil War. As women began attending colleges and universities as regular students or leaving farms for factories or stenographic pools in cities, their choices became the targets of arguments aimed at "correcting" the perceived demographic crisis caused by declining birthrates. The competitive aspect of race suicide that pitted white women against the more-fecund women of supposedly "inferior" races supports interpretations of race suicide in terms of anti-immigrant sentiment.[2] Nativist reactions against the growing numbers of immigrants from Asia and Southern and Eastern Europe during the late nineteenth century certainly fueled the perceived crisis. From the perspective of immigration, the demographic competition for future generations could be won with legislation restricting immigration. As a response to the choice of white women to have fewer children, anti-race suicide advocates urged that the demographic struggle could only be won if white women valued motherhood and realized a four-to-six-child family ideal.

For economist and sociologist Edward Alsworth Ross, who coined the term "race suicide," the campaign against it could not be reduced to a campaign against feminists or immigrants. Instead, I claim that, for Ross, regulating birthrates was a matter of regulating the social order in the image of a natural order. Ross idealized a natural order that nostalgically reconstructed the American rural family whose moral and physical character was thought to have been shaped by generations of experience on America's frontiers.

Where Mary Lease sought tropical colonization and George Maxwell wished to put homes on reclaimed land, Ross sought to restore his vision of natural order by altering the values of society itself. As the United States began to shift to a consumer society, Ross recognized the impact of images, ideals, and education on personal preferences and opinions. Ross, like other sociologists at the turn of the century, was particularly concerned with marking social change and then controlling that change. Like Ferdinand Tonnies and Emile Durkheim, Ross adopted a bifurcated view of society that posited a "nostalgic" vision of an earlier, more-homogeneous community with a more-mobile, heterogeneous capitalist present. Ross was intent, though, not simply on explicating these differences but on producing a manual for their control. Ross systematically investigated social influences and their impact under the rubric of what he termed social control. His groundbreaking book, Social Control (1901), was intended as a guide to social action as much as an analysis of social influences. Ross's vision had a profound impact. Not only did Ross influence policy with his sociological theory of social control, but by providing a clear template for manipulating the masses, he set forth a framework for the newly professionalizing field of advertising to follow. Indeed, the nostalgic projection of the rural family would become an unquestioned trope, sentimentally invoked as the "traditional American family." In the hands of Ross and others, the naturalized ideal of the rural family would be deployed as a tool of social control with the aim of raising the birthrate among "superior" white women.

Ever since Thomas Malthus's 1798 essay on population, political economists have been plying their trade in the bedroom. With his principle claim that populations increase at a geometric rate while their resources for subsistence increase at only an arithmetic rate, Malthus justified the systematic study of different means of checking "inevitable" overpopulation and the poverty that accompanied it. Given the brutality of natural checks to overpopulation, such as famine, Malthus advocated more-humane, socially imposed checks.[3] Malthus's vision of the social regulation of reproduction became a mainstay of Victorian culture in England as Harriet Martineau translated Malthus's economics into melodramatic tales of morality for popular audiences. In the United States, Malthus's warnings concerning unchecked reproduction did not have the same force. The United States in the mid-nineteenth century still imagined that it had free land with seemingly unlimited resources and was a destination for European immigrants as a result. By the turn of the century, however, statistics documenting the decline of the birthrate of "old stock" Americans and the large numbers of immigrants crowding American cities set the stage for a revival of the call for the regulation of reproduction.

In 1891, Francis Amasa Walker, director of the 1870 and 1880 U.S. census and an MIT professor of political economics, made decreasing birthrates an issue for national concern by linking it to immigration and declining standards in America's cities. Walker argued that the decline in the birthrates of "native" Americans from 1850 to 1890 had been caused by the presence of foreign immigrants. Where before the "the standard of material living, of general intelligence, of social decency, had been singularly high," the new immigrants brought a "vastly lower standard of living." When native-born Americans were brought face to face with immigrants, in Walker's words, "our people had to look upon houses that were mere shells for human habitations, the gate unhung, the shutters flapping or falling, green pools in the yard, babes and young children rolling about half naked or worse, neglected, dirty, unkempt." The sentimental "shock" of the native-born American to such a scene was enough to cause them to check their rate of increase, according to Walker.[4] Revulsion for the immigrant, a revulsion that Walker clearly felt himself, was powerful enough, he thought, to make native-born Americans want no contact with them. Rather than force their children to encounter such conditions or compete with such people, Walker believed that native-born Americans would not have children. From Walker's perspective, immigration had introduced a divide in American society between "natives and foreigners" with dire consequences for the "native" birthrate.[5]

Where Walker mourned the effects of the changes wrought by immigration on the whole fabric of society and urged immigration restriction, Ross used the same sense of alarm in 1901 as motivation for massive social reform. Even as Ross watched the social order changing, he understood this mutability as an opportunity to direct that change and remake society. The key to social reform then was to discover the means of social control.

Edward Ross was born in Virden, Illinois, on December 12, 1866. He was orphaned by the time he was ten and grew up with a farm family in Iowa. Described as intellectually gifted and motivated, Ross enrolled at Coe College in Cedar Rapids in 1882. Ross's enthusiasm for learning took him to Germany after graduation, where he studied in Berlin. When he returned in 1889, he decided to pursue a doctorate in economics with Richard T. Ely at Johns Hopkins University. Ely advocated a relationship between research and reform where economists offered moral guidance for the state. After writing a thesis on national debt, Ross worked his way through professorships at Indiana University, Cornell University, and Stanford University.[6]

Lester Frank Ward's *Dynamic Sociology* and Ward's niece, Rosamond Simons, influenced Ross's turn to sociology. Ross encountered both in graduate school and, according to his recollection, was smitten with each. He married Rosamond and began studying and eventually teaching sociology. With advice from Ely and Ward, Ross crafted a career in which he published tracts opposed to trusts and monopoly and advocated measures to aid farmers and labor unions, such as heavy taxation on corporations, public ownership of municipal transportation, and the free coinage of silver. In response to the laissez-faire Darwinism advocated by Herbert Spencer and William Graham Sumner, Ross saw the state as an important mechanism for advancing social progress and reigning in the worst impulses of an unregulated capitalist economy.[7] Ross's writings and teaching gained him the recognition of David Starr Jordan, who, as the new president of Stanford University, brought Ross to Palo Alto. Stanford, like the University of Chicago, opened in the early 1890s and immediately attracted a large number of female undergraduates, so many in fact that Jane Stanford, the university's benefactor, froze their enrollment at 500 lest the college dedicated to the memory of her son become thought of as a "female seminary."[8] If Stanford was not to be a female seminary, it was also not to be a sanctuary for the workingman or his sympathizers. Once at Stanford, Ross's Populist sentiments did not endear him to Jane Stanford.[9]

The speech in which Ross coined the term "race suicide" bridged the public and academic settings in a remarkable way. When Ross defended the supporters of Eugene V. Debs in the 1894 Pullman Strike and supported William Jennings Bryan in the 1896 election, he received word that Jane Stanford insisted that he be put on notice for his "erratic" and "unsound" behavior. His appointment at the university was shifted from economics to sociology, and a proviso was placed in his contract that he should resign in 1897 if the university deemed it advisable. Despite this warning, it was not Ross's speech on the money question in 1897, for which the *San Francisco Post* dubbed him "one of our most esteemed silver lunatics," nor his address before the Socialist Club of Oakland in 1898 that truly upset Stanford. Instead, it was his address before a labor audience on the subject of immigration restriction and differential birthrates, which became a celebrated cause both in university circles and in public forums.[10]

On May 7, 1900, Edward Ross addressed a San Francisco forum at the urging of David Starr Jordan on the subject of Japanese immigration. Ross argued that the "fecundity" of Japanese immigrants threatened both the "Anglo-Saxon character of American society" and the standard of living of "the American worker." The *San Francisco Call* quoted Ross as depicting the situation as so dire that he urged, "should the worst come to the worst it would be better for us to train our guns on every vessel bringing Japanese to our shores rather than to permit them to land." Though Ross claimed that this comment was not in fact in his text, in Jane Stanford's eyes, his nativist outburst was too reminiscent of the uniquely successful political mobilization of the Workingman's Party of California under Dennis Kearney. Kearney's partisans occupied San Francisco's sand lots, blasting railroad owners such as Leland Stanford for employing Chinese laborers until they effected the enactment of the Chinese Exclusion Act in 1882.[11]

The xenophobic statements made by Ross against Japanese workers not only evoked the "evil passions" in people, as Jane Stanford called them in her letter to Jordan demanding Ross's final termination, they echoed the particular virulence of campaigns for racial purity with a haunting twist. The Workingman's Party had used anti-Chinese slogans that were frighteningly violent. Kearney had proclaimed, "We will take them [Chinese workers] by the throat, squeeze their breath out, and throw them into the sea." Kearney's supporters used Darwinian rhetoric to attack exploitative labor practices and to naturalize anti-Chinese violence in slogans such as, "Anti-Coolie Club—Self Preservation is the First Law of Nature."[12] Even as the Workingman's Party of California used the rhetoric valorizing producers to foster tactical coalitions based on race, class, and gender, it asserted a reproductive role for white women. As Martha Gardner notes, the anti-Chinese movement in San Francisco included cross-class coalitions such as the Woman's Protective League, which mandated that members not employ Chinese men as domestic laborers and that they boycott Chinese-made products. The rationale was to improve the desperate plight of the white working girl depicted as displaced by the lower-paid Chinese worker and forced into prostitution in order to support herself. The racialized approach to labor organizing, according to Gardner, "subdued the potentially subversive image of the independent working girl" by representing her in relation to the family as a "mother to white children, and by positing the dire moral implications of her life adrift, prostitution, and tragic death."[13]

Ross's comment nearly twenty years after the Chinese Exclusion Act of 1882 came in light of the act's eminent expiration in 1902 and of a growing anti-Japanese sentiment in California. With the limitation of Chinese immigration into the United States, the numbers of Japanese immigrants had nearly caught up with the numbers of Chinese in some states. Indeed, by 1902, there would be 72,257 Japanese, compared to 71,531 Chinese. More important than the numbers of individuals of Japanese descent was their impact on agriculture in California. Where Japanese farmers were prohibited from owning or leasing productive farmlands within the state, they had adapted by farming intensively on the small, dry or nonproductive lands allocated them. This meant they enriched the soil by hand and planted small truck or produce farms.

The introduction of refrigerated train cars and the refiguring of vegetable and fruit crops as an important California export meant that Japanese farmers were in a prime location to benefit from the marketing of California produce.[14] The increase in profits from crops grown on the original nonproductive San Joaquin lands referred to as the "hog wallow" of the Sacramento Valley and desert lands of the Imperial Valley could be seen in the increase in acreage under lease to Japanese farmers. Nearly 5,000 acres in 1900 had grown to close to 62,000 acres by 1905.[15]

Ross concluded in his address that it was the Japanese population's *partial* adoption of American customs that made them "dangerous," and California governor Henry Gage repeated the claim in 1901. The "danger" Ross suggested lay not only in the agricultural and economic success of Japanese farmers, but in the implicit threat that they would continue to marry early and have more children than Americanized farmers. The California legislature in 1907 denied Japanese immigrants the right to own land, and President Roosevelt entered into a "gentleman's agreement" with the Japanese government in order to limit immigration and rights.

Ross's perception that the Japanese immigrant community only partially adapted to American standards of living was later contradicted by evidence on Asian assimilation produced by one of his own students. Mary Roberts Smith came to Stanford as a graduate student in 1893 to work with Ross as well as economist Amos Warner and historian George E. Howard. She completed her degree in 1896 and joined the faculty at Stanford as an assistant professor of sociology, teaching courses on the family. Her own research saw the American family evolving toward greater freedom and equality as women entered higher education. Smith's interpretation of Chinese family life in the United States insisted on seeing it as responsive to American mores, exemplified by the rapid adoption of the English language and of Western clothing, food, and often religion. Even as Smith altered her own family situation in 1903, divorcing her husband and marrying one of her students, Dane Coolidge, in 1906, she argued that Chinese immigrants conformed to the "civilized" constructions of gender relations. In direct contradiction to Ross, she used her book, *Chinese Immigration* (1909), to press to have the Page Law overturned. Passed by Congress in 1875, the Page Law prohibited the immigration of Chinese women under the guise of combating prostitution. Because very few Chinese women were able to immigrate, Mary Roberts Smith Coolidge argued that "normal" adaptation of Chinese immigrants to American standards was severely limited. Removing such obstacles, she claimed, would allow Chinese immigrants to assimilate as quickly as other immigrant groups to American standards.

Ross's early attacks on Asian immigration had recast "reactionary populist" anti-Asian slogans as social theory. Ross's statements attained a remarkable notoriety when his official resignation from Stanford was announced in the press. Jordan had waited to assure that Ross's book *Social Control* was being published to follow through on Jane Stanford's directive to fire Ross. In November, Ross gave a statement to the press that his academic freedom had been abridged. More than 800 newspapers applauded Ross (and his anti-Japanese comments).[16] He was depicted as a brave scholar, whose courageous testaments were "muted, and finally dismissed, by oppressive university officials."[17] The *San Francisco Call* lamented Ross's termination by concluding, "It is night." Faculty all over the country, including the presidents of Yale and Harvard, expressed support for Ross, with six of his fellow Stanford professors resigning their posts to demonstrate their sincerity. Historian George E. Howard compared Ross's dismissal to the excesses of absolute monarchy during a lecture on the French Revolution. When the Stanford administration insisted that he apologize for the comparison, Howard resigned.[18]

Amid the controversy and publicity surrounding Ross's dismissal, a committee of the American Economics Association convened to investigate the situation. Their report cleared Ross of "any defect in moral character," "incompetence," or "unfaithfulness in the discharge of his duties." Instead the committee blamed Mrs. Stanford for acting on her intolerance of Ross's views on "silver, on Japanese immigration, and public ownership of the railroads."[19] In 1901, Ross was hired at the University of Nebraska. In that same year, at the annual meeting of the American Academy of Political and Social Science, he reiterated his anti-Asian stance as he spelled out the threat of what he named race suicide, explaining it in terms of immigration, standards of living, and urbanization.

In 1901, Ross presented Americans with an apparent paradox of civilization.[20] Using statistical results from different nations, Ross argued that as nations or races became "more civilized" their birthrate declined. When understood in the framework of the social Darwinism then popular, lower birthrates and the competition among different races meant that "less-civilized" races would overwhelm and eventually replace "more-civilized" races. The slowing birthrate in France, for instance, was explained as a sign of "national degeneracy" and "failure to compete." America, how-ever, in the minds of its citizenry, was not degenerating; it was young and vigorous, indeed it was thought to be in its "prime." Ross and his readers were then faced with the question of why a highly civilized nation in its prime would have a declining birthrate.

For Ross the key to this paradox was the American "standard of de-cency" or standard of living. According to Ross, a sign of an advanced civilization and a superior race was a high standard of "decency or com-fort."[21] Where less-advanced societies would settle for minimum stan-dards of food and shelter, the more-advanced races demanded education, culture, and comforts well beyond the minimum necessities.[22] For Ross the American racial character and high standard of decency had been forged on the frontier and the farm where hardship selected a vigorous citizenry. While his infamous speech in California had concerned the partial assimilation of Japanese immigrants, this article spoke of Chinese immigrants or in more-general terms about "Orientals" or "Asiatics." According to Ross, these Asian immigrants who refused to assimilate and adopt American standards, instead retaining their own lower standards, would have more children sooner than their American counterparts. If left unchecked, competition would favor the "Asiatic," and the more-civilized American race would dwindle and disappear. Ross called this process "race suicide."

For Ross the term "race suicide" was apt because the "higher race" was not eliminated in an act of aggression or violence from the "lower race." Instead, in his words, "the higher race quietly and unmurmuringly elimi-nates itself rather than endure individually the bitter competition it has failed to ward off from itself by collective action."[23] Individual American families could not win out without lowering their standards, yet collective action by the race, or in this case more probably the state, had not been taken. Indeed Ross suggested that immigration of nonassimilating races was a problem that "high statesmanship" could solve.[24] Ross was clearly

The Political Economy of Sex

calling for immigration restriction, but in framing the causes of American racial superiority by idealizing the frontier experience and the farmer, Ross also suggested an interpretation of race suicide as a problem of urbanization.

In coining the term "race suicide," Ross created a new body metaphor by likening race to an individual capable of suicide. Such metaphors were a familiar element in sociology informed by social Darwinism and eugenics.[25] Indeed Ross reviewed the efforts of early sociologists such as Herbert Spencer to formulate laws of sociology as analogs to laws in biology or physics. Despite his willingness to allude to the "social body" in discussions of race suicide and the American type,[26] Ross was wary of the extensive analogies proposed by social Darwinists. Ross argued that "excessive reliance upon superficial analogies between social facts and other facts" was one of the "faulty methods" with which sociology had been burdened.[27] Analogy suggested what to look for, but scientific sociology had to be based upon investigation of the facts. In the case of the term "race suicide," Ross was not offering a sociological observation based upon analogy alone. He offered a metaphor of the social body, which allowed him to express a sociological conclusion that he believed he had reached by studying American society. The metaphor of suicide brought with it its own set of sociological and cultural associations. Indeed, Ross may have selected the term because suicide and race suicide had similar sociological implications. More specifically, invoking the term "suicide" had antiurban implications that reinforced Ross's own antiurban analysis of "race suicide."

In his *Foundations of Sociology*, Ross appealed to Emile Durkheim's work on suicide as an example of a natural law in sociology. Ross explained that according to Durkheim, "suicide of the egoistic type varies inversely with the degree of integration of the social group to which the individual belongs."[28] If Durkheim were correct, suicide should be more common in communities with less social integration. Such communities were typical of large cities producing what Durkheim called an experience of "anomie."[29] To be in a condition of anomie was to be lost in a new and changing world where tradition and experience were not reliable guides.

Although Durkheim's views would become more popular in the United

States in the 1920s, urban newspapers at the turn of the century frequently reported extensively on suicide, often with an antiurban tone. The story of Ada Baeker is a case in point.

In July of 1897, a female reporter from Joseph Pulitzer's New York paper, the *World*, was sent to the New York penitentiary to interview a young girl from Texas. Ada Baeker had been locked up because she had tried to kill herself on four separate occasions. She identified the cause of her actions as stemming in part from her migration from Texas to Brooklyn. At the urging of an aunt, Ada, the youngest child and only daughter in a family of five children, had left her home to try her luck "in the city." She did this explicitly against the will of her parents. After a course in typewriting and a brief employment stint, Ada decided that she did not particularly take to the city. She despaired that her family refused to answer her letters. When the small Christmas gifts she had mailed to her family were returned unopened, her disappointment became, in the words of the *World*'s headline, "a mania" and she made the first attempt on her life. Three tries later, she lamented to the reporter that she was especially unhappy in jail and had learned the lesson that "one's life belongs not to one's self, but to the state."[30]

What was crystal clear to Ada Baeker as she sat locked up in a New York jail cell was that the state had identified an interest in the very lives and deaths of its citizenry. Newspapers such as Pulitzer's had identified an interest as well. Indeed, the appearance of Baeker's story on the front page was not an unusual event; turn-of-the-century urban newspapers featured accounts of suicides and suicide attempts almost daily. The significance of this coverage lies in what it reveals about perceptions of the problems of urbanization and their solutions.

The extensive narrative of Ada Baeker's situation, like many of the suicide narratives, offered readers an explanation of why the young woman had tried to kill herself and of how such events could be prevented. In Baeker's case, the cause seemed to be the city itself. Though she had moved to the city at the urging of a female family member, had equipped herself through a typing course to enter the newly feminizing field of clerical work, and appeared to suffer from an intolerant family in Texas, the narrative ascribed Baeker's despair to her feelings of isolation. She had not been able to share her feelings of abandonment with anyone. Baeker had left what the narrative suggested was a sheltered, rural community for the anonymity and opportunity of the city. Had she been able to tell someone of her grief, the state would not have had to intervene.[31]

As a coda on urbanization, Ada Baeker's story perpetuated the image of the city as a site of opportunity and danger, while maintaining the image of the country as a place of safety, as home, even if it was stern. More important, Ada Baeker's story represents an important pattern in Progressive thought with its suggestion of a rural solution to an urban problem, implying that a rural sense of community and family would have eased the sense of isolation and despair that Baeker experienced in the city. It is in this sense that Baeker's story presents an important context for analyzing the metaphor of race suicide.

For Ross, race suicide, like suicide, was identified as at least in part an urban problem. Understood as a reference to Durkheim's theory of egoistic suicide, the term "race suicide" put the consequences of poor social integration on a racial or national scale. The suicide of a race occurred when a race with lower standards did not assimilate the values of a race with higher standards. Of course, Ross stated this lack of integration in terms of the failure of Chinese and Japanese immigrants to assimilate or Americanize—to conform to the Anglo-Saxon ideal that he championed as the "American" norm.

SOCIAL CONTROL AND THE AMERICAN TYPE

Throughout his career, Ross celebrated the farmer and castigated "the deteriorating influences of the city and factory." He idealized the Iowa farms of his own youth, distinguishing himself from eastern intellectuals with his frequent celebration of his rural midwestern origins.[32] This sympathy for the rural Midwest was clearly expressed in his defense of the Populists but later developed into an integral part of his social theory. Ross's rural orientation was linked to the power of the frontier experience in shaping and creating those features of Anglo-Saxon Americans that he admired.[33] As he put it, "The hardships of the pioneer life pitilessly screened out the weak and debilitated, leaving only the hardy and vigorous."[34] Selection on the frontier, according to Ross, had created an "American type." This "American breed" was superior to the European and Asian in "natural physique" and "energy of will."[35] At the same time, the "born American" had an innate sense of "native morality" that valued truth and fair play, and that, in Ross's words, "does not stick at corruption, fraud and grand larceny, yet keeps faith with foes and warns before striking."[36] As grand as this nostalgic vision of the past seemed to Ross, he realized that the frontier was closed and the same selective processes were no longer at work.

Worse than the closing of the frontier, however, was the migration from the country to the city. The "simple life" was being thrown over by young Americans for the "great glittering cities," but at a cost. Ross warned that "with shortened lives, bachelorhood, late and childless marriages, and small families, the cities constitute so many blast furnaces where the talented rise and become incandescent, to be sure, but for all that are incinerated without due replacement." According to Ross, the cities threatened to "run down" what two centuries of selection had created.[37] Ross would undoubtedly have agreed with William Jennings Bryan, his neighbor and friend in Nebraska, when he argued in his famous "Cross of Gold" speech, "Burn down your cities and leave our farms, and your cities will spring up again as if by magic; but destroy our farms and the grass will grow in the streets of every city in the country."[38]

Unlike other urban progressives who saw a solution to the city's problems in a return to the country or to the simple life, Ross allowed a broader range of possibilities. While he praised efforts to reclaim arid and abandoned land, he also praised the creation of "new margins" by "keeping open Oriental markets," reducing farm mortgages, restricting immigration, increasing labor solidarity, and encouraging conservation.[39] None of these measures could substitute for the effects of the frontier, because while they created opportunity, they did not create it for the "common man" or "plain people." The closing of the frontier created a tremendous challenge for the reform-oriented Ross as he tried to recreate the positive effects of the frontier through what he called "social control."

Ross feared that the natural bonds that "were many and firm when the rural neighborhood" of community was the norm would no longer be at work as the community transformed into the "huge and complex aggregate" that was urban society.[40] The transition from natural order and natural control to social order and social control required the "improve-

The Political Economy of Sex

ment of the instruments that constitute the apparatus of social control."[41] At the same time, Ross readily conceded that the means of social control were not flawless and were not necessarily a barrier to degeneration. As he put it, "No doubt the elimination of the savage still goes on among us, and the humane type of person will more and more predominate. But is it not possible that, as society ever more skillfully and lavishly provides braces for the weak spine, the fibre of character will soften, and the power to follow the good when one knows it will decline?"[42] This "decay of character," like the need for social control itself, was the result of the closing of the frontier and the nature of city life as the United States shifted from a rural to an urban society. Race suicide was a manifestation of this decline in character as urban, white families failed to reproduce at the rate Ross believed necessary.

THEODORE ROOSEVELT AND THE POPULARIZATION OF RACE SUICIDE

The elaboration of Ross's application of his principles of social control to the problems of regulating fecundity was complicated by Theodore Roosevelt's very public attack on what he thought were the causes of race suicide. Roosevelt was instrumental in bringing the issue of race suicide before the American people. As no other American could, Roosevelt used his various political offices to urge the "nation" to procreate. However, Roosevelt's rhetoric drew the race suicide debate away from the issues of economics, immigration, and urbanization that Ross had emphasized and recast it as an issue of women's duty to the state.

Roosevelt had a long-standing interest in racial reproduction and birthrates. First struck by declining birthrates reported in the 1890 census, Roosevelt developed his views on racial progress over the next ten years. Because he equated a high birthrate with racial progress and strength, Roosevelt believed that a declining birthrate implied racial decline or "decadence" as well. By 1903, he had translated his racial concerns into exhortations to women to breed as a patriotic duty.[43] Roosevelt became aware of Ross's written work on race suicide in 1904. By 1906, he was urging Congress to pass immigration restriction legislation, which they did in 1907, setting specific quotas for the first time.[44]

In 1906 Roosevelt used the occasion of his sixth annual address to express his presidential concern over "race suicide." Citing the low birthrate among white, upper-class women and the high birthrate of working-class immigrants, Roosevelt warned, "willful sterility is, from the standpoint of the nation, from the standpoint of the human race, the one sin for which the penalty is national death, race death." Roosevelt blasted women who chose to have small families or no children at all. In his eyes, "no man, no woman can shirk the primary duties of life." Indeed those of what he called the "best stock" who refused to procreate were castigated as "criminal," and those women who chose to avoid their "duty" were condemned for their "viciousness, coldness, and shallow-heartedness" as "race traitors."[45]

Roosevelt's comments on numerous occasions in the first decade of the twentieth century set an agenda that pulled the race suicide debate away from economics toward an antifeminist backlash. Instead of emphasizing immigration and urbanization, as Ross had, Roosevelt's rhetoric was directed at women. At the turn of the century, "new women" and working women were distinguishing themselves from the preceding generation. In the first decade of the twentieth century, one in five women worked. In New York City in 1910, over a third of all women worked. Independent and self-aware young women were celebrated and castigated as "new women."[46]

As women sought greater access to higher education, their opponents urged that so much education might actually be physically harmful for women. As early as 1872, Edward Clarke argued that college had a detrimental effect on women's "limited energy," endangering their chances of motherhood by harming their "female apparatus."[47] Redirecting the blood flow from the womb to the brain made it more difficult for women to reproduce, he claimed.[48] Female educational advocates fought back. In an essay awarded Harvard's Boylston Prize in 1876, Dr. Mary Putnam Jacobi disproved Clarke's contention, demonstrating that menstruation inhibited neither women's energy nor the possibility of their education.[49] The issue of reproduction and education was far from settled, however.[50]

An article from the *Cincinnati Medical Journal* in 1894 typifies the concern with the impact of college on women's bodies as experts answered the question of at what age women should optimally marry and, by implication, begin to bear children. Medical college professors urged women to wait at least until age eighteen or even twenty-two or twenty-four to become mothers. As Dr. Theophilius Parvin, a professor of obstetrics at Jefferson Medical College and the "highest of all authorities upon the subject," warned, girls must be "thorough and complete women, physically, mentally and morally, before they become wives. Very few are aware, that it is a rare exception to find a woman perfectly developed in all these respects until between 20 and 25 years of age."[51] Coinciding with reformers' advocacy of age-of-consent laws, this discussion of the appropriate age for reproduction purportedly was motivated entirely out of concern for the health of individual women.[52]

One of the most important responses to the problem of women's education and reproduction took the form of sustained, statistical studies of the possible correlation between higher education and declining birthrates. Beginning with the discussion of the effect of coeducation on the relationship between the sexes, early studies measured marriage statistics for different cohorts, locales, and types of schools. Starting with an 1895 study of American collegiate alumnae undertaken by Millicent Shinn, differences were marked in marriage rates among women attending western colleges, where they were fewer in number but demonstrated a "consequent superiority in the strategies of courtship," and those of women attending single-sex colleges in the East.[53] In subsequent years, the impact of cohort, age of marriage, schools studied, whether male rates of marriage coincided with female rates for the same institutions or for different ones, all refined the discussion of race suicide and its correlation with women's higher education and professionalization.[54]

In 1903, for example, G. Stanley Hall, president of Clark University and founder of the American Psychological Association worked with Theodate Smith, one of the first women admitted to Clark as a regular student, to demonstrate a drop in the rates of marriage and childbirth among female graduates from Vassar, Smith, and Wellesley. What Hall and Smith appeared to confirm was a correlation between increasing numbers of women attending colleges and a decreasing birthrate, with the first class at Vassar marrying at twice the rate of their successors (55.46 percent of the class of 1867 were married in 1903 compared to 28.92 percent of the class of 1896, with a corresponding decrease in the number of children born to alumnae).[55] Hall and Smith's study, as well as others like it, provided grounds for a lively debate as physicians, educators, and reformers considered the causes underlying this correlation and their possible solutions.

One response to the physiological "damage" predicted for women scholars was to increase women's participation in sport. The era that saw physicians arguing that too much blood was diverted to the brain to allow girls to adequately develop their reproductive organs saw an intensification of athletics in venues educating young women. The introduction of competitive sports in high schools and women's colleges offered one way to counter the medical establishment's pronouncements about the problems with women focusing too much on their studies. Wellesley, for example, was the first of the women's colleges to require physical activities beyond the gymnastics that had been a mainstay at places such as Mount Holyoke since their founding. Beginning in 1906, female scholars at Wellesley would assure that their vital organs received the blood that might be misdirected to the brain by playing basketball, hockey, and other active sports.[56]

Roosevelt increased public scrutiny of women's education and professionalization when he implicated them as causes of race suicide. In a speech reprinted in the *Ladies Home Journal*, Roosevelt argued that "no scheme of education, no social attitude, can be right unless it is based fundamentally upon the recognition of seeing that the girl is trained to understand the supreme dignity and the supreme usefulness of motherhood."[57] Roosevelt's comments were more pointedly antifeminist in a 1911 lecture at the Pacific Theological Union entitled "The Home and the Child." Commenting on an invitation from the Equal Suffrage Association to speak on the issue of women's suffrage, Roosevelt proclaimed, "I have always told my friends that it seemed to me that no man was worth his salt who did not think very deeply of woman's rights; and that no woman was worth her salt who did not think more of her duties than of her rights." This paternalistic stance was continued as Roosevelt argued that "the ideal woman of the future, just like the ideal woman of the past, must be the good wife, the good mother, the mother who is able to bear, and to rear, a number of healthy children."[58] Roosevelt's lecture notes indicated that "a large number of men" applauded this statement. Indeed a large number of men and women discussed and supported Roosevelt's analysis of race suicide.[59]

After Roosevelt took to his bully pulpit against race suicide, photographs of large families began to appear in newspapers with captions such as "No Race Suicide in This Indiana Family" or "the accompanying photograph shows what might be appropriately termed one of President Roosevelt's ideal families." Prior to Roosevelt's exhortations, newspaper photographs of large families were rare. Those that appeared before 1903 often served public health reformers' goals of reducing infant mortality by calling attention to the family's health. For example, a photograph of a family from Illinois was captioned: "A healthier family never lived in Clinton County. In the twenty-seven years there has not been a serious case of illness among the children. The medical bills for that period have not amounted to $40." After Roosevelt's campaign against race suicide, not only did photographs of large families appear more frequently with captions lauding them as fitting an ideal type, but even the form of the photographs changed. Significantly, children were often posed differently in these anti–race suicide photographs. Prior to this moment when the family become a tool of the nation in Roosevelt's hands, family portraiture emphasized the conventions of painting in terms of their composition: most family photographs clustered the children around their parents to produce a balanced arrangement. Anti–race suicide photos began to arrange the children by height forming a "stair-stepped" representation. Unlike grouped photographs, the stair-stepped photographs depicted not only the number of children, but their spacing.[60] The issue of race suicide refigured these photographs as testimonies to fecundity as well as health.[61]

Roosevelt's indictment of childless women found its way into mass culture, as evidenced by a letter to the Butterick Company's sewing magazine in 1907 written by a Michigan clergyman. Reverend Esper denounced the teddy bear as destructive of the instincts of real motherhood and perhaps leading to race suicide.[62] The toy had been inspired by Theodore Roosevelt's magnanimous gesture of conserving the life of a bear cub on a 1902 hunting trip in Mississippi. Three years later, the Steiff Toy Company

The Roosevelt cousins arranged in a stair-step pose.
(From Theodore Roosevelt, Autobiography [1913], 365)

was exporting the stuffed animals as toys for boys at a remarkable rate. Millions had been sold by the time Roosevelt left office.[63]

Esper's letter voiced a fear about the toy's destructive potential not because little girls had begun to favor the stuffed bears over dolls (which were thought to be more conducive to the development of maternal feelings) but because grown women had. The toy had been adopted by young women who were increasingly toting the bears in public, cuddling them at night, and using them for decoration. Teddy bears thus not only comforted children, they became a visible symbol of the transference of affection and sexuality out of the familial mold by a generation of new women. When Anna Held, the wife of Florenz Ziegfeld, belted out, "I've lost my Teddy Bear" in the 1908 musical ironically titled, Miss Innocence, or an unidentified singer lamented, "A poor black girl ain't got no teddy at all, but she's teddying just the same" a few years later in a blues tune, it was clear that what had begun as Teddy Roosevelt's symbol of paternal masculinity had become one of feminine sexual autonomy.[64]

Indeed, journalist Lydia Commander, who wrote extensively on race suicide, cast aspersions on some new women who chose to remain childless by attacking the grounds for their decisions. Comparing the frivolity of childless women to the anguish of Rachel in the Bible, Commander asked her readers in 1907,

> What kinship can you find between that fiery, Eastern nature-woman, furious at the denial of motherhood, and the soulless creature who turns coldly from a child to lavish caresses upon a pedigreed dog or cat? Instead of Rachel's fierce insistence, "Give me children, or I die!" you hear, in soft, lisping tones, "Give me a Teddy-bear, or I'll be out of fashion."
>
> Fortunately, the women to whom the cult of the dog or the Teddy bear is more than motherhood are much fewer than the attention they attract would lead us to suppose.[65]

The association of urban women's frivolity with their choice not to have children was even commented on by Ross. As he spoke on race suicide in 1905, Ross advocated a return to the simple life because in his opinion, "the patent-leather life of some people makes them want a piece of bric-a-brac instead of a child."[66] Expanding on Ross's remarks, the New York

Telegram celebrated Ross's "eagle-eyed" perception by noting that "it is told that in the early days of Nebraska the first man to wear patent leathers was lynched, the sturdy pioneers contending that the feet of men were too worthy to be profaned by such wanton profanity." Of course, the story was acknowledged to be apocryphal, but the phrase was "expressive." While "patent leather shrinks from a long hard journey," according to the *Telegram*, "Strong democratic leather" did not. Indeed, the column concluded, "Our forefathers wore cowhide boots . . . and wanted not of the decadent glory of the glazed thing called patent leather which seriously marks a period in social evolution."[67] The plainspoken *Sacramento Bee* simply commented, "In the days of cow-hide and grain-leather boots, large families were the rule."[68]

Ross's remarks on "patent-leather life" should not be taken as a sign of his agreement with Roosevelt's public conceptualization of race suicide. In the same year that Ross commented on women's frivolity as a cause of declining birthrates, he shifted the terms of debate by introducing the specter of overpopulation. In speeches and in print, Ross spread the word that having families with as many as ten children was as much a concern as having families without children.[69] Dropping mortality rates meant that people were living longer and that more infants were surviving into adulthood. This meant that families did not have to have as many children as in the past in order to replace themselves in the next generation.[70] Indeed, having too many children now posed a threat of overwhelming available resources. Newspapers made much of Ross's apparent disagreement with Roosevelt, pitting Roosevelt's call for large families against Ross's call for families with at least four children.[71] In fact, Ross and Roosevelt were in agreement. In a letter to Ross, Roosevelt commented that he did not think "that families of fifteen or twenty are possible or just in a high civilization; but, as you say, what is needed is to standardize a family of from four to six" as opposed to the one- or two-child ideal common among the middle class.[72]

Ross's more-nuanced approach to family size failed to temper the discussion over falling birthrates. In 1914, Congress passed a bill making Mother's Day a national holiday. The next year the scholarly debate was reinvigorated by a new set of statistical studies of birthrates among college women. Robert Sprague, an economist at the Massachusetts State Agricul-

The Political Economy of Sex

tural College in Amherst, drew a clear connection between education and race suicide with new birthrate statistics for graduates of women's colleges. With data from Mt. Holyoke College, Bryn Mawr College, Vassar College, and Wellesley College, Sprague revealed that the average number of children per graduate was always below one. In order to "sustain the present population," Sprague had calculated that each woman needed to bear 3.7 children. Rather than being "doomed to extinction" by these results, Sprague argued that colleges needed to face their "race responsibilities" and become "powerful agencies for race survival rather than race suicide."[73] Drawing a parallel between land and fertility, he continued, "The farmer that uses his land for golf links and deer preserves instead of for crops has but one agricultural fate; so the civilization that uses its women for stenographers, clerks and school-teachers instead of mothers has but one racial fate." The solution, Sprague thought, was to strengthen public opinion about the family and the home—create a curriculum that "would idealize and prepare for family and home life as the greatest work of the world and the highest goal of woman." Borrowing Roosevelt's language of patriotic duty, Sprague exhorted his readers to stop idealizing "individual independence" in favor of the family or face even more "portentous" race suicide statistics.[74]

Sprague's 1915 article was followed by a spate of statistical studies of marriage rates and birthrates among college graduates from Stanford University to Syracuse University.[75] Women's marriage rates at coeducational institutes were discovered to be higher than at women's colleges, with the exception of Stanford University. Stanford women tended to marry at about the rate of Wellesley women, but well below the rate for women at Iowa State. Stanford's low marriage rate was ascribed to its selectivity and its curriculum directed at "celibate careers" for women, but these things could be remedied by admitting more women using lower academic standards. The "superior students" would then be joined by "more socially-minded" students who would "exert a eugenic influence on them." Howard Banker's study of Syracuse women seconded both this diagnosis and the suggested cure. Banker posited that the similarity in marriage rates for Stanford and Wellesley women indicated that these schools were selecting for a type of woman with "purely intellectual aspirations." These women were acknowledged to have great value for society, but Banker argued that colleges and universities needed women who were "naturally more reproductive." "These normal, 'all-round,' 'red-blooded' women," Banker claimed, "are really the superior type and the college should provide a course of training attractive to their instincts and intended to develop all of their innate powers and capacities to the highest efficiency."[76] While home economics courses were being added to the college curriculum at this time, there is no evidence that reduced admission standards were ever adopted in order to encourage students to marry.

Compounding the problem of marriage rates, pursuing an education, a career, or both often delayed marriage and parenthood. To counter this trend, new studies argued that a mother's age had a distinct effect on the vitality of her child. An article describing Alexander Graham Bell's research urged young motherhood in order to guarantee child "vitality." Infant mortality statistics indicated that the best age for marriage was "between 20 and 25." This was a radical inversion of the approach to thinking about the age of motherhood thirty years earlier. Where earlier experts sought to protect adolescent females by urging that they be allowed to develop both physically and psychologically before marriage, by 1917 the emphatic narrative around the duty to reproduce had significantly altered the vision of what was at stake and what protections were owed to adolescent women. Bell's findings, based on a genealogical study of the Hyde family, concluded that young women needed to be reproducing by age twenty-five; the very age a panel of medical experts had earlier called the ideal age for marriage had become the last possible age to consider reproduction. Women were warned that every year they delayed childbearing past the age of twenty-five penalized their children.

In 1917, however, Luther Gulick urged a solution for encouraging young women to consider motherhood—Camp Fire Girls. Gulick proposed that the organization could "develop the home spirit and make it dominate the entire community." With the goal of creating "custom and fashion, habit and want" in young women, the Camp Fire Program would help instill the "concept of motherhood" in its members. Although eugenics was not explicitly mentioned in Camp Fire literature, Gulick believed that it was embodied in the program.[77] Adapting the tools of social control to eugenic ends, the *Journal of Heredity* article linking Camp Fire and eugenics acknowledged that "the work before the true promoter of Eugenics is that of social engineering which will make for the realization of desire in the wholesomest and quickest way."[78]

None of this fooled Leta Hollingworth.[79] She saw the manipulation inherent in the social control of reproduction for what it was; an attempt to induce young women to undertake the kind of sacrifice and suffering that made childbearing, in her words, "analogous to the work of soldiers," involving "danger," "suffering," and, in some cases, "the actual loss of life."[80] In an article that began with a quotation from Ross's *Social Control*, Hollingworth promised to explain the social devices for impelling women to bear children. Using Ross's categories for social control, Hollingworth reviewed how personal ideals, public opinion, law, belief, education, art, and illusion were used to persuade women of their reproductive duty. From scientific celebrations of the "normal woman" as the enthusiastic mother to newspapers' embrace of Roosevelt's letters of congratulations to large families, Hollingworth demonstrated how these different influences worked to reinforce the same maternal message. Hollingworth pointed out that infant mortality statistics were widely discussed, while maternal mortality statistics were rarely mentioned, for instance. In her words, "the pains, the dangers, and risks of child-bearing are tabooed," and "the drudgery, the monotonous labor, and other disagreeable features of child-rearing are minimized."[81] From her analysis, Hollingworth believed that it was clear that "all possible social devices" have been used to "re-enforce maternal instinct." The problem was that very soon, Hollingworth predicted, "all the most intelligent women of the community, who are the most desirable child-bearers, will become conscious of the methods of social control." Once "enlightened," childbearing would become voluntary. If the government for "national aggrandizement desired more children" Hollingworth argued, then they would have to provide "adequate compensation, either in money or in fame." Hollingworth's willingness to value women without reducing them to mothers appealed to a strong feminist tradition at the time. Her willingness to reveal the means of social control for reproduction and to frame it as coercive stands in stark contrast to the work of pronatalist champions such as Ross and Roosevelt.

Just as Hollingworth was trying to pull back the curtain on the social control of reproduction, eugenicists were embracing it explicitly. In 1926 California eugenicist Paul Popenoe followed his earlier book, *Applied Eugenics*, which he had coauthored with Roswell Johnson, with *The Conservation of the Family*.[82] Popenoe, like Hollingworth, used Ross's categories for social control to guide his analysis of the means to regulate reproduction eugenically. The last third of Popenoe's book concerned how education, public opinion, economic reforms, and community organization can be shaped to support large families among select individuals. Unlike many other eugenics tracts at this time, Popenoe was very concerned with promoting reproduction among those he considered to be "fit." Ross's analysis of social control provided a framework for organizing and developing a strategy of positive eugenics. For instance, Popenoe championed a "Back to the Farm" movement as a means of promoting larger families, or at least the creation of new playgrounds, day care centers, and kindergartens to make city and town life more conducive to family life. Popenoe evaluated a range of economic incentives, from "baby bounties" to family insurance. Combined with promotion of family ideals in art, education, and community life, Popenoe believed that eugenically "fit" couples would "voluntarily" seek and have larger families.[83]

Ross himself had become sympathetic to the eugenic movement by at least 1910. After Stanford, Ross had spent five years at the University of Nebraska before joining the faculty of the University of Wisconsin in 1906. In 1911 he sponsored the eugenics club at the University of Wisconsin and urged its members to discuss topics such as the sterilization of the feeble-minded and the implications of declining birthrates. In 1910 a newspaper reported that Ross advocated marriage restriction for "mental and physical defectives." Later he would advocate sterilization and, of course, immigration restriction, both important issues in the American eugenics movement.[84] The rise of eugenic thought also significantly changed the terms of the race suicide debate. Where earlier discussions had concerned rates of racial reproduction in a broad sense, the later revival of interest in birthrates by supporters of eugenics focused on college-educated women. The concern of anti–race suicide advocates had moved from racial competition to promoting the reproduction of supposedly "superior" individuals within the "American" race.

By the 1920s, Ross's idea of social control was in virtually every textbook of sociology produced in the United States. It had been the topic of the annual meeting of the American Sociological Association, and his book *Social Control* had sold over 18,000 copies by 1930.[85] The language of control and especially control of fecundity or birthrate would have been familiar to anyone reading American sociology in the early twentieth century.

Yet by 1920, Ross had significantly refined his views. Realizing the importance of both mortality rates and birthrates, Ross offered a more-nuanced consideration of when it was necessary to regulate reproduction in his book, *The Principles of Sociology* (1920). When the birthrate dropped below the death rate in a group, then that group was susceptible to being swamped by any other group with a higher birthrate and the same death rate. These were the conditions that would create race suicide and the conditions that necessitated the social control of reproduction. Significantly, the regulation of mortality rates was treated by Ross as a medical matter; their control depended on advances in medicine. The regulation of birthrates, however, was very much a matter of the type of social control with which Ross was concerned.

From the time he introduced the term "race suicide" in 1893, Ross had advocated immigration restriction as a means of solving the problem by preventing competition with more rapidly reproducing races. Immigration restriction was a major feature of the social reform agenda to which Ross devoted tremendous amounts of his time. To his mind, however, immigration restriction was not a means of socially controlling birthrates; in contrast to Walker, Ross did not believe restricting immigration would raise native-born birthrates. Immigration restriction was a solution to race suicide because it eliminated competition between groups with different standards of living and different birthrates. The causes of race suicide were not the causes of declining birthrates.

In his *Principles of Sociology*, Ross outlined the causes of declining birthrates and the means for their social control. Among the causes Ross cited was democracy, by which he meant the elimination of caste barriers such that men and women were free to "strain to reach a higher rung in the social ladder"; early marriage and a large family were a handicap to such ambition.[86] Similarly indicted was striving for new "economic wants," or in Thorstein Veblen's more-pointed language, the conspicuous consumption of luxuries,[87] as was the spread of birth control and the advancement of women, but without the opprobrium of Roosevelt's declarations.

Central among the correctives of Ross's principles of social control was to alter the social valuation of "a normal-sized, well-reared family." In effect, Ross urged substituting pride in a "normal-sized" family for what he considered the "selfish and frivolous ideals" behind the decline of the birthrate.[88] Ross agreed with Roosevelt to the extent that he thought that women should value motherhood, but he also recognized that women's education and equality was a feature of the higher standard of living he valued as a characteristic of the American racial type. As early as 1905, Ross acknowledged that the recognition of women's rights and higher education for women were significant causes of declining birthrates, because the "professions are more attractive than marriage." Ross did not propose closing the professions to women but instead showing them that they were "more capable of motherhood than of any profession."[89] Placing greater social value on motherhood was also part of Roosevelt's campaign, however crudely executed. Ross, however, chose to increase the onus on men to make home life more attractive for women. Projecting an ideal of the "normal" family was an additional means of changing the social value assigned to motherhood and is a topic to which I will return below.

Should a greater appreciation of children and motherhood not work, Ross also suggested economic inducements for child rearing, such as free medical care for school children, free schooling, free meals in school, and state allowances for children. Lest "shiftless elements" cash in on these incentives, Ross recommended mental testing to determine which "healthy" children came up to "standard." Ross also thought that there ought to be legislation to prevent child labor and mandate school attendance, thereby converting children in the mind of their parents from assets to be exploited into liabilities to be managed. Social opinion should also be enrolled to communicate praise for the large families of the "endowed" and resentment for the large families of the "subcommon."[90]

The object of social control was not to impose order directly upon others but to shape opinions, beliefs, and judgments such that desired conduct was encouraged and undesired conduct discouraged.[91] For Ross, mechanisms of social control were necessary because they made possible a "better order" with greater cooperation than the "rudimentary order" that might arise spontaneously. Moreover, in urban environments and societies with pronounced differences in the ownership of property and capital, orderly living required the codes, laws, and values furnished by a system of social control. Ross believed that social orders had to be created to replace natural orders. However, as in nature, the effect of creating order involved selection, and the process of social selection bore directly on the regulation of reproduction.

Social selection, according to Ross, occurs when "social processes and institutions in some measure react upon and modify a people by checking the increase of certain types or stimulating the increase of other types." Social selection was meant to be analogous to natural selection, except "while Nature eliminates the unfit, society eliminates the misfit." The major difference between natural and social selection was that natural selection was a matter of living or dying, while social selection was about reproducing or not. As a means for molding "the race," social selection acted "by influencing one or more of the following factors: (a) the inclination to marry; (b) amount of marriage—polygamy, monogamy, etc.; (c) the age of marriage; (d) the will to have children; (e) the ability to rear children to maturity."[92] The social control of fecundity was basically a means to regulate social selection. Ross's discussion of processes of social selection operating within his society offered a slightly different perspective on the social control of reproduction. Significantly, Ross's discussion of social selection processes made clearer what ideals of the family and womanhood he held.

For instance, consider Ross's discussion of economic success as a process of social selection. As he had in the context of race suicide, Ross argued that economically or socially successful individuals tended to have fewer children. However, in his discussion of success as a process of social selection, Ross tied the effects of success directly to the migration of the "best" individuals from the country to the city. As he put it, "the farm family whose members push on to college and rise into the higher callings does not multiply like the commonplace family which sticks to the soil."[93]

Ross called this phenomenon "folk depletion." With characteristic over-statement, he wrote that "in parts of southern Michigan, Illinois, Wisconsin, and even as far west as Missouri, there are communities which remind one of fished out ponds populated chiefly by bullheads and suckers."[94]

In *Principles of Sociology*, Ross's solution was to call for a return to a simple life such that financial gain was balanced with raising a larger family. Only two years later, Ross diagnosed the problem of folk depletion as the loss of leadership in the country, not the wholesale decline in the quality of the country population.[95] For Ross, leaders, whether social, religious, or political, were "radiant points of social control."[96] As such, these leaders set the standards or ideals for social order. The migration of such leaders to the city meant that country people had lost some of the enlightening influences that guaranteed their continued moral progress. Such conditions could be remedied by improving the conditions of farm life so that these leaders did not leave or by bolstering other sources of rural leadership and social control such as schools and churches.[97] For present purposes, what Ross's discussion of folk depletion reveals is his continued idealization of the farm family. Even as the problems of rural life were becoming the objects of entire fields of sociological research (rural sociology), Ross was reluctant to let go of the rural family as the ideal social and reproductive unit.[98]

A second example of social selection was equally revealing of Ross's attitudes. As he had before, Ross attributed declining birthrates to women's emancipation. Ross celebrated women's access to higher education and looked forward to the day when perhaps one in ten women would attend college. However, college tended to postpone marriage and led women into professions where they had to make a choice between career and children. To remedy these problems, Ross proposed that the standards of primary education be raised so that women could complete college within two years. The remaking of women's careers was acknowledged to be more difficult, but Ross proposed that "household work" be reorganized and women's workday limited to four or five hours in order to allow them time for both profession and family.[99] This kind of opportunity was held to be especially important for women teachers, who had previously been required to remain unmarried. In Ross's opinion, half-time positions would allow teachers to also be wives and mothers.[100]

In the context of the debate over race suicide, Ross's grappling with the problem of reconciling women's emancipation with the regulation of reproduction stands in sharp contrast to the standard depiction of Roosevelt's antifeminism or even Ross's nativism.[101] Through the influence of his close friend Charlotte Perkins Gilman, Ross had begun to regard the changing role of women and their social emancipation with considerable sympathy. In *The Principles of Sociology* and *The Social Trend*, Ross presented and defended Gilman's antimasculinist views serialized in *The Forerunner* as "The Man-Made World; or, Our Androcentric Culture" in 1909. Following Gilman, Ross argued that war and militarism were attributable to "male pugnacity," as was coercive government. Gilman had posited that women, as the first humans (she terms them "the race type"), had organized an early government that was female-centered, organized along maternal lines with love and nurturance as its primary characteristic. The androcentric era began when men organized hunting and other violent activities, which allowed them to subjugate women. Ross adopts Gilman's argument that masculinity produces control in governing institutions.[102] Similarly, masculine influence in business had "justified child labor, the wrecking of the health of working girls, the night work of women, [and] preventable work accidents." In addition, Ross described men as having less self-control and less common sense than women.[103] Even Ross's calls to redesign household work echoed arguments Gilman had raised against the effects of women's domesticity in her household reform.

While Ross looked forward to greater equality in marriage and encouraged the move away from the male domination of the family, his vision of social order remained grounded in an idealized conception of the rural family. Despite the new social order he was able to appreciate in Gilman's work or the reformed regulation of reproduction he articulated, his ability to reconstruct society remained limited by what could agree with his nostalgic agrarianism.

Although he retired from the University of Wisconsin in 1937, Ross continued to publish and travel widely in his retirement. In one of his last essays, the originator of the term "race suicide" turned back to Malthus and the question of population. Arguing that Malthus could not have imagined advances in agriculture, food distribution, transportation, and public health that had been realized, he acknowledged that the issue of population size and reproduction nevertheless remained. Moreover, Ross argued, the possibility of creating more tillable land through reclamation overlooked the fact that soon even that reclaimed land would be filled. Similarly, "safe, speedy, and cheap" long-distance travel opened up the possibility of migration and population redistribution but forgot that new lands could be filled just as old lands were. Despite opposition from "nationalists," "militarists," "employers," and "socialists," Ross championed family limitation and the conscious regulation of reproduction until his death in 1951 at the age of eighty-five.[104]

Edward Ross's vision of the ideal American was firmly rooted in his version of middle America. New immigrants from Europe and Asia threatened this vision, as did the migration of his cherished rural Midwesterners to the cities. Couched in terms of race suicide and standards of living, Ross objected to Japanese immigrants in California because they would not assimilate the "American" values he idealized. Ironically, the rural midwesterners who were leaving their farms in record numbers were not assimilating Ross's American values either. Ross was striving to regulate the nation's population, but his vision of the American family was so firmly rooted in an idealized past that even the majority of white farm families chose not to realize it.

5

MEN AS TREES WALKING

THEODORE ROOSEVELT AND THE
CONSERVATION OF THE RACE

Conservation and rural-life policies are
really two sides of the same policy; and down
at bottom this policy rests upon the fundamental
law that neither man nor nation can prosper
unless, in dealing with the present, thought
is steadily taken for the future.

THEODORE ROOSEVELT,
"Rural Life," 1910

The first National Conservation Congress in 1909 featured what in retrospect may seem like a surprising variety of papers on subjects ranging from conservation in lumber and electricity production to the conservation of child life and manhood. In addition to the expected papers on forestry, the public health and child labor efforts undertaken by the General Federation of Women's Clubs and the Daughters of the American Revolution (DAR) were both represented at the congress.[1] The DAR speaker was Mrs. J. Ellen Foster, chair of the DAR Committee on Child Labor. In her address on the conservation of child life, Foster argued that child-labor legislation was essential for the conservation of children as a national resource. In her words, "just as surely as a big tree is worth more than a growing slip, so a man is worth more than a child. . . . It is not only that we love the child and want him for ourselves, but it is because we know he is worth more to the country, if he is allowed to grow up. He makes a better tree out of which to cut lumber to build a house or a church or a school if he is allowed to grow up to full stature and to develop himself fully. He cannot do that if he is put in a factory at a too early age."[2] As the analogy between forests and children made clear, children were a natural resource that needed management as much as forests did to insure future prosperity.

For Theodore Roosevelt, conserving the nation's natural resources was integrally connected to the idea of conserving the "race." As a proponent of irrigation and land reclamation, Roosevelt had championed putting homes on the land. As he moved to nationalize his conservation policies beginning in 1907, however, he articulated his agenda for conservation in tandem with his agenda regarding country life. The country life movement, which Roosevelt supported, was a modernist program to economically and socially improve rural life. Roosevelt presented his case for conservation and country life by appealing to a racialized agrarianism that argued for the superiority of the small rural farmer and his family. Invoking nostalgic ideals of the farmer and the rural family allowed Roosevelt and his compatriots to claim that both the conservation and country life movements were relevant to the future of the "American race." The managing of natural resources were thus brought to bear on the management of the "race."

Men As Trees Walking

Born in 1858 to a wealthy New York family, Theodore Roosevelt developed his early interest in natural history into a real affinity for the countryside and the strenuous life he discovered there.[3] Roosevelt's father encouraged his son, who was afflicted with asthma as a child, to improve his health and body, building a gymnasium on the second floor of their house. At Harvard in the late 1870s Roosevelt had his eye on a lightweight boxing championship, but he was soundly defeated. More successful at romance, Roosevelt met Alice Lee and married her soon after his graduation in 1880.

Roosevelt was schooled in the exclusionary racial theories emerging in the social sciences following in the wake of Darwin's theory of evolution. Through his Harvard professor Nathaniel Shaler, Roosevelt learned theories of the social evolution thought to produce an "American race." The "old stocks" that made up this "race" constituted an "American type" whose character had been shaped by their experiences in the American environment.[4] Though he was not enrolled in Henry Adams's famous 1873 seminar that rooted American democratic practices in the tribal practices of the Anglo-Saxons and their German ancestors, Roosevelt was exposed to Teutonist theories during his years at Harvard through political science professor John Burgess. Burgess argued that Teutonic germs brought from the Black Forest to Great Britain could also be traced to Puritan New England. In addition, Roosevelt ascribed to the romanticization of historical and literary Anglo-Saxon roots of both American practices and individual genealogies as professed by the Harvard faculty. The end result for Roosevelt was a view of northern European racial superiority based on the profound influence of the frontier on the development of American character.[5]

Roosevelt gave over his interest in science to study law, but he was soon swept up into politics and was swiftly elected to the New York state assembly. Alice's death from complications during childbirth in 1894 had a devastating effect on Roosevelt, who left New York politics for the ranch he had purchased the year before in South Dakota. Roosevelt threw himself into ranch life and remade his image into that of a western hero. The transformation from Harvard-trained New Yorker to western ranchman was communicated through a series of books, *Hunting Trips of a Ranchman* (1885), *Ranch Life and the Hunting Trail* (1888), and *The Winning of the West* (1885–94).

His multivolume *The Winning of the West* continued Burgess's Teutonic trajectory by drawing explicit parallels between the hero of the *Nibelungenlied* and the American frontiersman.[6] Indeed, Roosevelt ascribed the success of the frontiersmen to their "blood and breeding." In his words, the frontiersmen's "inheritance of sturdy and self-reliant manhood helped them greatly."[7] This is not to say that Roosevelt believed that blood determined the frontiersman's success completely.

Roosevelt was deeply dedicated to the Lamarckian idea that the environment could profoundly influence an organism and that the results of that environmental influence could be passed from generation to generation. The highly valued character of the frontiersman was as much a result of blood as breeding, that is, living in the frontier environment. The ability of the environment to shape the character of an individual, family, or race was crucially important to Roosevelt because it allowed that altering the environment was a powerful and lasting means of social reform.[8]

With its emphasis on the influence of the environment, Roosevelt's view of race and racial development was much more flexible than that of the social Darwinist. Where Darwinists emphasized the struggle for existence as the means for the evolutionary progression of races, Roosevelt adopted a life cycle model of racial development. In his 1910 paper, "Biological Analogies in History," for instance, Roosevelt argued that races, like biological species, followed patterns of life and death, birth, change, and growth. Blurring the boundary between races and nations, Roosevelt applied the analogy to explain the birth of southern European races as well as the decline of the Romans into racial or national decadence. The Romans had "lost their fighting edge" by succumbing to "greed and luxury and sensuality"; but Roosevelt was careful to note that fallen races could rise again.[9] From a social reform standpoint, Roosevelt's racial scheme was not determinist; it was full of possibility. Any race was capable of improvement or decline. Nevertheless, at any given time, the worth of a race and its potential could be judged and pronounced either superior or deficient.

Men As Trees Walking

The status and development of American racial character was a particular concern for Roosevelt. As his political star began to rise again after his excursion in the West, Roosevelt's thinking about racial competition and race progress was expressed publicly in his imperialist vision of the "white man's burden" to advance civilization around the globe. Intertwined with his advocacy of virile masculinity and the "strenuous life," Roosevelt's imperialism was intended to demonstrate American racial superiority.[10] Racial competition was not restricted to the international arena, however. Roosevelt had long been concerned with race struggles within the United States, especially with increasing immigration. As I discussed in the preceding chapter, Roosevelt had shown concern over declining birthrates from the mid-1890s. As president after McKinley's assassination in 1901, Roosevelt developed his concern over race competition within the United States into an attack on race suicide.

As part of his campaign against race suicide, Roosevelt's pronouncements on national character and race were often generalized descriptions of men and women who embodied "decency, morality, virtue, clean living," as well as "the power to do, the power to dare, and the power to endure."[11] However, in his sixth and seventh annual addresses in 1906 and 1907, Roosevelt privileged the farmer as the typical American and the exemplar of American racial character. Acknowledging the rising prominence of the city and the increasing migration from the country, Roosevelt argued, "We cannot afford to lose that pre-eminently typical American, the farmer who owns his own medium sized farm." Roosevelt applauded the growth of American cities, but would not allow the growth of the cities to be "at the expense of the country farmer."[12] The full scope of Roosevelt's advocacy was spelled out in a speech celebrating the founding of America's agricultural colleges.

In "The Man Who Works With His Hands," Roosevelt clearly equated the status of the nation with the status of the rural family. "If there is any one lesson taught by history," Roosevelt argued, "it is that the permanent greatness of any state must ultimately depend more upon the character of its country population than upon anything else."[13] "It would be a calamity," Roosevelt continued, "to have our farms occupied by a lower type of people than the hard-working, self-respecting, independent, and essentially manly and womanly men and women who have hitherto constituted the most typically American, and on the whole the most valuable, element in our entire nation."[14]

Roosevelt's fears were based on the high rate at which young men and women were leaving the countryside for the city. Like others, Roosevelt feared that the country was losing its best and brightest. The dispersal of sons and daughters to jobs outside the home had challenged the patriarchal family of the nineteenth century and resulted in the creation of family reform groups who wished to restore "order." Roosevelt wished to restore the order by reforming the rural family.[15] The key, he thought, was to make country life as socially and culturally attractive as urban life, to build a sense of community in the countryside, and to improve the economic prospects of farm families.

An absolutely crucial element of his plan was the farmer's wife. After arguing that special attention should be given to the improvement of women's lives on the farm, Roosevelt fell back into a familiar celebration of motherhood and the home. "The best crop is the crop of children," Roosevelt proclaimed; "the best products of the farm are the men and women raised there."[16] These "pre-eminently American" farm women were charged to engage in the one "really indispensable industry," the "industry of the home." By arguing that nothing could take the place of the home, Roosevelt made clear that women's duty was within that home "doing her full housewife's work." Of course, the other duty to which Roosevelt felt all "American" women were bound was the duty to bear children in order to preserve the "race."[17] That Roosevelt would end this speech on the farmer with an overtly pronatalist proclamation of women's duty to the state and the race speaks to the extent to which his ideologies of the home and the rural family had been racialized. The year after this speech, Roosevelt put his racial ideology to work politically.

"ONE ORGANIC WHOLE": THE COMMISSIONS FOR CONSERVATION AND COUNTRY LIFE

In 1908, Theodore Roosevelt officially launched two major commissions: the National Conservation Commission and the Country Life Commission. Conservation of natural resources and the improvement of country life were conceived of as interdependent efforts by Roosevelt and by com-mission conveners Gifford Pinchot, the chief forester for the Department of Agriculture, and Sir Horace Plunkett, an Irish member of Parliament and sometime Wyoming rancher.[18] According to Plunkett, he and Pinchot regarded conservation and country life as "one organic whole."[19] A fact with which Roosevelt agreed when he wrote, "Conservation and rural-life policies are really two sides of the same policy; and down at bottom this policy rests upon the fundamental law that neither man nor nation can prosper unless, in dealing with the present, thought is steadily taken for the future."[20] Under Pinchot's direction, Roosevelt's conservation pro-gram promoted the development of natural resources as efficiently as possible for the common good. From Plunkett's perspective, Pinchot ar-gued that "*every* National resource must be husbanded." He did not view his job as "mere forestry administration," but "seemed to see men as trees walking."[21] Pinchot was explicit in The Fight For Conservation (1910) that the livelihood and living conditions of the farmer were of paramount impor-tance. For Pinchot, the farmer was of special value to the nation by virtue of his "attachment to the soil." This relationship to the land gave the farmer "his steadiness, his sanity, his simplicity and directness, and many of his other desirable qualities."[22] What was needed was a way of preserv-ing and maintaining that relationship.

Using Plunkett's experience organizing the Farm Cooperative System and the Department of Agriculture and other Industries and for Technical Instruction in Ireland, both Pinchot and Plunkett advocated education as a means to teach farmers the value of a cooperative system of agricultural production. This Irish model directly addressed economic issues such as land tenancy and the distribution of wealth away from producers. Cooper-ative organization was thought to offer greater economic stability and a greater sense of community.[23]

Plunkett did not expect to be able to apply directly the techniques he had used in Ireland to the United States. In fact, he expected to meet with significant resistance because of the American ideology of the individual-ism of small yeoman farmers.[24] Plunkett also imagined he would have more success if he approached groups whom he believed would be more pliable and less entrenched in their individualism. Early on, he advocated organizing African American farmers in the South, claiming they were a group in which "clan and tribal instincts seem to survive."[25] Because of this vision of American individualism, Plunkett and Pinchot tended to emphasize a social agenda based upon community building and education.

The National Conservation Commission was appointed in 1908 following Pinchot's well-orchestrated Governor's Conference on Conservation. This conference was extremely successful at rallying support for conservation and produced a mandate for a national, as well as thirty-six state, conservation commissions.[26] The National Conservation Commission was comprised of four sections—Waters, Forests, Lands, and Minerals—with W. J. McGee, Overton Price, George Woodruff, and Joseph Holmes as the respective section secretaries. Pinchot was the chairman of the Commissions Executive Committee and organized a systematic inventory of the nation's resources as the first order of business.

The Country Life Commission, like the National Conservation Commission, was a group of carefully chosen experts. Liberty Hyde Bailey, soon to be dean of the College of Agriculture at Cornell University, was appointed chairman. Other members included Henry Wallace, publisher of *Wallace's Farmer*; Kenyon Butterfield, a founder of rural sociology; Walter Hines Page, editor of the *World's Work*; C. S Barrett, president of the Farmer's Cooperative and Educational Union; William Beard, chairman of the National Irrigation Association and the Sacramento Valley Improvement Association; and Gifford Pinchot.[27] The commission was charged with reporting on conditions in the countryside, available remedies for any problems, and the best means of organizing a permanent investigative body. To compile their report commissioners surveyed country residents, toured and held hearing in twenty-nine states, and encouraged local meetings whose results could be forwarded to the commission.[28]

Conceived as "one organic whole," the Country Life and National Conservation Commissions both undertook surveys or inventories of the state of the nation. With significant overlap in their leadership, these two movements exerted a mutual influence on each other that created in each an element of what Samuel Hays has characterized as a "moral crusade." This emphasis on the social and cultural aspects of each movement would eventually create a rift in each as more economically oriented groups were founded.[29]

Men As Trees Walking

At a time of increasing migration to the cities from the countryside and from abroad, country life reformers thought it was essential to keep future generations on the farm. Plunkett argued that "the people of every State are largely bred in rural districts, and . . . the physical and moral well-being of those districts must consequently determine the quality of the whole people."[30] If America continued to drain the best and brightest from the country, Plunkett continued, "the raw material out of which urban society is made will be seriously deteriorated."[31] Plunkett's and Pinchot's plan to avoid this "national degeneracy" was to improve the conditions of rural life economically, socially, and culturally.

Economically, country life reformers wanted to make the farm more organized and efficient.[32] A number of means for this revitalization were proposed, including the introduction of scientific and mechanized agriculture, improved public roads, and improved systems of distribution of farm products using state and federal farm agencies. Education programs were also proposed on topics such as water and soil conservation and cooperative organization. Intensive agriculture of high cash value crops was proposed to bolster the small farm.[33] In addition, new farm-credit programs were introduced in order to reduce tenancy and increase the number of farmers who were also farm owners.[34]

These economic issues were not completely separate from the social issues of the country life movement. In the case of tenancy, the transient nature of tenant farmers was connected to the decline of the rural church, opposition to rural community improvement, and the deterioration of the physical appearance of rented farms. In many cases, tenant farmers were recent immigrants and became a target as a result of their "foreign ways." Increasing numbers of immigrant tenant farmers also contributed to fears that native-born Americans were abandoning the countryside. Tenant farms seemed to accelerate the process of folk depletion and racial decline. In the words of country life reformer William Rossiter, immigrant tenant farmers were not "in harmony with the spirit of the institutions created by native stock."[35]

More generally, country life reformers addressed social and cultural conditions with efforts directed at the country church, school, and home. These kinds of efforts were all overlaid with the agrarian myth of the yeoman farmer and farm family. While country life leaders urged rural churches to become more community oriented and include farmers as part of that community, educational efforts emphasized the farmer's relationship to the land through programs in nature study and agriculture. Efforts directed at the rural home sought to make it more convenient, less isolated, and more sociable.[36]

As part of his involvement in the country life movement, Gifford Pinchot collaborated with Charles Otis Gill to reach a scientific assessment of the status of the country church. Gill and Pinchot as well as others within the leadership of the country life movement had identified the country church as a key institution in the reform of rural life. As Gill and Pinchot put it, "Among the institutions available for the great task of restoring country life to its proper and necessary life of the nation, the country church holds or should hold a commanding place." The country church represented an important bulwark against the migration of the "best people" from the countryside and the subsequent "decline in the quality of the country population." The country church was credited with determining and vitalizing the "religious, moral, and social life of rural communities in the United States during whole periods in our national development," especially among the Pilgrims of New England. This was a recognition of the social role played by the church in defining a rural community by bringing people together regularly and focusing community resources. The problem was that the country church had declined and needed to be "restored to its old-time vitality."[37]

Gill and Pinchot took their task to be an accurate assessment of the condition of the country church since the 1880s. Focusing on a rural county in Vermont and another in New York, Gill, who had been a country minister in Vermont, systematically surveyed the Protestant rural churches in order to get an accurate accounting of their membership, involvement, and income in terms of both dollars and purchasing power. This survey method was a hallmark of the Country Life Commission's approach to studying the problems of rural life and agriculture. It characterized their approach to problem solving and planning as a scientific endeavor.[38] Incidentally, this was the same approach taken by Roosevelt when he ordered an inventory of the nation's resources in order to evaluate how best to conserve them. In this study of country churches, Pinchot used his experience surveying and assessing forest resources to prepare a plan of investigation that Gill then executed in the field.[39]

The results of their survey confirmed Gill and Pinchot's fears regarding the country church. In the twenty-year period they analyzed, church expenditures in both counties had increased in dollar amounts but had decreased when figured in terms of purchasing power. Moreover, small gains in membership did not make up for the "alarming reductions" in church attendance. In Gill and Pinchot's words, "the vitality and power of the country church in these two counties is in decline."[40]

Because the causes of the decline of the country church were numerous and varied, Gill and Pinchot were careful not to overgeneralize their proposed remedies. Instead they first presented an exemplar of the successful country church and built their general recommendations from this example and others in the two counties they studied.

The most successful church in Gill and Pinchot's study was a Vermont church oriented toward the community and governed by "principles of democracy and social service." Instead of promoting what was seen to be in the narrow interests of the church, this church put itself in service to the community by founding a civic league and boys club. More important for Gill and Pinchot, when the church ministers began to participate in the country life movement and extended their idea of community into the countryside, farmers began to attend regularly and "gave the church a new vitality and a new appeal."[41] For Gill and Pinchot, the successful country church was a force for community improvement.

When they began to generalize their remedies, social service and cooperation were acknowledged as crucial aspects of the revitalization of the church as a force within the community. Naturally, the improvement of country life was at the top of the list of remedies. In the past, according to Gill and Pinchot, the country church, the press, and the schools "helped to direct the attention of the country boy and girl to the city as a place of success."[42] The country church could take a role in making rural life a success by organizing cooperative ventures in crop production and marketing, milling, banking, and the purchasing of supplies. For Gill and Pinchot, country churches had to realize that part of their job was, using

Horace Plunkett's slogan, to promote "better farming, better business and better living"—to promote the country life movement.[43] Economic cooperation was the means to retain and promote the physical, intellectual, and moral health of the country population.

Improving farm conditions, agricultural practices, and business skills required reaching an adult population that was in many ways resistant to urban authority. The Country Life Commission decided that its best means to reach adults was through the home demonstration and extension system being established by the U.S. Department of Agriculture. Started in Texas by Seaman Knapp, extension work brought farm experts to the farmers, teaching them "economy, order, sanitation, patriotism, and a score of other wholesome lessons."[44] While farm agents dealt with agricultural issues, home demonstration agents usually addressed themselves to farm wives about home and family life. From its beginning in 1902, the extension system grew quickly and was federally supported by the Smith-Lever Act in 1914, which provided matching funds for farm and home demonstration programs.

Agricultural extension and home demonstration was also strongly supported among African American educators and farmers. Booker T. Washington's Tuskegee Institute established its Movable School in 1906. Thomas Monroe Campbell, who directed the Tuskegee effort, described the object of these Movable Schools as placing "before the farmers concrete illustrations proving to them that they can do better work; make more produce, on a smaller number of acres of land, at least expense, and at the same time, beautify their homes."[45] Campbell's vision for this type of educational outreach was motivated by his desire to help the people to whom he dedicated his autobiography: "the millions of rural dwellers of the nation, now struggling desperately to attain the established 'American standard of living,' and to the most costly, yet the most priceless commodity that any farmer can grow, namely a 'crop' of children."[46] While Campbell clearly celebrated the farm family, as an African American his work should be considered as part of a wider program of racial uplift promoted by Washington and other African American leaders at the time. Roosevelt famously supported Washington's efforts at Tuskegee, but it is not clear that his comments on race suicide and country life were intended for rural African Americans.[47]

Perhaps the largest piece of social reform undertaken on behalf of country life concerned education for children. When the Country Life Commission filed its report, fewer than one in four rural children completed the eighth grade. According to David Danbom, "unstandardized and locally controlled, marked by primitive physical facilities and unsanitary conditions, plagued by unprofessional instruction and poor attendance, the nation's one-room schools epitomized educational inefficiency to urban educators."[48] The proposed answer was to use professional supervision to enforce changes in curriculum, the school calendar, teacher qualifications, and school conditions. Beyond improvements in efficiency, country life reformers wanted to alter the goals of rural education. In order to keep children on farms, education stressed cooperation, technical agricultural training, and nature study.

Keeping the rural child, who was perceived to be closer to the earth and nature, in his or her environment was a fundamental goal of the Country Life Commission.[49] Cornell University College of Agriculture dean Liberty Hyde Bailey advocated nature study as a way of celebrating the farmer and country citizen as a naturalist.[50] Reinforcing rural children's relationship to nature, Bailey thought, would help keep them on the farm and out of the city when they got older. Bailey believed that one should start with the child's sympathies and develop the child, not the subject. Using the example of a children's garden, Bailey wrote that "the child is first interested in the whole plant, the whole bug, the whole bird, as a living, growing object. It is a most significant fact that most young children like plants, but that most youths dislike botany."[51] For Bailey, nature study was an appeal to make school match life. Something as simple as planting a garden would not only beautify the farm and possibly keep young people there as a result, it would help link them to the objects of their study. This connection to nature and to the land was what Roosevelt, Pinchot, and Bailey celebrated as the source of the farmer's character.

If the rural family was the foundation of the race or the nation, the farm wife was the foundation of the rural family. As they did for other aspects of rural life, country life reformers tried to ease the burdens of country women by introducing organization and efficiency into the rural home. Labor-saving devices such as washing machines, more-efficient cleaning, and simpler meals were promoted. Farmer's wives' courses became a popular means of engaging rural women in the ideas of domestic science and home economics. Telephones, improved roads, parcel post, and rural free delivery were meant to ease the isolation of the farm wife and convince her of the attractiveness of farm life. By encouraging women to become farmers' wives, Roosevelt sought to keep women in the dependent relationship he thought essential to the reproduction of the race. The challenge for him was to improve rural living conditions without altering the family structure or relationship to the land that made the country population the wellspring for the city.

What is crucial to understand is that the effort on behalf of the family farm and especially of farm women and children was linked by Roosevelt and others explicitly to the good of the race and the dangers of race degeneration. In language common to the country life movement and the conservation movement, the country was heralded as the "reservoir" for the city and the race.[52]

As Roosevelt turned to the public for support of conservation in 1908, the ideology of the home and family that made the country life movement relevant to the future of the race was extended to the conservation movement, thus contributing to a racialized understanding of the implications of the management of natural resources.[53]

THE CONSERVATION MOVEMENT

Under Roosevelt's administration, conservation efforts succeeded as individual pieces of legislation, such as the Reclamation Act of 1902. However, by 1909 Congress began to seriously oppose Roosevelt's conservation legislation. The National Conservation Commission had compiled a massive inventory of the nation's natural resources and argued for a comprehensive conservation policy.[54] Tensions between Congress and Roosevelt's allies over who should control conservation legislation reached a high point in 1909 when Congress refused to appropriate funds to support any further work by the commission. Despite support from President Taft and members of the Senate, Congress put an end to the National Conservation Commission.[55]

Pinchot had begun rallying popular support for forestry and conservation in 1905, when he first experienced resistance from Congress. In order to generate popular support and bring it to bear on Congress, Pinchot organized the National Conservation Association in 1909.[56] However, as public interest increased, the emphasis in the National Conservation Association shifted from primarily economic concerns regarding resources to a "moral crusade" dedicated to preserving nature in the face of the increasing artificiality and social instability of urban life.[57] As was forcefully expressed at the National Conservation Congresses, the conservation of children was taken to be a crucial part of the goal of ensuring the future well-being of the country by assuring an abundance of natural resources.[58]

After the summer of 1908, the scope of the conservation movement expanded dramatically.[59] This expansion to encompass issues of national health and vitality was encouraged by Roosevelt and backed with academic authority by the contributions of Irving Fisher, a professor of political economy at Yale. Although an expert on income and interest, a bout with tuberculosis beginning in 1898 left him with a keen interest in the value of healthy living. Public health became an agenda item under Fisher's direction.[60] Fisher advocated a eugenic program to improve the nation's heredity but emphasized the need to address public health concerns that would lower rates of infant mortality. Fisher framed his discussion by illustrating differential mortality rates among native-born Americans and immigrants, among different races, and between urban and rural populations. Fisher was concerned with issues of race degeneracy as a cause of poverty. Conserving natural resources, including the "national stock," were seen as a means of preventing that degeneracy and the host of social ills associated with it. Fisher's extensive report on national vitality published in the 1909 Report of the National Conservation Commission led to the establishment of a standing committee on vital resources at the 1910 National Conservation Congress.[61] By 1912, the entire annual meeting of the congress was devoted to the "conservation of human life."[62]

The broad scope of the early conservation movement was widely supported by women drawn from the General Federation of Women's Clubs to the DAR and the Audubon movement. The General Federation of Women's Clubs had forestry and waterway committees that lobbied for protective legislation and informed the federation's 800,000 members of the most pressing conservation issues. Women addressed national conferences and congresses and penned articles, editorials, and letters in support of various conservation causes. Even Gifford Pinchot's mother was involved as chair of the DAR's Conservation Committee in 1909.[63]

In the hands of these women, conservation was presented in terms of the conservation of womanhood, the home, and children. As with other maternalist reforms, women made issues of forestry, soil, and water relevant to their roles as protectors of future generations and of the home.[64] At the Second National Conservation Congress in 1911, DAR president Mrs. Matthew T. Scott addressed conservation in terms of race and motherhood. Likening immigrants to pollutants, Scott urged her audience to keep "our race" pure: "We must conserve the sources of our race in the Anglo-Saxon line, Mother of Liberty and Self-Government in the modern world." Scott's assumption that her audience shared her racial background and her interest in its supremacy were further accentuated as she continued by arguing, "We, the mothers of this generation—ancestresses of future generations—have a right to insist upon the conserving not only of soil, forest, bird, minerals, fishes, waterways, in the interest of our future home-makers, but also upon the conservation of the supremacy of the Caucasian race in our land. This Conservation, second to none in pressing importance, may and should be insured in the best interests of all races concerned; and the sooner attention is turned upon it the better (great applause)."[65] The effect of Scott's comments and others like them was to make the future status of the Anglo-Saxon race as important to the future homemaker or home builder as the conservation of any other natural resource.

While the broadening of the conservation agenda has struck historians as a departure from the real business of resource management relevant to forestry or the mining industry, the social agenda of the "moral crusade" was a crucial component of the culture of the conservation movement.[66] The women of the DAR connected conservation to the home and to child labor. Irving Fisher connected conservation to public health or national vitality. Even the business-oriented chief forester, Gifford Pinchot, was engaged on behalf of the broadened social agenda, as evidenced by his work on the country church and his service as one of the American vice presidents to the first International Congress of Eugenics in 1912. The importance of this social agenda is that it laid bare the racial ideology embraced by many proponents of conservation and country life.

In 1927, Leon Whitney, executive secretary of the American Eugenics Society, began a study of four Massachusetts towns: Shutesbury, Prescott, Pelham, and Leverett. The motivation for Whitney's study in Massachusetts was "to make a study of a degenerate community and compare it with a prosperous one."[67] Indeed, he was probably drawn to the region by its reputation as a rural area in decline. Unlike earlier Country Life Commission surveys that had helped established the patterns and effects of rural to urban migration, Whitney sought to understand the eugenic consequences of migration for rural life.

In the early twentieth century, a favorite device of eugenicists was the family study. Because they were interested in demonstrating the hereditary basis of social ills ranging from feeblemindedness to poverty, the study of the supposed patterns of inheritance across several generations was taken to be compelling evidence for both a eugenic diagnosis to the problem as well as a eugenic solution. Henry Goddards's infamous study of the Kallikak family, for instance, purports to demonstrate the hereditary basis of their feeblemindedness and the necessity of segregating feebleminded individuals in institutions such as the Vineland Training Home, which Goddard just happened to direct. The vast majority of family studies were of families from rural areas.

The Swift River valley, and the town of Shutesbury in particular, first became an object of eugenic investigation in 1912 when Isabelle Kendig was asked to research the family of "Sammy Huck" so that he might be committed to a local hospital. A field worker trained at the Eugenics Record Office, Kendig conducted a "careful study" of the Huck family during the summer of 1913.[68] As was the practice in these kinds of eugenic family studies, Kendig had invented the name "Huck" in order to protect the identity of her subjects. Historian Nicole Rafter has shown that these pseudonyms also protected field-workers from criticism by making it more difficult to discover that the "families" or "tribes" they discussed were often composites of individuals from different families.[69]

Kendig described the "notorious Huck family of S——" as a "net-work of degeneracy." Of course, one of the distinguishing features of the family studies undertaken by field-workers for the Eugenics Record Office is that they never failed to find degeneracy once they set out to look for it. Despite the commitment of Sammy Huck, it took considerable effort for Kendig to substantiate her "net-work of degeneracy."

According to Kendig, the Huck family was descended from Pilgrims who came to Plymouth in 1623. Two Huck brothers settled along the coast, and their descendants became "eminent men of affairs" who were "honored throughout the State." The family of a third brother went west and settled around what is now Shutesbury.[70] Indeed, Kendig found the Hucks to be "a sturdy race" well known for their "shrewdness" and their "iron constitution." If not for "an appalling amount of alcoholism and immorality," Kendig wondered whether the Hucks could be "called degenerates at all."[71]

Kendig's family study placed 436 individuals in the Huck genealogy. The most "conspicuous" degenerate trait in this genealogy was alcoholism. Kendig counted 50 members of the family, or 11.4 percent, as "intemperate." Because the Hucks were unwilling to discuss how much they drank with her, Kendig "adopted an arbitrary rule and pronounced everyone alcoholic who has been known on more than one occasion to drink to the point of intoxication."[72] The second "degenerate" trait of the Huck family was "immorality." Although Kendig did not have "an arbitrary rule" to define immorality, she apparently meant having sex and/or children out of wedlock. By her count the Huck genealogy included 52 "immoral individuals," or 11.9 percent of the family. This percentage is not higher than that found in a number of other eugenic family studies, but what made it stand out for Kendig is that despite their immorality the Huck family enjoyed good social standing. The "fact that such a situation excites little comment" was taken by Kendig to be an indictment of the morality of the entire community, where almost everyone was a Huck or was related to one.

When Leon Whitney came to Shutesbury in 1928, he had read Kendig's report on the "Hucks" but preferred to call them by their proper name, the Pratts. It was the Pratts who had captured Whitney's imagination. As he explained to a professor at the Massachusetts Agricultural College, "there are a few most excellent families which have gone out of Shutesbury and that vicinity and there is a direct connection between, so I am told, the Standard Oil Pratt family and the Pratts of Shutesbury. We expect to make a study of both the minus and plus families, therefore, and learn the reasons of their present condition."[73] Where Kendig focused her attention on degeneracy, Whitney was more interested in the contrast between "good" and "bad" branches of the Pratt family. This contrast was valued because it bore on the question of the impact of migration on rural decline. The decline of Shutesbury could be explained in part by those Pratts who were left behind.

To reformers and politicians who idealized rural life in a kind of romantic agrarianism, rural decline resulting from the migration of the "best elements" of the country to the city was cause for alarm—witness Edward Ross's description of certain "depleted" midwestern "communities which remind one of fished out ponds populated chiefly by bullheads and suckers."[74] Addressing the causes of rural decline led Roosevelt to form the Country Life Commission. It led eugenicists to places like Shutesbury.

Whitney's study of Shutesbury, Leverett, Prescott, and Pelham may have started with the Pratts, but it quickly diverged from the typical eugenic family study. In early family studies, the environment was not seriously considered as a cause of degeneracy. Whitney, however, defined eugenics as "a study of the effects of environment upon the quality of human stock." In other words, he believed that eugenics was as much about environment as heredity. Whitney made it clear that he was not studying the Pratts per se; he was studying the four Massachusetts villages in their entirety. In Whitney's words, "We were observing Shutesbury. . . . The town was the people and their properties and their activities. . . . There were the forces of the environment acting upon the quality of the stock and that was why Shutesbury . . . makes to us so fascinating a history."[75]

Shutesbury itself was acknowledged to be in decline. In correspondence, Whitney commented that "at one time there were 1,100 people there, but at present only 200 due to the adverse environment."[76] His description of the town in the introduction to his study is even more dramatic.

Shutesbury, now consists of a large number of cellar holes, a few new homes and many older ones in process of becoming cellar holes. These cellar holes and houses reflect to a remarkable degree the whole tenor of the town. Indeed it is possible, almost, to indicate the character of the people at various times, even the general character of the town itself by the rise and fall of the homes. Something happened which caused the beginning of Shutesbury. Something happened which caused its rise and something happened which caused its depletion. Some internal and external forces were exerted which made the town what it was in progressive periods.[77]

Whitney attributed this decline to a combination of economic, environmental, and hereditary factors. On the one hand, Whitney conceded that "there was no good way to earn a living so the ambitious young folks drifted away." On the other hand, Whitney described the remaining inhabitants as unmotivated and disorderly. To illustrate this judgment, Whitney told the story of Carry Pratt, who during court testimony was asked by the judge, "What do you raise in Shutesbury?" She answered, "Judge, in summer we raise blueberries and in winter we raise hell." Whitney noted that blueberries grew wild in the untended pastures around Shutesbury.[78] The moral that he drew from this story was that this kind of rebelliousness was an undesirable, constitutional feature of the inhabitants of Shutesbury.

Shutesbury residents did not share Whitney's interpretation of Carry Pratt's answer. In fact, soon after Pratt's testimony, "Hell'-en Winter" became the local nickname for Shutesbury. In addition, some residents founded a "Hell'en Winter" Club that held meetings during fishing and hunting season.[79] Local pride in their reputation for rebelliousness was also traced back to Shay's Rebellion.

Daniel Shays had lived in Shutesbury and then Pelham. A veteran of the Revolutionary War, Shays led an armed rebellion in 1787. "Shay's Army" was a group of local farmers and veterans who opposed an increasing tax burden that they could not meet without having their property seized by the state.[80] In the spirit of the Sons of Liberty, they closed courthouses and marched on Springfield, Massachusetts, before the militia put them down.

Contrary to Whitney's judgment, the residents of Shutesbury had "village pride," but they were proud of the kinds of traits and history that Whitney believed to be undesirable. Whitney held an ideal of rural life and the New England village that he expected towns such as Shutesbury to live up to. Whitney's praise for Shutesbury's fine church and village green located on a small hill at the center of the town suggests that Whitney held a ideal of the New England landscape common to urban reformers in the Northeast. Whitney was invoking an invented tradition of the New England village that depicted the ideal colonial or Puritan settlement as an agricultural village with two-story houses neatly ordered around the village green.[81] This village ideal transformed Thomas Jefferson's praise for the yeoman farmer into a regionally based ideal of the community, which preserved the equally idealized values and heritage of Puritan colonists.

In the hands of eugenicists such as Whitney, the New England village became a biological ideal as well as a geographic or environmental ideal. Maintaining the New England village was therefore a means of maintaining the "old stock" of New England. Whitney was not so much of an idealist, however, that he thought villages such as those to be flooded by the Quabbin Reservoir ought to be maintained at any cost.[82] Instead, Whitney's analysis of successful New England villages such as Sunderland and declining New England villages such as Shutesbury advocated the relocation of farmers and rural residents to better farmland and more-prosperous villages.

As executive secretary of the American Eugenics Society, Whitney had been working closely with Henry Perkins, who would become the society's president in 1931. Perkins was a native of Vermont and especially concerned with implementing a eugenic program to preserve the rural "old stock" Vermonter. Drawing on Elin Anderson's study of three Vermont towns, in 1931 Perkins proposed the relocation of Vermont farmers from "declining" towns to "progressive communities."[83] In Perkins's report to the Vermont legislature, he wrote: "Deterioration can take place only in poor isolated communities where the potential capacities of the people are not challenged into use. If then Vermont wishes its future citizens to have the same fine qualities of character that marked the early builders of the state, it must . . . provide a social environment that will continue to bring out all the fine qualities in the character of its people."[84] In the mid-1930s the Federal Emergency Relief Administration's Rural Rehabilitation Division advocated this resettlement plan, but the Vermont legislature was unwilling to fund the proposed program. Perkins did successfully gain legislative support for a number of other rural eugenics efforts in Vermont, however. Significantly, the organization that coordinated and advocated these efforts was the Vermont Commission on Country Life.[85]

Roosevelt idealized the past and sought to manage the conditions of rural life in order to maintain the rural family as the "reservoir" for the nation and the race. In the words of Samuel Hays, Roosevelt "faced two directions at once, accepting the technical requirements of an increasingly organized society, but fearing its social consequences . . . he sought Jeffersonian ends through Hamiltonian means."[86] The national conservation and country life movements combined social and economic agendas in an effort to organize and efficiently manage the nation's resources. The nationalization of resource management was a significant expansion of the scope of government. More important, because of the interconnection between conservation and country life, management of the rural family became part of the national regulation of resources. The scale of this intervention and its intrusion into the lives of rural families was masked and made more acceptable by framing it in terms of nostalgia for the farm family. The racial and agrarian image of the family Roosevelt deployed was meant to invoke a sense of stability, a sense of naturalized order to be recreated by governmental management on a national scale.

6

FITTER FAMILIES FOR
FUTURE FIRESIDES

FLORENCE SHERBON
AND POPULAR EUGENICS

Yea, I have a goodly heritage.
Psalms 16:6

The 1911 "Million Dollar Parade" of prize livestock and other agricultural products at the Iowa State Fair concluded with an automobile filled with preschool children. A runner on the side of the car proclaimed them to be "Iowa's Best Crop." A later report on the event noted that these children had participated in a preschool health examination competition in which the examiners followed the only criterion available to them at the time: the methods of observing used by stock judges for determining prize livestock.[1]

Charles Davenport, head of the Eugenics Record Office, wrote a post card to the Iowa contest-organizers stating that stock judges always took inheritance into account, warning, "You should score 50 percent for heredity before you begin to examine a baby." The next year, Davenport admonished even more dramatically, "A prize winner at two may be an epileptic at ten."[2] The Iowa administrators took note of this caution but did not change the way they thought of their better baby contests until they observed for themselves how calves were sometimes judged. At Iowa county fairs, a calf would be examined on its own and then carefully compared to each of its parents. To contest organizer Dr. Florence Sherbon, this comparison suggested that perhaps they needed to judge entire families instead of just individual children.[3] Over the course of the next decade Sherbon and Mary T. Watts transformed their Iowa better baby contest into Kansas's fitter family contests. In Watts's words, "It remained for the Kansas Free Fair to give the Better Baby a Pedigree. It is now demanded that the Better Baby be supported by a Family, fit both in their inheritance and in the development of their mental, moral, and physical traits."[4]

Where better baby contests had been developed as part of the U.S. Children's Bureau campaign against infant mortality, fitter family contests were developed as part of the popular education campaigns of the American eugenics movement.[5] Eugenicists' concern with heredity certainly broadened the scope of these contests from "healthy" children to "fitter families," but the infusion of hereditarian thinking did not displace earlier concerns with diet, exercise, and home environment. The fitter family contests merged eugenics with expansive and intrusive public health campaigns and practices. The result was a much more expansive type of eugenic reform encompassing heredity and environment within an ideal of the family and the home.[6]

Florence Sherbon, Mary Watts, and Leon Whitney in front of the Eugenics
Building at the Kansas Free Fair in 1924. (American Eugenics Society Papers,
American Philosophical Society Archives, Philadelphia, Pa.)

Watts and Sherbon deliberately chose to hold these contests at agricultural fairs. Fitter family contests appealed to a deeply rooted sense of nostalgia for the rural family at a time when the nation was becoming increasingly urban, when rural children were choosing not to stay on the farm, and when the culture of the Roaring Twenties challenged "traditional values." Introducing fitter family contests as human livestock competitions encouraged families to reimagine their histories as pedigrees subject to scientific analysis and control. As such, these contests fused nostalgia for the farm family with a modernist promise of scientific control.[7]

BETTER BABIES AND THE CHILDREN'S BUREAU

The Children's Bureau was initiated as a government clearinghouse for information on child hygiene and rearing.[8] The legend of the founding of the Children's Bureau holds that over breakfast one morning in 1903 settlement leaders Lillian Wald and Florence Kelley were reading their mail and the morning newspaper when Kelley read a letter asking her for information on the high summer death rates among children. Neither Kelley nor Wald had an answer. After reading a newspaper article on the secretary of agriculture's trip to the South to survey damage to the cotton crop from the boll weevil, Wald is said to have remarked: "If the government can have a department to take such an interest in what is happening to the cotton crop, why can't it have a bureau to look after the nation's child crop?"[9]

Ten years later the Children's Bureau was officially established through the efforts of settlement house workers and residents, a vast network of club women, and, notably, the National Child Labor Committee.[10] In 1909 the campaign for a federal agency received its biggest boost when Theodore Roosevelt held the White House Conference on the Care of Dependent Children. Although the key advocates for the Children's Bureau were maternalist reformers such as Wald, Kelley, Julia Lathrop, and others, they shared some of Roosevelt's concern with the "American family" and the purported erosion of Anglo-American standards of living.[11] Roosevelt's endorsement brought the campaign for a government agency before the federal government, even if it would be President Taft who would sign the bill marking its creation.

The bureau's mandate included "all matters pertaining to the welfare of children and child life among all classes of people," though infant mortality and the birthrate were highlighted as concerns of the agency.[12] Toward this end, the Children's Bureau officially created Baby Day in 1915, Baby Week in 1916, and Children's Year in 1918 to publicize the need for better infant and maternal care, although the Children's Bureau pamphlet introducing the Baby Week campaigns makes it clear that such events had been organized on the local level for years out of growing interest in the welfare of babies.[13] The bureau's efforts culminated in the 1921 Sheppard-Towner Act promoting infant and maternal health.[14]

In 1916, the Children's Bureau commissioned a number of studies of different communities in order to assess the relative rates and causes of infant mortality in rural and urban settings. While the director of the Children's Bureau, Julia Lathrop, was trained at Hull House and more familiar with problems of child welfare in urban settings, she thought the comparison of rural and urban, as well as native and immigrant, communities to be an important part of the bureau's approach to infant mortality. Part of Lathrop's and her successor, Grace Abbot's, agenda was ending child labor. Opposition to this agenda, especially from southern textile manufacturers, miners, and farmers, meant that it was politically expedient to focus on the deaths of infants rather than intervene on behalf of child workers.[15]

Florence Sherbon was hired by the Children's Bureau in 1915 to conduct a series of children's health conferences in rural communities throughout Indiana and Wisconsin.[16] Born in Iowa in 1869, Sherbon earned a nursing degree from the Iowa State Hospital, where she later worked as a nurse and superintendent of the Training School in the 1890s. She entered medical school at Iowa State University at the turn of the century and earned her M.D. in 1904. That same year she married classmate James Bayard Sherbon. With her husband and father, Sherbon moved to Colfax, Iowa, where the three took over the Victoria Sanitarium and Mineral Spring. The sanitarium filled the first year and would be expanded and renovated by the Sherbons.[17] At some point, it began losing money, or perhaps the Sherbons could not pay off the cost of renovations or of a new annex. When her father died in 1912, Sherbon was counting on his estate to pay outstanding liens.[18] The value of the estate was much less than expected, however, and when the estate was settled in 1916 Sherbon was forced to sell the sanitarium. Moreover, her husband had gone, leaving Sherbon a single mother of twin girls, Alice and Elizabeth, born in 1908.[19]

Perhaps inspired by her own interest in her daughters, in 1911 Sherbon joined Mary T. Watts to organize a better baby contest that year in Iowa.[20] Once again, the disparity between the care provided to livestock and that given children evident at an agricultural fair was credited in popular accounts with inspiring Watts to begin judging babies at agricultural fairs.[21] The Iowa contest was sponsored by members of the American Medical Association's Committee for Public Health Among Women and the Iowa Congress of Mothers.[22] The success of the first contest spurred its organizers to form the American Baby Health Organization with both Watts and Sherbon as officers. In 1913 Watts wrote to Julia Lathrop at the Children's Bureau of the contest's popularity and, interestingly, noted that they usually tried to have "Eugenic Expositions" associated with the contests.[23] Iowa organizers quickly developed their own scorecard and instituted rural and urban categories. The sudden popularity of better baby contests after 1911 was remarkable thanks in part to publicity and organization of similar contests by the *Woman's Home Companion*.[24] In fact in 1913, the *Woman's Home Companion* reported that their Better Babies Bureau had examined almost 150,000 babies during that fair season alone.[25] The popularity of these child health contests and Sherbon's experience with them certainly helped her land a job at the Children's Bureau in 1915.

Sherbon's new position at the Children's Bureau required her to travel extensively, focusing specifically on infant and maternal health. Fourteen conferences in three months with twins in tow was clearly not feasible, so Sherbon persuaded her sister, Maud, to move to Iowa and join in the "joint mothering" of her daughters while she was in the field.[26] Maud Brown had trained to teach high school sciences by getting a master's in biology and psychology at the University of Iowa in 1901. She returned in 1908 to get a credential in educational administration, which allowed her to use her experience teaching high school science in Butte, Montana, and Des Moines, Iowa, to move into curriculum development. From 1912 to 1916, she served as the supervisor of nature study for the Los Angeles public school system. Later, as the supervisor of hygiene in Kansas City, Missouri, she started the first work in health education linked to measurements in public schools. She is credited with originating the "first permanent record cards recording height, weight, immunizations, [and] growth records" now routine in public schools.[27]

When Florence Sherbon began her fieldwork in Wisconsin, she carried with her a medical ideal of child and maternal health backed by her authority as a physician. She had an agenda for reducing infant mortality and improving the health care of both infant and mother that was based on institutionalized and medically supervised obstetric care. Sherbon reports that when she began in 1916 she was certain that "midwives had to go."[28] Her imposition of urban medical standards was frequently resisted, however, and with good reason. As other field-workers reported, local practices of obstetric care were often safer.[29] After observing midwives and maternity practices in rural Wisconsin in the summer of 1916, Sherbon abandoned her earlier preconceptions of what constituted medically appropriate obstetric care.[30] She did not surrender her authority as a physician with this shift in attitude, however. Instead, her appreciation of local medical practices signifies her understanding that she was entering already existing health networks. Her effectiveness at communicating health standards depended on this understanding.[31]

One of the most important lessons for Sherbon and the Children's Bureau concerned the way in which they communicated their message about child health and hygiene. In 1915 Dr. Lydia DeVilbiss from the Kansas Department of Health persuaded Julia Lathrop of the value of using contests by arguing, "Instead of going into the country districts and trying to persuade the farmer folk to do what we want them to do, this plan proposes to put them on their mettle and let them do for themselves what we want them to do and what we should have difficulty in getting them to do in any other way."[32] DeVilbiss's suggestion to use contests as an indirect means of social control was persuasive within the Children's Bureau, and Sherbon's experience with the Iowa better baby contests reinforced her confidence in this approach. In 1916 Sherbon held conferences where infants and children were examined and their mothers interviewed. Not all contests were the same, however. Sherbon complained to the

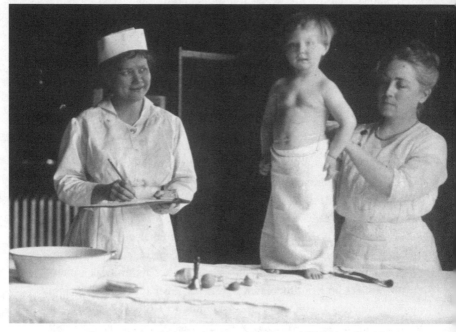

Florence Sherbon (right) and a nurse measuring a child during a health examination, no date. (Florence Sherbon Papers, Kenneth Spencer Research Library, University of Kansas, Lawrence, Kans.)

Children's Bureau that Better Baby Contests sponsored by the *Woman's Home Companion* produced a situation in Wausau with "disorderly mobs of crying babies coming without appointments—more than one hundred a day."[33] Sherbon preferred a more orderly format where fewer children would be seen, but she could spend at least twenty minutes with each one and then work with a local follow-up committee. Sherbon wanted to promote child health, but she also wanted to carefully document and communicate health standards in individual medical exams. The Children's Bureau wanted Sherbon to reach as many people as possible. In fact, Sherbon's mission of surveying a large number of rural communities in Indiana and Wisconsin had proven much more expensive than originally anticipated. Lathrop and Meigs had wanted Sherbon and her "crew" to travel by horse and buggy, but Sherbon was forced to rent a car and driver to keep on schedule. In the end, the Children's Bureau decided to cut expenses by letting Sherbon go and instead promoted child health contests nationally through networks of women's clubs as part of their Baby Week campaign.[34]

FLORENCE SHERBON AND THE FITTER FAMILIES CONTESTS

When Sherbon found out in 1916 that her work for the Children's Bureau would not be extended past the next year, she admitted to Julia Lathrop that child welfare work had "got" her. Sherbon dreamed of settling with her sister and daughters in a small town in rural Wisconsin in order to conduct a complete study of every woman from "one day to ninety year" with regard to the manifold effects of maternity on a woman's life. It is clear that Sherbon wanted to continue her survey work, but there was no further appropriation for her at the Children's Bureau, her mortgage was in foreclosure, and she had decided not to leave her daughters again. As a result, Sherbon applied to state boards of health and extension services throughout the Midwest in order to continue her work on child hygiene.[35]

In 1917 Sherbon was brought to Kansas by Dr. Samuel Crumbine and the Kansas State Board of Health to temporarily replace Dr. Lydia DeVilbiss, who was on a lecture tour.[36] By the fall she was named the director of physical education for women at the University of Kansas in Lawrence. Her duties included teaching courses on the physical development of the child, physical examination technique, and hygiene. She also supervised physical examinations for every woman student and gave advice on exercise and nutrition.[37] Her position was moved in 1920 to the Department of Home Economics, where she was appointed professor of child care.[38] This new position appropriately reflected her work in the better baby contests and for the Children's Bureau. However, just as she was appointed to this position, she greatly expanded the scope of her earlier contest work.

In 1920 Sherbon and Watts orchestrated the first fitter family contest. By this time, both were experts at using the contest format to reach rural communities. Their goal was to "stimulate" the "interest of intelligent families" and arouse a "family consciousness by which each family will conceive of itself as a genetic unit with a definite obligation to study its heredity and build up its health status."[39] As will be discussed below, the format and design of the fitter family contests had special appeal, but eugenics in general was enormously popular during the 1920s.

Eugenics in the United States had been growing in popularity since the turn of the century despite increasing scientific criticism. By 1928, 376 universities and colleges in the United States offered courses in eugenics.[40] During the first three decades of the twentieth century, eugenicists in the United States successfully pressed for national legislation restricting immigration as well as state legislation for marriage restriction and institutionalization and sterilization of the "unfit."[41]

Florence Sherbon's brand of eugenics was not typical of mainstream eugenics, however. In the first two decades of the twentieth century, Charles Davenport led the American eugenics movement as he combined research on patterns of human inheritance with a desire to preserve the sanctity of the germ plasm.[42] Davenport, like most geneticists who were also eugenicists, was a strict hereditarian who allocated a relatively minor role to the environment in the determination of biological traits. As director of the Eugenics Record Office from 1910 to 1934, Davenport promoted eugenic research including the collection and organization of family pedigree data collected by trained eugenic field-workers. In the 1920s, however, organization of the American eugenics movement began to shift away from Davenport's efforts in the Eugenics Record Office toward the activities of the American Eugenics Society.[43]

The American Eugenics Society (AES) arose from the 1921 Second International Congress of Eugenics.[44] Unlike the Eugenics Record Office, the AES emphasized education and the promotion of eugenics in American society more than scientific research. The AES chairman from 1922 to 1926 was Irving Fisher, a professor of political economy at Yale University and founder of the Life Extension Institute. Fisher's interests were very broad. An expert on monetary policy, he had a long-standing involvement in public health policy, chairing the Committee of One Hundred, which had proposed a national health service in 1908. The Life Extension Institute, which he founded in 1914, promoted health practices through annual health exams and related literature on healthy living and lifestyles distributed through insurance companies such as Metropolitan Life.[45] Guided by Fisher and later by Frederick Osborn, the AES would significantly broaden the scope of what was considered to be eugenic reform.[46] The broader goals of the AES were reflected in the motto from their letterhead from 1935, which read, "The children of the United States must be born of parents who will provide the essentials necessary for the development of character, physique and intelligence."[47] This motto "disturbed" more-hereditarian eugenicists such as Charles Davenport, who thought that the motto placed too much emphasis on "conditioning" when it should be emphasizing "racial" and "genetical" traits. Indeed, Davenport worried that he would not "be welcome" at meetings of the AES any longer, because, as a result of their change in emphasis, his opinions would "cause enmity rather than promote friendship."[48]

From their headquarters in New Haven, Connecticut, the AES organized conferences, contests, and publications on a wide range of topics related to eugenics. Indeed throughout the 1920s and into the 1930s the American Eugenics Society became much more oriented toward improving the environment and extended the domain of eugenic reform to living conditions, nutrition, home life, and social life more generally. In many ways, the organization's understanding of heredity was more in line with popular concepts of heredity, which incorporated both nature and nurture. As historian Martin Pernick argues, when most Americans spoke of "good breeding" they meant the combination of good ancestry and good upbringing. The fitter family contests appealed to and embodied this popular conception.[49]

Sherbon and many leaders in American eugenics saw the fitter family contests as opportunities for education and the promotion of eugenics. Together with sermon contests and traveling exhibits, the contests became central parts of the publicity effort of the American Eugenics Society in the 1920s.[50] At the same time, the fitter family contests were a means to collect detailed family information that could be used for research. These two goals came into conflict when Watts and Sherbon tried to standardize the procedures and the forms for the contests. As they prepared for their third contest in 1922, Watts asked permission to send Davenport a copy of the family history form they had been using for his criticism and feedback.[51] Davenport replied that he approved of the contests' emphasis on the family over the individual and asked that copies of the completed forms be placed on file at the Eugenics Record Office.[52] Once Davenport had received a copy of the form, he responded with detailed comments on the categories, the types of measurements, and the instructions for taking the measurements. Davenport was especially impressed with the length of the examination, because his goal of collecting a database of hereditary information for all human traits required as much information as he could reliably gather. The information from the fitter family contests was raw data that eventually could provide a basis for eugenic manipulation. Davenport was eager to have the contest data and repeatedly offered to analyze it statistically for Sherbon.[53]

The length of the exams became an issue between Watts and Sherbon in 1924. Watts favored a shorter exam that would have more appeal and so be more effective as a popularizing tool for eugenics. Sherbon believed that a shorter form taking anything less than an hour and a half to complete would not be a "fair test." Invoking the industrial ideal of assembly-line automation, Watts exclaimed, "This is the day of the Ford," and urged Davenport to intervene and propose a form that would be both quick and thorough.[54] Davenport, like Sherbon, favored more data rather than less. In letters to Irving Fisher and Davenport, Sherbon praised Watts's ability to forge an "indispensable link between science and the public," but she argued that a short form that would "sell the goods" would not be grounds for awarding prizes or collecting scientific information.[55] Sherbon's goal, however, was to synthesize efforts by Davenport's Eugenics Record Office, Fisher's Life Extension Institute, John Harvey Kellogg's

Race Betterment Foundation, and many different preschool and elementary school health examinations. She wanted a "unified procedure" for studying the family group.[56] Davenport agreed and, over the course of the next year, they exchanged many letters as they standardized the fitter family contest forms to include a wide range of eugenic and medical information. Watts agreed to the longer forms rather than alienate Sherbon and weaken the medical authority associated with the contests.[57] She pressed Davenport for funds to print copies of the forms, and in 1925 he urged the Eugenics Society (soon to become the AES) to fund the printing of the examination forms and instructions.[58] With Watts and Sherbon already serving on the society's exhibits committee, the eugenics committee agreed to sponsor the fitter family contests in 1925. Watts's advocacy of short forms was not lost on Sherbon. After Watts's death in 1928, Sherbon advocated three types of exams: a short popular exam for fairs, an official exam used in fitter family examination centers, and a eugenics registry exam for those who passed the official exam and wished to deposit their family records in a registry.[59] Despite the time involved in completing it, the longer form remained in use at fitter family contests into the 1930s.

MAKING THE GRADE

In 1925 forty families participated in the Fitter Families for Future Firesides contest at the Kansas Free Fair. These families were interviewed about their social and medical history and were examined by psychiatrists, psychometricists, physicians, nutritionists, nurses, and dentists. They had their bodily fluids collected and analyzed, along with a "eugenic history" of family members, including those not at the fair. The participants came from a range of occupations, although two-thirds had some experience with farming and listed multiple occupations. While 26 percent reported having immigrant grandparents and 10 percent reported having immigrant parents, all of these had originated in England, Canada, or Northern Europe. Several participants had apparently competed in similar contests in previous years, and the majority of them were encouraged to return again the following year, promised by contest officials that if corrections were made to the family diet that their child would likely medal the next year.

To enter the contest, a family made an appointment for a particular time and day. Upon arrival at the tent or exhibit building, the family (no individuals were seen and few childless couples unless they were seeking "eugenic" marriage counseling before they paired off) might have taken in a show at the "Mendel Theater," in which marionettes were used to illustrate Mendelian principles, seen the cage of black and white guinea pigs used as a live demonstration of dominant and recessive inheritable traits, or read the chart on literacy in which literacy rates for "native-born," "foreign-born," and "negroes" were compared.[60] The contestant family then entered the building through an entrance designed to remind them of why they were participating in the health examination. In Watts's words, "We use the words 'Eugenics' as a sign over the door of the building at the Kansas Fair where we test human stock and it causes considerable discussion. When someone asks what it is all about, we say, 'While the stock judges are testing the Holsteins, Jerseys, and White-faces in the stock pavilion, we are testing the Joneses, Smiths, and the Johnsons,' and nearly every one replies: 'I think it is about time people had a little of the attention that is given to animals.' "[61] One historian took a "eugenic family history" encompassing members not seen at the fair, while clerks filled in a "social and other history" section of each family member's individual form. (Each member had her or his own form. Questions differed only in the section pertaining to reproductive history, with a special form for children under three.) The social section was designed to establish the educational, occupational, and social background (meaning participation in religious, political, fraternal, or other organizations) an included a query about the individual's size and condition at birth, illnesses, accidents, and inoculations. Mental condition was evaluated in psychometric and psychiatric sections based on mental test scores and an exam evaluating reflexes, personality, and temperament. Physical condition was evaluated first with an anthropometric structural assessment, a medical exam, and laboratory tests including blood tests, urinalysis, and a Wasserman test for syphilis. A dental exam, vision test, and hearing test rounded out the physical condition survey. The last section concerned health habits and focused on nutrition, including how much meat and coffee a person consumed, as well as work, sleep, exercise, and recreation habits. Completing all of the ten sections took about three and a half hours.

Fitter Families for Future Firesides

The large family winners from the fitter family contest at the 1925 Texas
State Fair. (American Eugenics Society Papers, American Philosophical
Society Archives, Philadelphia, Pa.)

An expert graded each section, and an overall individual score was assigned at the end.[62] At the 1925 fair, experts included Dr. James Naismith, inventor of basketball, who conducted the structural exams, and Karl Menninger, founder of the Menninger Clinic, who conducted the psychometric exams. Winning families inevitably had their pictures published in the local newspaper, while winning individuals were awarded a medal inscribed with a verse from the 16th Psalm, "Yea, I have a goodly heritage."[63]

The fact that the range of items comprising the fitter family contest form could have been considered as "grade-able" points to both the "stock"-judging and public health origins of this activity as well as Sherbon's resistance to have it reduced to "merely a study of heredity," as some eugenicists would have preferred.[64] As interest in the American Kennel Club (begun in 1884), the fad of poultry breeding, or stock-breeders clubs attests, the concern with breeding was fairly widespread in the nineteenth century. After the late 1880s, it became almost a passion. Until that time, for example, a hunting dog was simply a big dog with a good nose. With the spread of dog fancying in the twentieth century, specific breed clubs proliferated. The breed concept had ideological ramifications as it codified traits and, according to Enrique De Cal, ascribed "to a given combination certain moral values (a breed that is, for example, inherently 'loyal')." Breeds were also nationalized, as they were "increasingly conceived of as 'national' types ('German' shepherds versus 'Alsatians', to cite an obvious case)."[65] Some leading eugenicists, such as Leon Whitney of the American Eugenics Society, were also animal breeders. In fact, Whitney used dog breeds at fairs and exhibits to demonstrate eugenic principles.[66]

Similar concern with "normalcy" came to dominate aspects of public health education in the 1920s. The practice of weighing and measuring children using growth charts was popularized by Emmett Holt's manual on child care in 1894 and institutionalized by the Children's Bureau in their guidelines for evaluating child health. Sherbon, who had authored the 1917 Children's Bureau guidelines for child measurement, had helped inaugurate these weighing and measuring procedures in child health contests. Her sister Maud helped promote the statistical norms embodied in growth charts as social norms for students in school health programs. One five-year child health study supported by the Commonwealth Fund

Fitter Families for Future Firesides

Fitter family medal awarded by the American Eugenics Society. (American
Eugenics Society Papers, American Philosophical Society Archives,
Philadelphia, Pa.)

sought to remake hygiene education for rural populations. Maud Brown was the health education consultant in Fargo, North Dakota, from 1923 to 1928, where she supervised the measurement of 6,000 children. Weight and height were measured every six weeks, and a weight-height-age ratio was compared to a scale produced by the Minnesota State Board of Health. Frequent measurement allowed the teacher or nurse to "confront" the student with their actual weight. As Brown put it, "the few words of encouragement or of caution from teacher or nurse, mutually reinforced, make this the most important single health event of the six weeks' period." Weight gain was emphasized, and almost every grade graphed student weights in their classrooms. In addition weight reports were sent home, but with some safeguards. Parents and children were told that growth was a complex process and that following all the "health rules" taught in school did not guarantee "satisfactory growth."[67] Because these statistical norms for growth rarely incorporated differences in race and class, there were well-known deviations from normalcy that could not be easily explained within the rubric of growth charts. The problems of establishing a robust statistical norm did not stop educators from using growth charts to help construct and communicate norms about body size. How individual children measured up was made public in growth charts and classroom displays. Social standards of a "normal body" were reinforced by comparisons to classmates, by comments from teachers and nurses, and by weight reports sent home. These actions contributed to a growing awareness of body size and deviations from purported scientific norms of health.[68]

Shifting attitudes toward body norms and scientific standardization of health and diet were also reflected in changing attitudes toward fitter family contests. In 1920 the contest at the Kansas State Fair was greeted with some skepticism from fair officials: "The notion of judging human livestock was so novel, . . . that Mr. Eastman [the manager of the Fair] did not deem it wise to place human stock first on the [Fair] program." Instead the fitter family contest was sandwiched between the "Pet Stock" and the "Milch Goat" categories.[69] By 1925, however, the situation had changed; contests were now held at the Michigan State Fair, the Kansas Free Fair, the Eastern States Exposition in Massachusetts, the Oklahoma Free State Fair, the Arkansas State Fair, the Texas State Fair, and the Texas

Fitter Families for Future Firesides

Cotton Palace Exposition. In fact, in 1926, the committee on exhibits of the American Eugenics Society, then headed by Mary Watts, was receiving so many requests from fairs to run fitter family contests that they decided to limit the number of fairs to those that could be personally supervised by committee members (about twenty-five).[70] Moreover, the contests were getting rave reviews from fair organizers. Ethel Simonds from the Oklahoma Free State Fair claimed, "The Entrants and Winners at our last years' contest seem very enthusiastic about it and state that it is one of the best things that we had." The Arkansas State Fair doubled the space available for the contest, and a number of organizers credited the contest with drawing the interest of the local medical community, educators, and professionals.[71]

Sinclair Lewis lampooned the "Eugenic Family" in his attack upon the medical and public health professions in his 1925 novel, Arrowsmith. The contests were such a widely recognized cultural phenomena that the protagonist's boss, a "two-fisted fighting poet doc" decides to cement his political ambitions by sponsoring a health fair. Chief among the exhibits, which also highlight the Boy Scouts, antinicotine information, and teeth-brushing demonstrations, is the Eugenic Family, "who had volunteered to give, for a mere forty dollars a day, an example of the benefits of healthful living." As Lewis describes the "beautiful and powerful" group of a mother, father, and five children, none of whom "smoked, drank, spit upon pavements, used foul language, or ate meat," it becomes clear that it is the dysgenic practices that are most important in defining the family. The irony of the scene, of course, emerges from the reader's understanding of the principles of inheritance. When the detective sergeant recognizes the Eugenic Family as the Holton gang ("the man and the woman ain't married, and only one of them kids is theirs"), who have served time for "selling licker to the Indians," the reader is supposed to understand the principles of inheritance that saw criminality or feeblemindedness as the result of 'bad breeding.' This line is further developed when the "youngest blossom" of the fraudulent family collapses on stage in an epileptic fit.[72] Epilepsy was assumed to be an inherited "weakness" or outward manifestation of weakness. For Lewis, the public zealotry of eugenics seemed to have a shaky foundation at best.

The public enthusiasm for fitter family contests, however, brought them to fairs in over forty states by the 1930s. John Harvey Kellogg, popularizer of corn flakes, decided to promote eugenic contests as well at the Third Race Betterment Conference held in January 1928 at his Battle Creek Sanitarium, where Sherbon orchestrated the demonstration competition. Working with Luther S. West, a professor of biology and eugenics at Battle Creek College, Sherbon and Leon Whitney ran a fitter family contest for a group of preselected "desirable families."[73] Sherbon admitted that this contest was a "unique experience" in that 125 "superior individuals" were evaluated. The "velvet carpets" and "exquisite food" helped set it apart from the country fairgrounds, as well.[74]

The Battle Creek contest was meant to promote the contests within the particularly well-endowed Race Betterment Foundation. The supposedly superior families that served as contestants raised a number of issues, however. As Luther West noted, it was difficult for judges to give low social scores to families considered locally imminent and even harder to give anything below an A in the psychiatric test without the participant demanding a "lengthy explanation."[75] In fact, the only category with consistently low scores was dental, and these were explained away in terms of the "low survival value" of good teeth in a modern environment.[76] Under the auspices of the Battle Creek Sanitarium, West wanted to continue examining selected families over at least five years. He hoped that the data from such a study would help distinguish a "normal" individual, as in "ideal norm," from an "average" individual. This distinction would allow him to define what he considered to be genuine superiority and "true aristocracy" based on genetic principles. Individuals from "superior stock" would then be placed in a eugenic registry. The fitter family contests remained with the AES until 1931 in part because the AES was reluctant to lose control of one of their most effective means of popular education.[77]

While the fitter family contests were certainly popular, they should not be interpreted as a piece of mass culture deftly produced for passive consumption. The contests tapped a widely shared interest in genealogy and especially in having ancestors of "sturdy pioneer stock." The contest forms included a five- to ten-page section where contest participants provided insight into their families' histories. The 1925 contestants frequently described their relations for contest officials in highly nostalgic terms. Most of these descriptions reflect an idealized type, with the "sturdy, pioneer type" or "rugged type" being the descriptions that were repeated most often. One of the contestants identified her father as a "splendid pioneer in the early days of Kansas," while four families explained their love of order and discipline as descending from their parents who kept well-bred livestock. Families also identified themselves as inheriting their inventive, musical, or prohibitionist tendencies from their predecessors. This interest in ancestry was translated by the fitter family contest into a nostalgic vision of the rural family. The contests provided self-selected participants with an opportunity to celebrate their families at a time when America was becoming increasingly more urban, more mobile, and more industrialized.

For the eugenicists, the end product of popular campaigns such as Kansas contest was a denial of the individual as a unit in favor of the family. Their writings specifically identified modernity with the individual in opposition to the traditional family. Eugenicists were not alone in this identification. As a series of farm newspapers in the Midwest noted, the migration of rural youth to the city was a rejection of the cooperative unit of the family farm for the uncaring and atomized modernity of the city. If contestants privileged the family unit over modernity's celebration of the individual, then the family began to signify a constant amid changing circumstances. The contestants were people on the move. Even as their sons and daughters forsook the family farm for Chicago and other urban centers, the contestants and their parents also moved often: only nine out of twenty-four families in the 1925 Kansas contest had not moved in the preceding twenty years. Knowing one's ancestors, or at least stories of one's ancestors, provided a sense of constancy to people whose immediate circumstances may have been in flux.

Eugenicists in particular idealized the rural family. Consider, for instance, the first president's report for the American Eugenics Society written by Irving Fisher in 1926. Noting that "rural districts supply a disproportionately large part of the future population" because of larger family sizes, Fisher's report urges greater control over rural-urban migration. Because the AES wanted to keep the "best stocks" in the country and attract "new good stocks" from the city, the society urged a set of policies to improve rural life. From its perspective, "farm credits, farmer's cooperatives, community art, suburban life for city workers, favorable agricultural legislation, agricultural colleges and schools, abolition of tariffs, etc., would appear to be eugenic measures par excellence." Automobile travel was also relevant to this "rural-urban problem," because "it tends to reduce in-breeding from propinquity and to widen the range of marriage selection in rural districts."[78] Writing as secretary of the AES in 1926, Leon Whitney made the usual demographic case for the value of the farm family. In his words, "the average farm family is at least sufficient to carry on the goodly heritage, while the average city family is too small." But farmers had a deeper appreciation of eugenics, because they were animal breeders themselves.[79] Indeed, Mary Watts frequently emphasized the farm families that attended the fitter family contests. "The farmer," she wrote, "is easiest to reach because he is the best posted on stock raising."[80] It is not surprising that in 1929, Sherbon could report that "Farm families are again in the majority among the winners, five first and second places going to families of farmers, two to ministers, one to a physician, one to a salesman, one to a banker, and one to a hatchery manager."[81] Farmers may have had a greater appreciation of the value of breeding, but it is not clear that they shared eugenicists' demographic concerns. In fact, a short note in the *New York Times* noted that in 1927 the large family competition at the Kansas Free Fair had to be canceled because no families with more than five children applied.[82]

POSITIVE EUGENICS AND SHERBON'S
"SCIENCE OF PARENTHOOD"

For Sherbon, the fitter family contests were also a tool for advancing her own research agenda as a child researcher and professor at the University of Kansas. From a professional standpoint, these contests became part of her larger program to study the modern family, child development, children's health, and education. This program resonated with the direction that would be charted by the AES in the 1930s.

By 1920 Sherbon was a permanent member of the faculty in the Department of Home Economics at the University of Kansas. Sherbon's program of child research marked a significant shift in the direction of the home economics program toward child welfare.[83] The emphasis within home economics on the home and the family simultaneously pushed Sherbon to redefine her research in terms of the extended environment of the child, especially its family.[84] This institutional context was very supportive of the fitter family contests. Indeed, the success of the contests spurred Sherbon to envision what she called a "science of parenthood." In conjunction with Luther West and the Race Betterment Foundation, Sherbon had proposed an ambitious program including a School of Family Life with courses of instruction, a community forum, a preschool health center, a research division, and a fitter family extension service modeled on the Agricultural Extension and Home Demonstration Services. In an overview of her research, Sherbon proclaimed, "Eventually I see this movement spread until it ought to contribute to the strengthening of the family as the organic racial and social unit."[85] In effect, Sherbon advocated a "positive eugenics" program that sought to encourage the spread of desired traits by supporting supposedly "worthy" families and eugenic marriages.[86]

Sherbon's department of scientific parenthood never came to be, but her professional agenda of blending child study, eugenics, and home economics continued to develop in the 1920s. Sherbon held workshops for graduate students on the fitter family contests, which culminated in at least one master's thesis.[87] At the request of the Federal Board for Vocational Education, Sherbon developed a self-study program concerning family health in relation to the home and the community.[88] More far-reaching were Sherbon's courses on the child and the family, which advocated a philosophy of the whole child; i.e., the child as the complex whole emerging from the combination of its ancestry, its biology, its parents, society, and environment. These courses led to her successful textbook, The Child. Aimed at parents as well as students, The Child was intended to be a comprehensive scientific treatment of parenthood from conception to birth and beyond.[89] In 1934 Parent's magazine awarded it an honorable mention in its contest for the Most Helpful Book of the Year.

The fitter family contests were not discussed in The Child, but the medal given in the contests served as the book's frontispiece. Sherbon's caption reads, " 'Fitter Families' Medal formerly presented by the American Eugenics Society to families meeting certain standards of mental, physical, and hereditary excellence. The artist here has well expressed the spirit of this book."[90] Eugenics, heredity, and evolution were prominent features of Sherbon's philosophy of the child. Sherbon made the study of the child scientific by representing the child as a product of biological and social evolution. This perspective was crucial. In her words, "It makes an essential and illuminating difference whether one views a child in his relation to the entire past and to the future of the human race, or as a personal possession, a personal miracle, who too often develops a baffling, uncontrollable personality."[91] Full consideration of a child's heritage in Sherbon's view allowed her to claim, "There is no break from soil to soul."[92] Accordingly, in her discussion of eugenics, Sherbon appealed to social evolution to further delineate the child's "inheritance" in terms of not only the mother and father, but the units of the child's evolving society—its family, state, country, and race.[93] This holistic view of the body and society was a fundamental feature of Sherbon's science and allowed her to replace the dichotomous debate over nature and nurture within a more-complex and interactive model of human development.

Sherbon's holistic approach to integrating the body, society, and the physical environment allowed her to extend the domain of her science beyond the body. For instance, in 1937, Sherbon produced a second book for McGraw-Hill's series on euthenics. *The Family in Health and Illness* was based upon her university lectures. Sherbon's aim was to educate young women on the best means for creating and maintaining a healthy family. As such, the book's topics ranged from how to select a home to how to care for the ill. Sherbon's definition of health integrated the individual with the larger society and environment in such a way as to make community organization and social experience directly relevant to bodily health. Health, according to Sherbon, involved "not only a chemically efficient body but socially efficient relationships with other human biochemical organisms." Put another way, according to Sherbon, "the human being is a unity within himself, and he is also a unit within a complexly integrated organization of human beings known as society. So intimate is this integration that his social experiences may definitely effect his body chemistry."[94] The health of the family, therefore, necessarily involved ancestry and environment. Securing the health of the family required women to be actively concerned with the condition of their homes, communities, and states as well as their bodily traits.[95]

Sherbon's concern with environmental and domestic reforms, commonly associated with home economics, represent a popular conception of eugenics as well as a fusion of approaches from public health and mainstream eugenics.[96] Her efforts were widely acknowledged by the AES in the 1920s, but the Great Depression led the AES to cut its funding severely—it ceased publishing the journal *Eugenics* and ended financial support for the fitter family contests. When the AES emerged from the depression, Sherbon was no longer officially associated with it, but positive eugenics was.[97]

Most historians of eugenics agree that within the United States the eugenics movement underwent significant changes in its outlook and leadership during the late 1920s and 1930s. Daniel Kevles describes this shift as a move from mainline eugenics to reform eugenics, which was associated with increasing scientific criticism of the genetic basis for eugenic claims about mental and racial differences.[98] During the same period, eugenicists associated with the American Eugenics Society embraced the importance of environmental conditions and began to consider programs dedicated to encouraging reproduction among those thought to be "fit." This move toward positive eugenics coincides temporally with the rise of reform eugenics but is not usually included in its description. My account of this transition period emphasizes the continuity and increasing prominence of positive eugenics.[99]

From its incorporation in 1926, leaders of the AES were interested in a range of reforms that would promote reproduction and large families among those they considered to be "superior" people. The president's report for 1926, for instance, called for action against declining birthrates by making rural life more "economically and culturally attractive" through programs advocating "farm credits, farmer's cooperatives, community art, suburban life for city workers, favorable agricultural legislation, agricultural colleges and schools, abolition of pro-tariffs, etc." In addition, the automobile was singled out for attention as a "eugenic measure" since it allowed for greater access and mate selection in rural communities.[100] This interest in positive eugenics became much more pronounced after the Great Depression. From 1934 to 1938, the president of the AES was Ellsworth Huntington, a professor of geography at Yale University well known for his advocacy of the place of evolution in geography.[101] Huntington articulated and advocated a new positive eugenics program that he hoped would "produce actual results measurable in the number and quality of children."[102] From his perspective, negative eugenic efforts of the 1920s such as segregation and sterilization had produced "concrete" changes that education about the "desirability of large families," marriage advice, and medical exams had not.

Huntington's advocacy of positive eugenics had been influenced by AES secretary Frederick Osborn, whose notes on eugenics programs included the warning to Huntington that "there is no evidence that preaching large families as a matter of individual morality has any effect. This should be avoided."[103] Among the "practical steps" to promote larger families urged by Osborn were the "elimination of city slums," raising economic standards on farms, encouraging "endowment and dowry systems," and supporting marriage and childbearing among college students. These practical steps were all in support of a four-child ideal of the family meant to replace the "dysgenic" small family ideal.[104]

Huntington transformed this advice into a set of three positive eugenic programs, which he proposed to the AES board of directors in December 1934. Huntington's first programmatic proposal was to create a eugenic insurance company, called the Family Insurance Corporation, that would, for a small premium, provide coverage for the mother's health care during pregnancy, the costs of childbirth and care in early infancy, and perhaps postnatal unemployment. Young couples interested in purchasing this insurance would have to pass a set of exams to establish their eugenic worth. As with his other programs, Huntington wanted this program to take advantage of similar kinds of social programs but turn them toward eugenic goals.

Next Huntington argued for a system of nursery schools and collective parenting that he called "maternal cooperation." These voluntary associations would ease the "nervous strain" of mothering and make larger families more attractive. Moreover, Huntington believed that "the mothers who carried out the plan would have to be the cooperative, efficient, tactful type who are the very best material from which to construct a high grade community."[105] Successful cooperative nurseries would therefore be eugenically self-screening.

Lastly Huntington proposed eugenic housing. Starting from the assumption that urbanization lowers birthrate, Huntington proposed forming a building corporation to design communities and houses for the kinds of young couples that took out eugenic insurance. The key element of these suburban and rural communities would be their rural character, "which seem[s] to be favorable not only to the growth of children themselves, but to the production of comparatively large families." Such communities would have communal facilities for laundry, cooperative nurseries, and playgrounds for the hordes of supposedly superior children.[106]

The eugenic housing scheme was particularly noteworthy. Huntington's enthusiasm for housing was produced by New Deal spending on housing and community development.[107] Huntington wished to act immediately and put federal funds in the service of a "eugenic ideal" of housing. To this end, he sought to "secure the appointment of a representative of the American Eugenics Society upon the President's Housing Commission."[108] It is not clear that he succeeded in this, but Irving Fisher did begin writing to the Federal Subsistence Homesteads Corporation urging them to adopt child-friendly community designs that would meet eugenic goals. Miles Colean, technical director of the Federal Housing Administration, responded, "we heartily approve the idea [of] . . . day nurseries, playgrounds, and other desirable social features."[109]

Huntington's eugenic housing scheme called for suburban development because suburbs were close to urban employment opportunities yet offered "the rural conditions which seem favorable not only to growth of children themselves, but to the production of comparatively large families." Huntington himself began promoting the eugenic housing idea in an essay entitled "A Family Community" for the *Atlantic Monthly*'s Million Dollar Community Contest in 1936. Huntington's ideal community promoted childbearing by "enabling high-grade parents to have families of reasonable size without lowering their standard of living." The keys to this community were fourfold: "(1) young parents, (2) suburban homes, (3) co-operative enterprises, and (4) expert trustees." Subsidized health care and scholarships would lighten the economic cost of child rearing, while communal laundries, garages, groundskeeping, health services, and housekeeping would both making parenting easier and discourage excess individualism. The family-oriented community that Huntington imagined would supposedly create a model city while physically improving its population.

Huntington further promoted his ideas for eugenic housing in his book *Tomorrow's Children* (1935).[110] Although Huntington is listed as author, the book was a revision of Leon Whitney's *A Eugenics Catechism* (1923) and had received considerable input from AES directors. The discussion of housing in *Tomorrow's Children* reflects Huntington's proposal to the board and his article on "A Family Community." Clearly, by 1935 promoting the idea of eugenic housing had become part of the American Eugenics Society's educational program.

Reflecting recommendations for popular education that Sherbon had advocated throughout the 1920s, the remaking of the *Eugenics Catechism*, the extension of *Tomorrow's Children* into a series of regional conferences, and the production of a film of the same title signaled a greater appreciation of positive eugenics and its popularization. Perhaps as an acknowledgement of Sherbon's recommendations, the AES retained the medal developed for the fitter family contests and placed it on the cover of all issues of their journal, *Eugenics*. Sherbon's role in the AES popular education committee was taken over by Dr. Willystine Goodsell, who would eventually become vice president of the AES. Goodsell, a professor at the Teacher's College of Columbia University, shared something of Sherbon's vision for family studies in higher education. Goodsell's *The Education of Women* (1923) carefully reviewed the literature on women's education and the controversy over the effects of education on marriage and birthrates, for instance. As vice president of the AES, Goodsell organized the "outreach conferences" in 1937 and 1938 seeking to forge links to recreation experts, housing planners, religious leaders, "family relations" experts, birth control advocates, educators, nurses, physicians, and publicists—all with the aim of promoting larger and fitter families.

The AES housing conference attempted to articulate and strengthen the relationship between eugenics and community planners.[111] Speakers such as Warren S. Thompson of the Scripps Foundation for Research in Population Problems connected the need for housing subsidies to increased family size. Where children and "good living quarters" are "competing choices in family budgets," Thompson argued, the decision to limit family size reflects the housing a family can afford. He urged that "the cost of adequate housing" be considered in terms of its effect "in determining the number of children that will be raised in many families." For Thompson, a longstanding member of the AES, the "city-village-rural differentials in reproduction" should frame U.S. housing considerations. With the rural birthrate higher than the urban birthrate, "even if housing in cities is greatly improved and cheapened for the moderate sized family, it is quite uncertain whether . . . [city-based subsidies] alone will have any very marked effect on the birthrate of the urban population." Location mattered. As Thompson noted, "the maintenance of a birth rate high enough to insure even a stationary population may be dependent on providing living quarters in rural or semi-rural areas for an increasing proportion of our people who now live in highly congested urban areas." Thompson, like Huntington and others, saw the eugenic implications of suburban development and believed that it had to be taken into account as new communities were planned.

In his presentation at the AES housing conference, Russell Black, a past president of the American City Planning Institute, agreed that suburban development was the best way to achieve population redistribution away from urban centers. As a developer of Radburn, New Jersey, Black had been involved in the planning of a new greenbelt community. Unlike Thompson, however, Black was more cautious about the causes of declining birthrates and seemed reluctant to claim that suburbs would arrest population trends. However, he did embrace eugenic ideology, arguing, in his words, "We have great mutual concern that the quality of the American people shall not be forced out by degrading and unhealthful environment nor bred out by unfortunate inheritance." For Black, the most planners and housing experts could do was shape the environment to "make the most of whatever human material is at hand."[112]

Housing activist Edith Elmer Wood was more willing than Black to find eugenic implications in housing. Wood had been advocating slum clearance and redevelopment since at least 1931, when she advocated giving "every American child something like an even break to show the stuff that was in him."[113] As a member of the Regional Planning Association of America, she helped redefine residential neighborhoods and influenced the greenbelt developments of the Resettlement Administration.[114] At the housing conference, she recognized that the issues that concerned her and other planners were better described as "eugenics and euthenics." Of particular concern for Wood was the nature of governmental support for housing. Limiting spending on public housing limited the size of that housing and so limited the size of families that could healthily inhabit those quarters. Wood argued that the population effects of spending limitations in the Wagner-Steagall Act were understood and referred to in the congressional debate as the "race suicide amendment." Without more government support, Wood feared that housing for larger families would not be possible. Moreover, the National Housing Act of 1934, which established the Federal Housing Administration (FHA), and the Home Owner Loan Corporation (HOLC) helped secure loans for housing generated by the vagaries of the private market. HOLC standards for awarding loans ranked properties from grade A, described as the "best" because of their "homogeneous" population of "American business and professional men," to grade C, described as "definitely declining" and marked by "infiltration of lower grade populations."[115] While this grading system imposed racial restrictions on housing, it was not explicitly eugenic. Nevertheless, Wood claimed that the private housing system should be under the influence of organizations such as the AES. It was up to eugenicists, Wood claimed, to "change the ideology and family-size habits" of those who could afford to use the FHA system. Wood herself advocated a "three-bed-room standard as a family norm" for both its social and eugenic consequences.[116]

After the eugenic housing conference, Wood's advocacy of housing reform continued to emphasize health and "a normal family life." In her words, "houses are also like factories. Their output is children—the citizens of tomorrow."[117] While lacking the eugenicists' emphasis on hereditary fitness, Wood and other housing advocates certainly embraced a pronatalist vision of the suburbs, putting a different spin on their identification as "bedroom communities."

The eugenic housing conference did not have an arguably causal effect; it is not possible to trace its direct impact on U.S. housing policy. While Averell Harriman, one of the seven officials sitting on the Home Owner Loan Corporation board may have been somehow influenced by the eugenic interests of his mother, who funded the Eugenic Record Office, this is only conjecture. Some of the conference attendees, such as Thompson or Wood, were already interested in eugenics. Others, such as Woodbury and Black, were identifying parallel goals between their planning specialty and eugenics. What is important to note is the way in which a faith in

Fitter Families for Future Firesides

positive modeling around the family was taken for granted. Promoting an ideal of the suburban family as one with three or more children coincided with promotion of homes of a certain size and communities with family-friendly features. Eugenic and housing ideals were understood as mutually reinforcing, but the means to their implementation was understood in terms of promoting an ideal as much as actual legislation of support for housing.

The fitter family contests were a campaign of popular education that lent scientific credence to a nostalgic vision of the rural family. Sherbon tapped an antimodernist sentiment that capitalized on a nostalgic moral order centered in the family, but the ability to realize that nostalgic ideal depended crucially on modern knowledge and her idea of innovation. Sherbon's success as a eugenicist lay in her ability to articulate her modern and scientific agenda in these antimodernist and nostalgic terms. Although we now think of Sherbon's efforts as seriously misguided, at the time, this nostalgic modernism simultaneously legitimated Sherbon's reform and research agenda as well as the participation of those seeking to reaffirm their identity and value as fitter families.

Some historians of eugenics consider fitter family contests to have been a "piddling" achievement given the goals of American eugenicists.[118] Others recognize them as "a source of amusing anecdotes" in contrast to the more-horrific eugenic campaigns of segregation, immigration restriction, sterilization, and euthanasia.[119] The fitter family contests do stand in contrast to the eugenic actions against the supposedly "unfit." They represent the first national effort by American eugenicists to promote selective reproduction, and they exemplify "positive eugenics" in the 1920s. Indeed, their success contributed to a shift toward positive eugenics by the American eugenics movement as a whole in the 1930s.

7

AMERICAN PRONATALISM

In all viable societies social control has
operated to organize human beings into
childbearing and childrearing groups—families
—that, by definition, have proven to be highly
efficient reproductive machines.

JUDITH BLAKE,
"Coercive Pronatalism and American
Population Policy," 1974

On October 18, 1940, the Leathers family of Clarendon, Texas, became the "nation's most typical American family" as judged by a committee at the New York World's Fair. White, with two children, nineteen-year-old John and sixteen-year-old Margaret Jean, the Leathers were described as "champion stock farmers" living on a "200-acre homestead" in Texas. A photograph in the *Christian Science Monitor* showed them gathered around the family tractor. The Leathers had been chosen in May by the *Fort Worth Star-Telegram* as part of a contest to represent the typical American family from West Texas. Like forty-seven other families from across the United States, when the Leathers won their state contest, they received an all-expense paid trip to the New York World's Fair, where they stayed for a week in a house built by the Federal Housing Authority on the fairgrounds. When they were selected the "most typical" of the typical American family winners, they received another trip to the fair, a new sedan from the Ford Motor Company, a trip to Henry Ford's Greenfield Village, and a meeting with President Roosevelt.[1]

The criteria by which any of the "typical American families" were judged is not entirely clear. Historian Robert Rydell sees this competition as a continuation of the eugenic fitter family contests popular at state fairs throughout the 1920s.[2] However, there is no evidence of a direct link between the typical family contests and any eugenics organization. Indeed it is doubtful that the kinds of detailed physical, mental, and genealogical information collected in the fitter family contests entered into the deliberations of the various committees appointed by local newspapers that judged the families. Rydell notes that a questionnaire supplied by the World's Fair requested information on race and sought two-child families, since only four people could fit into the FHA houses at the fairgrounds.[3] Not surprisingly, then, the "typical families" all were white and had children, usually one boy and one girl.

The FHA houses were added to the Town of Tomorrow section of the fair. The Town of Tomorrow itself had been planned to represent "a rebirth in modern form of new type of the old New England type village, which, it is universally conceded, was as perfect a form of democracy as the world has known."[4] The FHA model homes represented more than a recommendation for a better built environment; they also conveyed the belief that Americans should live as families—FHA housing was family housing. Unlike the fifteen houses built for the Fair's opening in 1939, the FHA houses were affordable to lower- and middle-class families. Built to meet FHA guidelines, these two-bedroom houses would have sold for between $2,500 and $3,500. Paul Roche, a developer from Long Island, New York, built both houses in a colonial style characteristic of the Stephen Manor development that he was then constructing.[5] The FHA homes were intended to promote home ownership, support the construction industry, and advertise the new "green cities" being planned and built as part of the New Deal.

The green city model was more explicitly articulated by the Regional Planning Association of America's (RPAA) film, The City, written by Lewis Mumford and produced by Pare Lorentz for the World's Fair. Contrasting rural idyll with urban industry, the film begins with a retrospective on rural life set in the Shirley Shaker Village north of Boston. Rural life close to the land is dramatically contrasted with the industrial landscape of Pittsburgh. Over images of smoke-covered houses rising up the hillside above the factories, the narrator intones that there are prisons that offer better living conditions than those that these workers can offer their children. Motivated by urban conditions, the opening titles in the film proclaim that "we must remold our old cities and build new communities." These new communities were "green cities—built into the countryside" and represented by images of Radburn, New Jersey—a new suburban community planned by members of the RPAA. Billed as a "modern city" that worked as well as "an old New England town," these "green cities" remade the industrial community on a smaller scale in a suburban setting. Tellingly, the juxtaposition between urban decay and suburban opportunity is depicted largely with children. Images of children playing in rubbish-filled alleys and congested streets are posed against children playing in the open green spaces between Radburn's houses. Indeed, The City nears its end with children's drawings of the suburb set against drawings of an urban tenement as Aaron Copland's score strikes a strident chord and the narrator urges viewers to make a choice between "wasted years of childhood" in the city and the "order and life" of the suburbs.[6]

The typical American family contests were intended to promote the World's Fair. But with the families ensconced in their FHA houses and with The City extolling their virtues, such contests also promoted a suburban family ideal.[7] Even if the contests were not explicitly eugenic, they were certainly pronatalist. The colonial style of the FHA homes, the selection of a rural farm family as the "most typical," and the reverence for the "old New England village" in The City all suggest the appeal that nostalgia and tradition had, even as city planners imagined the towns of tomorrow. The suburban family celebrated at the New York World's Fair was pronatalist in its promotion of home ownership and the child-friendly environment imagined in new suburban communities.

In the early twentieth century, regulating and promoting reproduction acquired several distinctive associations—with a tradition of American agrarianism, with Populist and Progressive reforms, and with racist and essentialist beliefs in biologically based social hierarchies. The association of agrarianism, the modernist promise of reform, racism, and reproduction were expressed through icons of "American tradition"—the family, the mother, and the home. These cultural icons or ideals were expressions of American pronatalism, but to understand the nature of that pronatalism one must understand what was associated with efforts to promote reproduction that rendered it appealing to some even as it discriminated against others.

Partly driven by census measurements demonstrating larger rural families, the agrarian dimension of American pronatalism strongly invoked the image of the virtuous farmer-citizen and the redemptive value of rural life. Celebrations of the yeoman farmer as a source of American virtue stem from Thomas Jefferson's particular brand of nationalism. During the Populist campaigns of the 1890s, celebration of the farmer was put to work as part of a political agenda meant to benefit the producer family. In the hands of skilled orators such as Mary Lease, the image of the virtuous farmer exploited by bankers and tycoons gained a new association with the family. Claiming her right to speak as a woman and mother, Lease justified her political actions by reframing the farm family as the objects of exploitation. Lease could articulate a Populist political economy because starving children created by overproduction were exactly what she should be concerned with as a mother. Lease's particular maternalist agenda did more than simply associate agrarianism and the family; it also gave that agrarian family a biological basis. Lease framed her understanding of the strengths and virtues of agrarianism and the agrarian family in Darwinian terms that appealed to the influence of ancestry and environment. For Lease, working the land became a source of virtue and biological improvement, although the potential for improvement did not obviate racial difference and her commitment to a racial hierarchy. Accordingly, Lease's views blended her beliefs in agrarianism, maternalism, and biological difference. This amalgam was expressed as she championed the cause of the producer family.

In contrast, George Maxwell shared Lease's belief in agrarian values but expressed them through an icon of the home on the land. Maxwell's various homecroft efforts sought to recreate the environment of the frontier and in doing so create the conditions for a more-virtuous citizenry. The homecroft was intended to place every industrial worker back into contact with the land, even if only in their backyard garden. In making every worker into a Jeffersonian yeoman, Maxwell also sought to protect them economically from the fluctuations of a wage-labor system. Literally, Maxwell's homecroft scheme would remake its inhabitants in the image of an agrarian producer. The homecroft was an instrument for a kind of reform campaign aimed at fundamentally altering the American landscape and the possibilities for families who came into contact with that landscape.

Of course, not just producers but producer families inhabited Maxwell's homecrofts. Unlike Lease, with her commitment to maternalism and women's resulting political agency, Maxwell seemed much more comfortable assuming a male breadwinner model of the family where women and children worked in guilds and gardens to create a buffer against industry yet themselves did not directly enter into industry or political life, for that matter. Because women were imagined in productive and reproductive roles within the household economy, Maxwell's homecrofts became sites of both agrarian and reproductive labor.

The expressions of agrarianism in the ideals of the family and home by Lease and Maxwell promoted reproduction indirectly in that their agendas had pronatalist consequences but were not driven by pronatalism as a goal. With the rise of eugenic thinking and the concern over race suicide, more-direct forms of pronatalism become associated with agrarianism and expressed as ideals of the rural family, home, and mother. When Edward A. Ross, for instance, articulated his concern with the supposed threat of race suicide, he also articulated a deliberately pronatalist program for the regulation of reproduction using the methods that he would so carefully explain in his sociological treatise, *Social Control*. Ross's ideal of the American family was expressed in terms of family size and standards of living. This centered the issue of promoting reproduction even as Ross's family ideal invoked familiar agrarian themes that valorized especially the midwestern farmer.

While Lease embraced racial hierarchies in her book, *The Problem of Civilization Solved*, and Maxwell saw America's greatest threat in a Japanese invasion, Ross, Roosevelt, and eugenicists such as Florence Sherbon associated race with agrarianism and reproduction much more strongly. Ross's concern with race suicide was motivated by ideas of racial competition that led him to become a lifelong and virulent advocate of immigration restriction. His valorized farmer, like Theodore Roosevelt's, was a product of biological selection. For Ross, generations of improvement had refined the American standard of living such that less-evolved races with lower standards could win the reproductive struggle for future generations by providing less for more.

Because rural families tended to be larger than urban families, preserving the family farm by bettering conditions for the entire farm family became an act of racial preservation. The association of Roosevelt's conservation and country life movements was not accidental—farm families were a resource to be managed and cultivated. The large size of rural families justified their reproductive regulation for reformers such as Ross and Roosevelt, yet rural families were typically celebrated for their virtue and character, both supposedly products of an agrarian life.

While Ross's and Roosevelt's pronatalism was more direct than that of Lease and Maxwell, it was not legislated, although Roosevelt certainly was in a position to foster new laws. Instead, Ross and Roosevelt understood and used social and cultural influence to promote reproduction. Roosevelt's exhortations from his bully pulpit urging women to breed as a national duty exemplified social control as codified by Ross. Ever an astute observer of social customs and practices, Ross understood the effects of social ideals on individual behavior. Celebrating a rural family ideal became a way of promoting reproduction, but because that ideal expressed associations with agrarianism and a biological understanding of racial difference, it was also exclusionary. Ross's and Roosevelt's pronatalism were racially motivated, and the family ideal that they used was not intended to encourage those who did not emulate the "racial character" of their imagined rural family.

The most direct expression of American pronatalism that blended agrarian and racist ideals was that of the eugenics movement. Francis Galton recognized the task of improving human heredity as having both "positive" and "negative" aspects in the nineteenth century. In the United States, however, negative enactments aimed at limiting reproduction among those believed to be "unfit" dominated the early eugenic movement. Historians have justifiably focused our attention on programs of sterilization and segregation in the United States and mass killing in Nazi Germany. Through popular education efforts, however, American eugenicists also promoted a "positive" program of promoting reproduction among those imagined to be the most fit. Beginning in the 1920s, Florence Sherbon's fitter family contests represented a significant "positive" eugenic enactment. These contests deliberately sought to forge an agrarian association in their format and their venue at state fairs. Spurred by the success of these contests, the American Eugenics Society sought other ways of promoting selective reproduction. Their deep interest in eugenic housing significantly extended their positive eugenics campaign in the 1930s while strengthening the association between agrarianism and eugenics. While leaders of the American Eugenics Society would try to distance themselves from racist biological hierarchies, especially after the Holocaust, the positive eugenics campaigns of the 1920s and 1930s employed a white family ideal. Leading eugenicists could claim that they did not discriminate on the basis of race while freely admitting that they discriminated on supposedly more biologically sound eugenic grounds, but the family ideal promoted in their positive eugenics programs did not reflect this special pleading. The resulting form of eugenic pronatalism was not simply coercive but designed to discriminate, racially and otherwise.

Eugenic pronatalism represents the culmination of a trend toward direct forms of pronatalism in the United States during the twentieth century. As such it has been the obvious focal point for scholarship seeking to document American pronatalism before World War II.[8] In the five historical cases considered in this book, I have revealed a much more pervasive expression of pronatalism associated with American agrarianism. Eugenic pronatalism was an important form of agrarian pronatalism, but it is essential to realize that the direct promotion of reproduction was relatively short lived in the United States. This does not mean that pronatalism and its association with agrarian family ideals was also short lived. The more-lasting and more-influential expression of agrarian pronatalism was indirect and noneugenic although still discriminatory—it was the triumph of suburbia. Eugenicists such as Ellsworth Huntington recognized the new suburban communities of the 1930s as pronatalist and sought to ally them with positive eugenics. The regional planners and housing experts that attended the American Eugenics Society conference on housing also saw the potential common cause of the child-friendly suburb. In the end, however, the "typical family" in their FHA house was not necessarily a "eugenic family." Both blended agrarian ideals and biologically based exclusionary doctrines, but the pronatalism of the "green city" suburbs was more indirect than that of the fitter family contests. As a result, suburban pronatalism bore a closer resemblance to the pronatalism of Maxwell's homecroft communities.

The demographic increase sought by American pronatalists coincided with the spread of the suburbs, but the baby boom that began with the Second World War had many causes. Patriotism may have started the boom, but postwar subsidies for education and housing and economic growth sustained it into the 1950s.[9] The "normal" or "nuclear" family became enshrined in the postwar culture of conformity. As feminists in the 1970s began to speak out against this ideal of domesticity, they found that the pressure to reproduce was pervasive in American culture. Motherhood as a feminine ideal and large families as a domestic norm were promoted in magazines, television shows, advertising, home economics textbooks, and military housing allowances.[10] The cultural norms were deemed coercive in so far as they did not represent reproduction as a choice. To consciously decide to remain childless meant confronting a pervasive and overwhelming culture that equated bliss, domestic or otherwise, with procreation.

In order to create a new population policy, feminists in the 1970s sought to name the pronatalism they saw perpetuated in the ideal of the traditional family commonly associated with postwar suburbia. This book reveals the deep roots of these kinds of pronatalist ideals. American pronatalism in the early twentieth century emerged from a modernist conviction that reproduction and population could be regulated. The instruments for that regulation were not laws as much as ideals of home, motherhood, and the family that invoked an American agrarian tradition. By their nature, these ideals were not universal, and the pronatalism produced by them was exclusionary. Understanding the historical circumstances that associated agrarianism, racism, and pronatalism reveals how reproductive conformity was manufactured, how it was promoted, and why it was coercive.

NOTES

ABBREVIATIONS

AES Papers

American Eugenics Society Papers, American Philosophical Society Archives, Philadelphia, Pa.

Children's Bureau Papers

U.S. Children's Bureau Papers, National Archives II, College Park, Md.

Davenport Papers

Charles Davenport Papers, American Philosophical Society Archives, Philadelphia, Pa.

Huntington Papers

Ellsworth Huntington Papers, Yale University Library, New Haven, Conn.

Lindley Papers

E. H. Lindley Papers, University Archives, Kenneth Spencer Research Library, University of Kansas, Lawrence, Kans.

Maxwell Papers

George H. Maxwell Papers, Arizona State Archives, Phoenix, Ariz.

Ross Papers

Edward A. Ross Papers (microfilm), State Historical Society of Wisconsin, Madison, Wis.

CHAPTER ONE

1. Blake, "Coercive Pronatalism."

2. Camiscioli, "Producing Citizens"; King, " 'France Needs Children,' " "From Pronatalism to Social Welfare?" and "Demographic Trends"; Klaus, *Every Child a Lion*; Koonz, *Mothers in the Fatherland*.

3. See Klaus, *Every Child a Lion*, for an important comparative study of the United States and France.

4. Heitlinger, *Women's Equality*, 129.

5. Ibid., 121.

6. Dorr quoted in Mink, "The Lady and the Tramp."

7. Berg, *Mothering the Race*; Delegard, "Women's Movements"; Mink, "The Lady and the Tramp."

8. Dorr quoted in Mink, "The Lady and the Tramp."

9. See also Newman, *White Women's Rights*.

10. Abramovitz, *Regulating the Lives of Women*; Gordon, "Putting Children First"; Gordon and Skocpol, "Gender, State, and Society"; Koven and Michel, *Mothers of a New World*; Ladd-Taylor, *Mother-Work*; Muncy, *Creating a Female Dominion*; Skocpol, *Protecting Mothers and Soldiers*.

no11. Gordon, *Pitied But Not Entitled*, 55.

12. Misra and Akins, "The Welfare State and Women," 264.

13. Abramovitz, *Regulating the Lives of Women*, 111.

14. Boris and Bardaglio, "The Transformation of Patriarchy," 80–81, 85.

15. Heitlinger, *Women's Equality*, 127.

16. Weiner, "Maternalism as a Paradigm," 97.

17. Mintz and Kellogg, *Domestic Revolutions*, 108–9.

18. The various approaches to whiteness and race during the time period will be a theme developed in later portions of this book. See Gossett, *Race*.

19. Danbom, *The Resisted Revolution*.

20. Thomas Jefferson to George Washington, March 15, 1784, in Boyd, *The Papers of Thomas Jefferson*, 7: 25. See Bradley, "Cultivating the Terrain," 43; Montmarquet, *The Idea of Agrarianism*.

21. Kuhl, *The Nazi Connection*.

22. Kevles, *In the Name of Eugenics*; Paul, *Controlling Human Heredity*.

23. Cooke, "Duty or Dream?"; Kevles, *In the Name of Eugenics*; Kline, *Building a Better Race*; Paul, *Controlling Human Heredity*; Pernick, *The Black Stork*.

24. Heitlinger, *Women's Equality*, 1.

25. Kline, *Building a Better Race*, 4.

26. Ibid., 96.

27. Ibid., 123, 189 n. 125.

28. Popenoe, *The Conservation of the Family*.

29. Put a slightly different way, modernism was embodied in the realization of and reaction to the "modern predicament"; namely, the realization that "knowledge of the external world is not easy to come by, that contradictions persist in human experience, that a real price was paid for the benefits of bureaucratic rationality, that a large measure of uncertainty was an enduring

condition of life, that human beings had a propensity to act irrationally, that it was difficult to find an unchanging standard for moral judgments, that God might be dead, and that many sensitive individuals felt alienated from industrial society." Hollinger, "The Knower and the Artificer," 38.

30. Singal, "Toward a Definition," 12.

31. Ross, "Modernist Social Science in the Land of the New/Old," 188–89.

32. Berman, *All That Is Solid*, 1–36; Ross, "Modernism Reconsidered"; Singal, "Toward a Definition."

33. Lawrence Levine argues that nostalgia was a major historical force in early twentieth century culture. Levine, *The Unpredictable Past*.

34. Kammen, *Mystic Chords of Memory*, 295.

35. On tradition, see Cotkin, *Reluctant Modernism*; Levine, *The Unpredictable Past*. On antimodernism, see Lears, *No Place of Grace*.

36. Burns, *Pastoral Inventions*; Crunden, *Ministers of Reform*; Kammen, *Mystic Chords of Memory*.

37. Slotkin, "Nostalgia and Progress."

38. Levine, *The Unpredictable Past*.

39. Kammen, *Mystic Chords of Memory*, 295.

40. Coontz, *The Way We Never Were*; Kammen, *Mystic Chords of Memory*, 295; Levine, *The Unpredictable Past*, 189–205.

41. For a history of ideas of agrarianism see Montmarquet, *The Idea of Agrarianism*.

42. Stephanie Coontz astutely recognizes that western settlement and later suburban development deploy an image of the self-reliant family. Rather than focus on issues of individualism, I address how this celebration of the family was used to promote reproduction of certain types of families. Coontz, *The Way We Never Were*, 73–79.

43. Klaus recognizes the pronatalism of Roosevelt's conservation movement but does not discuss its appeal to agrarian nostalgia. See Klaus, *Every Child a Lion*, 32.

44. For a historiographic review of agrarianism see Brownell, "The Agrarian and Urban Ideals."

CHAPTER TWO

1. Hofstadter, *The Age of Reform*, 129–30.

2. Unlike any preceding political party, the People's Party was very inclusive

of women. Until the Progressive Party of 1912, female political organizers and members were more prominent in the People's Party than in any other party (Brady, "Populism and Feminism"; Edwards, *Angels in the Machinery*; Jeffery, "Southern Farmer's Alliance"; Wagner, "Farms, Families, and Reform"). Among the few published works concerning women in Populism, Michael Goldberg's *An Army of Women* is the most detailed and extensive. Goldberg carefully traces women's growing political participation in Kansas from their roles in the Farmer's Alliance to their very complicated disputes over the place of suffrage and temperance in party platforms (Goldberg, *An Army of Women*).

3. Goldberg, *An Army of Women*.

4. Ibid., 159–60.

5. Nugent, *The Tolerant Populists*; Clanton, "Intolerant Populist?"

6. Wagner, "Farms, Families, and Reform."

7. Goldberg, *An Army of Women*, 161–83, 244–50.

8. Brooke Orr has written a richly detailed biography of Lease that surpasses earlier efforts by Stiller and Blumberg (Blumberg, "Mary Elizabeth Lease"; Orr, "Mary Elizabeth Lease"; Stiller, *Queen of the Populists*).

9. As historian Richard Stiller puts it: "The grasshoppers brought religion back into Kansas politics. Unwilling to pay a minister to open the state legislative meetings in 1874, the Kansas State Legislature declined to renew the contract of a clerical representative. Following the plague, the legislature paid not one but two clergy on a consistent basis." Stiller, *Queen of the Populists*.

10. Ibid., 53–60.

11. Ibid., 62–66.

12. Orr, "Mary Elizabeth Lease," 34.

13. Lease was not the only female Populist writer who drew parallels between American mortgages and farm debt and Irish tenants. Sarah Brigham serialized a fictional comparison between Irish tenants and American farmers who, according to "Waverland: A Tale of the Coming Landlords," had much in common. In fact, this 1886 account pointed to the American farmers as worse off than the Irish tenants. According to historian Mary Jo Wagner's summary of Brigham's story, benevolent Irish landlords traveling to the United States saw the dire circumstances of farmers in Illinois and South Dakota as a warning of how important it was to support home rule for Ireland. After learning of the hard economic situation exacerbated by the bad legislation, corrupt financial institutions holding mortgages, and criminal outrages of the

railroads, the Irish hero of the story vowed to return to Ireland, run for Parliament, and support the Irish Land League. Brigham, "Waverland"; summarized in Wagner, "Farms, Families, and Reform," 103.

14. Mary Elizabeth Lease, "School Hygiene." Proceedings, Addresses, and Discussions at the Sanitary Convention 1886. Kansas State Historical Society, Topeka, Kans.

15. Rebecca Edwards notes the parallel between the courses of Willard's and Lease's careers in Angels in the Machinery, 103. Indeed her analysis of women and Populism emphasizes both political participation and the use of "the 'scientific' vocabulary of economics in their bid to protect the home." Edwards, Angels in the Machinery, 110.

16. Willard, "Tenth Annual Address, 1889."

17. Ibid.

18. Ibid., 154.

19. Ibid., 155. My italics.

20. Figures on debt in Kansas from Argesinger, Populism and Politics, 11.

21. Ibid., 1–21.

22. Peffer, "Editorial."

23. Lease, "Editorial Department."

24. Anthony and Harper, The History of Woman Suffrage, 641.

25. As Laura Johns, president of the Kansas Suffrage Association, put it in her motion for adopting the yellow ribbon, the sunflower that "follows the wheel track and the plough, as woman's enfranchisement should follow civilization." Ibid., 640.

26. Lease, "Editorial Department."

27. Laura Johns quoted in Anthony and Harper, The History of Woman Suffrage, 641. For a detailed analysis of Johns see Goldberg, An Army of Women.

28. Wichita Independent, November 24, 1888, 2.

29. Ibid., December 8, 1888, 1.

30. Ibid., November 24, 1888, 2.

31. The Kansas State Historical Society listed 721 weeklies, 6 semiweeklies, 49 dailies, 45 monthlies, 1 bimonthly, 4 quarterlies, 3 occasionals, and 19 others in a state survey in 1888. See Wilder, The Annals of Kansas, 63, 69.

32. Orr, "Mary Elizabeth Lease," 51.

33. Argesinger, The Limits of Agrarian Radicalism, 51.

34. Lease was erroneously reported as having coined this remarkable

phrase. Only years later would she admit that it was actually the result of inaccurate reporting. She did not object, she claims, because she thought it was good advice. Clinton, "What Did You Say."

35. Argesinger, *Populism and Politics*, 87.

36. While historians during the first decades of the twentieth century celebrated the "farmer's revolt" of the 1890s for its democratic curbs on corporate capitalism following the depression of 1893, later historians during the middle of the twentieth century posited a very different vision of the Populists (Hicks, *Populist Revolt*; Hofstadter, *The Age of Reform*). Richard Hofstadter and others noted the xenophobic, anti-Semitic, racist, and anti-immigrant rhetoric of the Populist campaigns. For Hofstadter, the small midwestern and southern farmer, valorized in the rhetoric of the yeoman farmer, was in fact a single-crop exporter entangled in an international market for agricultural goods. The brief flourishing of wheat markets during the 1870s and 1880s, which benefited the U.S. farmer because of European market problems, was an anomaly. Once the Russian wheat recovered, the American farmer who had mortgaged the farm to grow more of the staple crop was choked by the false promise of foreign markets. According to Hofstadter, the subsequent decline in crop prices was falsely construed in the writings of the Populists as an attack on the backbone of America.

The next twenty years witnessed another reversal of the status of the Populist in the minds of historians. Where Hofstadter saw the Populist as the predecessor of the McCarthyite anti-intellectual, Steven Hahn, Walter T. K. Nugent, Lawrence Goodwyn, and others did not (Goodwyn, *The Populist Moment*; Hahn, *The Roots of Southern Populism*; Nugent, *The Tolerant Populists*). Indeed writing in 1963, Nugent titled his book *The Tolerant Populists* to emphasize his disagreement with Hofstadter's characterization of the People's Party (Nugent, *The Tolerant Populists*). The movements for popular democracy, which characterized many student movements in the 1960s and 1970s, recast the Populists as a model of an early movement culture for democratic control. This interpretation of the People's Party privileged its popular methods of local organization as well as those of its predecessors, the Alliance and the Grange. Goodwyn, for example, described a vibrant political and social movement characterized by picnics, marches, schools, and lectures (Goodwyn, *The Populist Moment*).

37. Elizabeth N. Barr, "The Populist Uprising," cited in Hicks, *Populist Revolt*.

38. Morgan, "Over-production."

39. Ibid., 16.

40. Reprinted from the *Kansas City Star*, April 1, 1891, in Clanton, *Kansas Populism*, 77.

41. This choice of depictive element built on and reinforced the emphasis on the farm family at the heart of the Grange movement (Goldberg, *An Army of Women*, 39). The fate of the farm girl in the city would later become the subject of popular novels such as Theodore Dreiser's *Sister Carrie* (1900).

42. Lease, "Do Kansas Women Want to Vote?"

43. Lease, "Legal Disabilities of Women."

44. Goldberg, *An Army of Women*, 179. *Topeka Capital*, July 11 and 15, 1891. Mary Elizabeth Lease Clippings File, Kansas State Historical Society, Topeka, Kans.

45. White, *Autobiography of William Allen White*, 218–19. As historian Gene Clanton has suggested, this description written later had resonances of descriptions written at the time. One Populist newspaper, the *Kansas City Star*, described her in terms that seemed to anticipate White's description: "Mrs. Lease is a tall woman—fully five feet ten inches, and rather slender. Her face is strong, good, not pretty, and very feminine. There is no mark of masculinity about her. She is woman all over. Her hair is a dark brown and evenly parted in the center and smoothed down at the sides with neat care. Her nose, chin and cheek bones announce themselves strongly. However, they give no sense of harshness to her face." *Kansas City Star*, April 1, 1891, 39. Mary Elizabeth Lease Clippings File, Kansas State Historical Society, Topeka, Kans. Also see Goldberg, *An Army of Women*, 177–79.

46. *Wellington (Kans.) Monitor*, October 3, 1890; cited in Clanton, *Kansas Populism*, 76.

47. Clanton, *Kansas Populism*, 127–50. On Lease see 142–46.

48. Clanton, "Intolerant Populist?" 195. This dispute was first mentioned in Hicks, *Populist Revolt*, 281.

49. Trattner, *Poor Law to Welfare State*, 86, 94.

50. Minutes, State Board of Charities, December 11–13, 1893, Kansas State Historical Society, Topeka, Kans.

51. Lease had Householder propose most appointments and made sure that the newspapers knew it, probably to avoid the impression that she was as bad as Lewelling at using appointments to pay off political obligations. *Farmer's Wife* 11, no. 9 (April 1893): 4.

52. See Brady, "Populism and Feminism," 283.

53. *Annals of Kansas* 1 (November 1894): 45.

54. Willard, "Tenth Annual Address, 1889," 157.

55. The 1887 *Union Signal* described the efforts of the Mississippi WCTU in taking this approach when the education bill mandating the study of physiology and hygiene failed. *Union Signal*, January 20, 1887.

56. Willard, "Tenth Annual Address, 1889," 154–55.

57. This decision was accompanied by an editorial comment about the significance of accepting these individuals as unteachable. Indeed, Lease's reform had the effect of turning Winfield into a facility used to segregate and remove these individuals away from the population (the Populace) rather than perhaps viewing the children sent there as teachable and malleable. This would have clearly fit with Lease's protoeugenical ideas. "At the institution for imbecile youth, at Winfield, high priced teachers have been employed to teach the inmates the common English branches. After six or seven years of school work some of the idiots can now distinguish the first three or four letters of the alphabet, but can make no further progress. The present board, recognizing the folly of attempting to educate beings absolutely destitute of mind, have discharged the professors and now employ attendants at lower wages." *Topeka Advocate*, January 17, 1894. Mary Elizabeth Lease Clippings File, Kansas State Historical Society, Topeka, Kans.

58. Ibid.

59. In introducing the program of the 1889 WCTU, Frances Willard made sure to introduce by name Mrs. Col. F. W. Parker of Englewood as a well-known Delsartean and Dress Reformer. Francois Delsart was a French actor and teacher who lived from 1811 to 1871 and advocated a method of studying human behavior by observing body movement. Willard, "Tenth Annual Address, 1889."

60. Goldberg, *An Army of Women*; Nugent, *The Tolerant Populists*; Orr, "Mary Elizabeth Lease."

61. Bellamy, *Looking Backward*; see Chapter 5 on the Sphinx's Riddle. Lease, *The Problem of Civilization Solved*, 11.

62. Lease, *The Problem of Civilization Solved*, 4.

63. Ibid., 17.

64. Ibid., 349.

65. Ibid., 354.

66. Ibid., 353.

67. Ibid., 249.

68. Ibid., 250–55.

69. Ostler, "The Rhetoric of Conspiracy."

70. "Mrs. Lease's Debts."

71. Takaki, *Iron Cages*.

72. Reynolds, *Cat'spaw Utopia*.

73. "Mrs. Lease Likens It to Barnum's Circus," July 3, 1898, Mary Elizabeth Lease Clippings File, Kansas State Historical Society, Topeka, Kans.

74. LaFeber, *The New Empire*; Love, *Race Over Empire*.

75. Orr, "Mary Elizabeth Lease"; Stiller, *Queen of the Populists*.

76. "In Ernest Now."

77. Stiller, *Queen of the Populists*, 171–72.

78. Clanton, *Kansas Populism*, 224–25.

79. Socialist Literary Guild flyer, April 3, 1904, Labor Archives, New York University, New York, N.Y.

80. "Mrs. Lease Beards the Red Dragon."

81. F. L. Shellabarger, "Mary Elizabeth Lease Eager to Run for U.S. Senator Here," 42–52, Mary Elizabeth Lease Clippings File, Kansas State Historical Society, Topeka, Kans.

82. Lease, "Address," 37.

83. "Sore on Reporters."

84. "Mrs. Lease, 'Who Pursues Man.' "

85. "Advice to Raise 'Less Corn.' "

CHAPTER THREE

1. Gilman, *Herland*, 13–14.

2. Banta, *Taylored Lives*; Wright, *Building the Dream*, 21.

3. Gilman, *What Diantha Did*. This serialized novel was written at the same time as "The Man-Made World; or, Our Androcentric Culture" and contains a male character named Ross who calls Diantha to take her place within the traditional home. Since Edward Ross wrote an essay in response, "Women in

the Man Made World," in *The Social Trend*, it seems logical that this must have been something she was discussing with him at the time. See Chapter 4, "The Political Economy of Sex: Edward A. Ross and Race Suicide."

4. Lane, *To Herland and Beyond*, 141–58. Gilman, in fact, penned a short story between the two utopian accounts acclaiming the wonders of irrigation. In "The Devout Farmers," written for her magazine, *The Forerunner*, Gilman contrasted the pious and devout farmers with their irreverent and profane neighbors. Both lived in the "Dry West" where the devout prayed for rain that did not come and the profane built dams and reservoirs and dug canals. The devout became poor and the profane prospered, for "the Lord sendeth rain in due season. And it is also true that men can dig." In this short parable, Gilman captured the modernist sense of the possibility of remaking the landscape. Gilman, "The Devout Farmer."

5. Gilman asserts the fragility of such a vision by including among the male explorers one who represents the innate lower instincts when he attempts to rape one of the inhabitants of Herland. See Gail Bederman on this aspect of the novel. Bederman, *Manliness and Civilization*, 166.

6. Philip Ethington argues that Gilman's political imagination was also produced by a particularly western phenomenon. Her early activity in the public life of San Francisco in the 1890s helped to shape her configuration of the way in which women would be enabled to enter political leadership. This was the case, Ethington argues, because Progressive Era San Francisco was a notoriously "public city," one that offered the opportunity for pluralist public participation in its governance. See Ethington, *The Public City*.

7. Pisani, "Reclamation and Social Engineering."

8. Taylor, *The Turner Thesis*; Turner, "Significance of the Frontier."

9. Maxwell, "Makes Homes of Desert Wastes." For a history of the safety-valve idea in relation to the West see Smith, *Virgin Land*.

10. Autobee, "Every Child a Garden," 196.

11. This vision of reclaiming the land for small homeowners touches upon some of the most important issues in western history, especially as it is being rewritten in response to Frederick Jackson Turner. The New Western History has focused much of its organizational effort on defining the problems with Turner's frontier thesis, which argued that "free land" available on the frontier was fundamentally responsible for reshaping Europeans into a new people committed to individualism, community, and democracy. As he put it, the

frontier was "the outer edge of the wave—the meeting point between savagery and civilization"; it was thus, "the line of most effective and rapid American- ization." The process of coming to terms with the American "wilderness" produced a new kind of a nation, according to Turner. Turner, "Significance of the Frontier."

Critics of Turner's thesis have pointed out that Turner posits the Midwest as the West and that though he argues that environment significantly shapes human behavior, he ignores the aridity of the West, arguably its most defining feature. Most significantly, Turner ignored the people who lived in the West who did not meet his white male settler model and romanticized the role of the economic pursuits of that settler in the mines, in settlements, or on public lands in creating the uniqueness of the West. Issues of capitalism and class as well as environmental exploitation were also ignored.

Still, critics of Turner have maintained that there is something unique about the western part of the United States even if it was not defined in terms of a "frontier." Patricia Limerick, in proposing a new framework for thinking about the West, suggests defining the region as unique in terms of its central process of "conquest," itself historically dependent on the region's aridity. In contrast, Donald Worster argues for the West's adaptation to its arid environs as its central defining process, while William Cronon and Richard White insist that it is the interaction between humans and the environment that are par- ticularly unique to the region. Cronon, Nature's Metropolis; Limerick, The Legacy of Conquest; White, "It's Your Misfortune"; Worster, Rivers of Empire.

12. Hill's motives are not wholly ascribable to profit; he maintained an interest in scientific farming and ran several experimental farm sites. He may truly have been interested in how the land could be improved. See Malone, James J. Hill; Martin, James J. Hill.

13. Hibbard, Public Land Policies, 248. On the value of these land grants and how they initially functioned as a basis of credit, see Henry, "The Railroad Land Grant Legend." Comments on Henry collected in Carstensen, The Public Lands, 145–80. The impact of later trying to sell the land, especially after the foreclosures of the 1890s, would suggest the significance of reclamation later rather than earlier.

14. White, "Main Street," 95.

15. Lilley and Gould, "The Western Irrigation Movement." Pisani, From the Family Farm, eloquently urges a consideration of the diversity of local control,

politics, and economics in any attempt to discuss national irrigation; Davison, *Leadership of the Reclamation Movement*.

16. Lilley and Gould, "The Western Irrigation Movement"; Pisani, *From the Family Farm*; Reisner, *Cadillac Desert*. On economic dependence of the West on national intervention, see Limerick, *The Legacy of Conquest*.

17. Pisani, "Reclamation and Social Engineering," 52.

18. Marion Bannister, *The Lands Ye Possess: Who Shall Administer Them?* (Washington, D.C.; Democratic National Party, n.d.). Theodore Roosevelt Collection, Widener Library, Harvard University, Cambridge, Mass.

19. Pisani, *Water and American Government*.

20. In fact James J. Hill, the railroad magnate and Maxwell's benefactor for a number of years, was nicknamed "the Empire-builder."

21. Smythe, *The Conquest of Arid America*, frontispiece.

22. Smythe's imagery fits within a tradition of depicting the western land as a virgin wilderness or unspoiled Eve to be taken by force. See Kolodny, *The Lay of the Land*.

23. *National Irrigation* 6 (August 1901): 99.

24. Ibid. 6 (October 1901): 129.

25. Kaplan, "Manifest Domesticity."

26. Heston, "The American Farmer's Future."

27. As quoted in Pisani, *Water and American Government*, 2. The scale of change wrought by reclamation was often captured in "before" and "after" photographs used in various reclamation publications. Indeed, Maxwell's magazines are filled with photographs of projects or rivers, often unconnected to the topic of the article in which they appear. The scale of these images, which take up much of the pages in which they are reprinted, make clear Maxwell's concern with presenting irrigation in the most vivid terms possible to his readers.

28. George H. Maxwell, "National Irrigation," *National Irrigation* 6 (October 1901): 128.

29. Reisner, *Cadillac Desert*, 81. Roosevelt made clear his equation of the strength of the home and the nation in a lecture at the Berkeley Theological Seminary in the spring of 1911 when he claimed that home building such as Maxwell proposed and homemaking by women were the strength of the country. Roosevelt, *Realizable Ideals*. See Chapter 5, "Men As Trees Walking: Theodore Roosevelt and the Conservation of the Race."

30. Roosevelt, "First Annual Message."

31. Pinchot, Breaking New Ground, 188.

32. Higham, Strangers in the Land, 148–49.

33. Heston, "The American Farmer's Future."

34. Later Maxwell would articulate a racial motivation for homemaking when he identified the supposed threat of invasion from Mexico by Japanese farmers. While Maxwell's comments were strongly anti-Japanese, they were not explicitly Anglo-Saxonist.

35. Heston, "The American Farmer's Future."

36. Bush, "The Way We Weren't."

37. Armitage, "Through Women's Eyes." The implications of constructing these elements as "natural" have been frequently and thoroughly discussed for a long time.

38. Maxwell, "A Problem for the Statesman."

39. Cott, The Bonds of Womanhood, 64.

40. Ibid.; Kaplan, "Manifest Domesticity."

41. Handlin, The American Home, 3–89. See also Clark, The American Family Home.

42. William E. Smythe, Irrigation Age 10 (August 1896): 55. Cited in Pisani, "Reclamation and Social Engineering."

43. Ibid.

44. Anderson, "The Little Landers' Colonies"; Lee, "The Little Landers of San Ysidro."

45. Many housing reform efforts in the United States were informed by English and European models of community development that incorporated space for gardens and playgrounds. See Rodgers, Atlantic Crossings.

46. George H. Maxwell, "Peace or War," ms., 15. Maxwell Papers.

47. The slogan continues: "And that until he owns such a Home, the concentrated purpose and chief inspiration to labor in the life of every wage worker should be his determination to 'Get an Acre and live on it.' " This appeared as the frontispiece in each edition of Maxwell's Talisman.

48. Ibid.

49. George Maxwell, "Be a Homecrofter," Maxwell's Talisman (April 1906): 5.

50. Maxwell, First Book of the Homecrofters, 26. For more on the gardening movement in the United States see Lawson, City Bountiful.

51. Christensen, *The American Garden City*, 29–35.

52. Ibid., 35–40.

53. Marsh, "City Planning in Justice"; as quoted in Scott, *American City Planning Since 1890*, 80.

54. Class Directories, 1904–8, Massachusetts Institute of Technology Archives, Cambridge, Mass.

55. "The Homecroft Weavers of Watertown, Mass.," *Maxwell's Talisman* (August 1906): 20.

56. George H. Maxwell, "Educational Inspiration at Watertown, The 'Back to the Land Movement,'" Series 9—Miscellaneous, Maxwell Papers.

57. It was through the image of the home that postwar reformers often approached issues of social inequity. Edward Bellamy's popular novel *Looking Backward* was just one example of a utopian vision of the future imaged in terms of idealized domiciles where the individual kitchens were replaced by a communal kitchen with optional individual dining rooms. He argued that eliminating the need to care for the home would allow for changes in society. The "home feeling" would be maintained by separable apartments while the drudgery of keeping the sweet home clean would be eliminated.

58. Boris, *Art and Labor*, 11.

59. Quoted in ibid., 157.

60. Ibid., 156–57.

61. Brady, *The Book of the Roycrofters*; Hamilton, *As Bees in Honey Drown*; Via and Searle, *Head, Heart and Hand*.

62. Elbert Hubbard, "A Social and Industrial Experiment," *Cosmopolitan* (1902), quoted in Boris, *Art and Labor*, 148. The *Homemaker* also ran an article by Hubbard commenting on the value of the farmer and irrigation to Montana. Hubbard, "Agriculture Montana's Great Resource."

63. Addams's role in the generation of new social science ideas should not be ignored. Critic Mary Jo Deegan points out the tendency to reduce the intellectual significance of the practice of social science in Hull House and argues that it deserves the same appreciation as the theorizing of the Chicago School. See Deegan, *Jane Addams*.

64. Addams, *Twenty Years at Hull House*, 75–89, 274–75.

65. Boris, *Art and Labor*, 46. The same claims about the role of traditional crafts in assimilation and financial adjustment is still made in the United

States among new immigrant communities such as the Hmong, who were encouraged to organize in needlecraft cooperatives upon arrival in the country.

66. George H. Maxwell, mss., Maxwell Papers.

67. Boris, *Art and Labor*, 157–62. I'm thankful to Eileen Boris for drawing my attention to these Massachusetts communities.

68. Elizabeth S. Hill, "The School Garden Movement," *Maxwell's Talisman* (October 1905): 11–13; and "Nature Study and Gardening," *Maxwell's Talisman* (April 1906): 11. The implications of nature study are discussed in Chapter 5 as part of the country life movement.

69. See the "Special Women's Club Garden School Number" of *Maxwell's Talisman* (July 1906).

70. One in three Americans lived in cities in 1910 according to the census. Quotation from Clifton F. Hodge, *Nature Study and Life* (Boston: Ginn, 1902), 132; as quoted in Schmitt, *Back to Nature*, 91.

71. George H. Maxwell, "Platform of *The Talisman*." Reprinted in Maxwell, *First Book of the Homecrofters*, 92.

72. See Banta, *Taylored Lives*, on Christine Frederick.

73. Seaton, "Making the Best of Circumstances," 90–104.

74. Maxwell, *First Book of the Homecrofters*, 33.

75. George H. Maxwell, "The Future of the Middle West," *Maxwell's Talisman* (August 1905): 9–12. Also George H. Maxwell, "The Japanese Situation," *Maxwell's Talisman* 5 (September 1905): 3–4.

76. In later years, Maxwell was convinced that the Japanese were establishing colonies in Mexico and were a serious invasion threat. Maxwell reasoned that if the highline canal was not built, then water would go to Mexico "to create there an Asiatic Colony and establish a ruinous competition in every product of the soil of Arizona and Southern California." This colony "will be the entering wedge for making Mexico an Asiatic country. It will transplant from Asia to America every friction point, every competitive struggle, and every military menace growing out of the racial and economic differences between the people of the two continents who are now separated by 5000 miles of ocean. It will make an Asiatic-American war inevitable." George Maxwell to C. P. Cronon, March 13, 1922, Maxwell Papers. Also see Maxwell, *Our Nation's Defense*.

77. Hudanick, "George Hebard Maxwell," 117–19.

78. George H. Maxwell, "Homecroft: The Making of a Word," *Maxwell's Talisman* 6 (April 1906): 5.

79. Pisani, "Reclamation and Social Engineering," 61.

80. George H. Maxwell, "The National Homecroft Bill," *Maxwell's Talisman* (February 1907): 45–46; Pisani, "Reclamation and Social Engineering," 62.

81. Pisani, "Reclamation and Social Engineering," 62.

82. See Skocpol, *Protecting Soldiers and Mothers*, for more on Civil War soldier's pensions.

83. Conkin, *Tomorrow a New World*; Hibbard, *Public Land Policies*, 133; O'Callaghan, "The War Veteran," 109–20; Shi, *The Simple Life*, 222–26.

84. George H. Maxwell, "Soldier's Adjusted Compensation," *Maxwell's Talisman* 16 (June 1920): 3–7.

85. Ibid.

86. Conkin, *Tomorrow a New World*, 53.

87. Mead, *Helping Men Own Farms*. Mead was explicit in his desire to see what he called "white families" become landowners and farmers in order to give them an advantage over the Japanese and "Hindoo" farmers in the Central Valley, whom Mead saw as threatening.

88. Rodgers, *Atlantic Crossings*.

89. Mead, *Helping Men Own Farms*.

90. Autobee, "Every Child a Garden," 201.

91. American Homecroft Society, Indiana Plan Newspaper Clippings, Reclamation Bureau Papers, RG 115-58, vol. 1, National Archives, Denver, Colo.

92. Autobee, "Every Child a Garden," 202.

93. F. A. Silcox, "Our Adventure in Conservation: The CCC"; in "George H. Maxwell: Conservation Pioneer," Mss. compiled in 1948, Reclamation Bureau Papers, RG 115, National Archives, Denver, Colo.

94. Autobee, "Every Child a Garden," 206; Pisani, *Water and American Government*, 20.

95. Reisner claims that the Reclamation Act of 1902, turned the western United States into the "first and most durable example of the modern welfare state." Reisner, *Cadillac Desert*, 111.

96. Danbom, *The Resisted Revolution*.

97. Abramovitz, *Regulating the Lives of Women*.

98. Misra and Akins, "The Welfare State and Women," 264.

99. Abramovitz, *Regulating the Lives of Women*, 111.

100. Boris and Bardaglio, "The Transformation of Patriarchy," 80–81, 85.

101. In the literature on welfare, this independence from the wage system is called decommodification. Maxwell's homecroft system was a form of decommodification.

102. Esping-Andersen, *Three Worlds of Welfare Capitalism*; Lewis, "Development of Welfare Regimes," and "Gender and Welfare Regimes"; Orloff, "Social Rights of Citizenship."

103. Lewis, "Development of Welfare Regimes."

104. Autobee, "Every Child a Garden"; Conkin, *Tomorrow a New World*.

105. Historians Katherine Jellison and Mary Neth demonstrate that a model of the rural family similar to that proposed by Maxwell was in fact widespread throughout the rural Midwest in the early twentieth century. Jellison, *Entitled to Power*; Neth, *Preserving the Farm Family*, 214–15.

CHAPTER FOUR

1. Lovett, "The *Popeye* Principle"; Richards, "True Cause of Race Suicide."

2. Gordon, *Woman's Body, Woman's Right*, 136–58. Additionally, Gail Bederman offers an analysis in terms of ideals of masculinity. Bederman, *Manliness and Civilization*. Also see Horowitz, *Alma Mater*; Newman, *White Women's Rights*; Solomon, *Ancestors and Immigrants*.

3. Malthus, *The Principle of Population*.

4. Walker, "Immigration and Degradation"; reprinted in *Discussions in Economics and Statistics*, vol. 2 (New York: Henry Holt, 1899), 417–26; quotes from 424.

5. For more on Walker see Reed, *From Private Vice*, 198–201. Walker was not alone in his demographic concerns. See Hodgson, "Ideological Origins of the Population Association"; Solomon, *Ancestors and Immigrants*; and Leonard, " 'More Merciful.' "

6. McMahon, *Social Control and Public Intellect*; Ross, *Seventy Years of It*.

7. For more on the history of sociology in the United States see Ross, *Origins of American Social Science*; Schwendinger and Schwendinger, *The Sociologists of the Chair*.

8. Rosenberg, *Beyond Separate Spheres*.

9. On Ross's career, see McMahon, *Social Control and Public Intellect*; Ross, *Seventy Years of It*; Weinberg, *Edward Alsworth Ross*.

10. On the controversy with Jane Stanford, which Jordan referred to as the

"regrettable Ross affair," see Burns, *David Starr Jordan*; Hofstadter and Metzger, *The Development of Academic Freedom*.

11. Burns, *David Starr Jordan*, 15–16; Weinberg, *Edward Alsworth Ross*, 47.

12. The assessment of the political success of Dennis Kearney's Workingman's Party as well as the centrality of anti-Asian sentiment in class and racial definition is discussed in Kazin, *The Populist Persuasion*; Ryan, *Civic Wars*; Takaki, *Strangers from a Different Shore*.

13. Gardner, "Working on White Womanhood," 78.

14. Stoll, *The Fruits of Natural Advantage*.

15. Takaki, *Strangers from a Different Shore*, 180–81, 189, 200.

16. In fact, Ross's anti-Japanese comments were part of a larger national debate. See response and summary of the discussion in Iyenaga and Sato, *Japan and the California Problem*.

17. Weinberg, *Edward Alsworth Ross*, 50.

18. Rosenberg, *Beyond Separate Spheres*.

19. Weinberg, *Edward Alsworth Ross*, 52–53.

20. Gail Bederman notes that the term "civilization was protean in its applications"; there were many ways that it was used during this era to "legitimate different claims to power." As Ross's comments make clear, one of the most significant ways the term was used was to construct an argument about racial and cultural superiority. Bederman, *Manliness and Civilization*, 23.

21. Ross, "The Causes of Race Superiority," 87.

22. Public health reformers such as Ellen Richards were also standardizing and raising minimum conditions for healthy living. Duffy, *The Sanitarians*; Hoy, *Chasing Dirt*; Levenstein, *Revolution at the Table*; Shapiro, *Perfection Salad*; Tomes, *The Gospel of Germs*.

23. Ross, "The Causes of Race Superiority," 88.

24. Ibid., 89.

25. Yeo, *The Contest for Social Science*, 183–203.

26. Ross, *Foundations of Sociology*, 387.

27. Ibid., 42.

28. Ibid., 65. Ross quoted Durkheim's *Le Suicide*.

29. Durkheim, *Suicide*.

30. *New York World*, July 18, 1897, 1. The reporting of Ada Baeker's story on the front page with an illustration was not unusual. Suicide involving women was frequently highlighted by relatively long and detailed stories that were

likely to be illustrated and run on the front page. Indeed, James Gundlach and Steven Stack have argued that during the early twentieth century there was "hyper media coverage" of suicide, meaning that disproportionately large numbers of suicide stories were run in the newspapers. See Gundlach and Stack, "Impact of Hyper Media Coverage."

31. As of 1880, women made up 40 percent of all stenographers and typists. By 1900, they filled more than 75 percent of jobs in these fields and a quarter of all clerical positions. A continuing debate in the 1890s about the appropriateness of such work for women attested to the newness of this development. Davies, *Woman's Place.*

32. Weinberg, *Edward Alsworth Ross.* Ross's attitude stands in contrast, for instance, to that of most of the intellectuals described in Solomon, *Ancestors and Immigrants.*

33. Ross, *Foundations of Sociology,* 353–95, see especially 360–363; and *The Social Trend,* 52–77.

34. Ross, *Foundations of Sociology,* 387.

35. Ibid., 389–90.

36. Ibid., 391.

37. Ibid., 394. This characterization of Americans and Ross's warning were widely reported. See, for instance, "'Lesser Breeds' vs. American Stock," *Washington (D.C.) National,* December 8, 1904, scrapbook, vol. 7, Ross Papers.

38. Bryan, "Cross of Gold."

39. E. A. Ross, "The Frontier," ms., ca. 1909, 10, Ross Papers.

40. Ross, *Social Control,* 432–33.

41. Ibid., 437.

42. Ibid., 437–38.

43. Dyer, *Theodore Roosevelt,* 143–67.

44. McMahon, *Social Control and Public Intellect.*

45. Roosevelt, "Sixth Annual Address to Congress." See Dyer, *Theodore Roosevelt;* May, *Barren in the Promised Land,* 61–62. Roosevelt had expressed concerns about declining birthrates much earlier.

46. Gordon, *Woman's Body, Woman's Right,* 189.

47. Newman, *White Women's Rights;* Rosenberg, *Beyond Separate Spheres;* Clarke as quoted in Solomon, *In the Company of Educated Women,* 56.

48. Clarke, *Sex in Education,* 43.

49. Solomon, *In the Company of Educated Women,* 57.

50. An 1889 symposium on the "co-education of the sexes" was still wrapped in the labeled brown paper that a Yale professor had used to protect his young charges from accidental exposure to the biological description of the impact of college on women's bodies. Clippings on Marriage, Family, Intercourse and Prostitution, Zeta File, Mudd Library, Yale University, New Haven, Conn.

51. "The Age to Marry.—Physically Considered," *Cincinnati Medical Journal* (1894), Clippings on Marriage, Family, Intercourse and Prostitution, Zeta File, Mudd Library, Yale University, New Haven, Conn.

52. For age-of-consent campaigns see Odem, *Delinquent Daughters*; Ullman, *Sex Seen*; Bordin, *Women and Temperance*; Pivar, *Purity Crusade*; Robertson, "Age of Consent Law."

53. Shinn, "Marriage Rate of College Women."

54. Historian Nancy Cott ascribes a decline in the number of women entering what were defined as male-dominated professions (medicine, law, professoriate) in the 1920s to an increasingly professionalized ideology that was in tension with a feminist ideology even as it allowed women to enter professions. The first women to enter the legal profession on behalf of women, for example, were increasingly displaced by professional lawyers who could themselves be women. See Cott, *The Grounding of Modern Feminism*, 213–40.

55. Table of Hall and Smith's results reproduced in Goodsell, *The Education of Women*, 36.

56. On the introduction of women's sports, see Cahn, *Coming on Strong*; Inness, " 'It Is Pluck' "; Verbrugge, "Recreating the Body."

57. Roosevelt, "The Successful Mother."

58. Roosevelt, *Realizable Ideals*, 48–50.

59. Numerous references to the widespread discussion of race suicide are included in Calhoun, *A Social History*; Gordon, *Woman's Body, Woman's Right*.

60. On the impact of infant mortality on the family see Curry, *Modern Mothers in the Heartland*; Klaus, *Every Child a Lion*.

61. "No Race Suicide in this Indiana Family," December 1905; "President Roosevelt's Ideal Family," *Louisville-Courier Journal*, July 9, 1905. Both in Clippings on Marriage, Family, Intercourse, and Prostitution, Zeta File, Mudd Library, Yale University, New Haven, Conn.

62. Calhoun, *A Social History*. Esper, "Letter to the Editor," 6.

63. Forman-Brunell, *Made to Play House*.

64. Calhoun makes reference to the "teddy bear controversy" as a fairly widespread or at least recognizable issue to his audience. See Calhoun, *A Social History*. Esper's letter from the December 1907 *Delineator* appears to be the only primary reference to the issue discussed in contemporary secondary sources. See Tamony, "The Teddy Bear."

65. Commander, "The Home Without a Child," 723.

66. E. A. Ross, "Race Suicide and the Simple Life," *Canton (Ohio) Repository*, August 20, 1905. Also reported in "The Patent-Leather Life," *Charleston News*, August 20, 1905.

67. "The Patent Leather Life," *Charleston News*, August 20, 1905.

68. "Patent Leather and Babeless Marriage," *Sacramento Bee*, August 20, 1905.

69. "Race Suicide vs. Race Homicide," *Richmond Dispatch*, August 9, 1905. "Upholds Race Suicide," *New York Daily People*, August 6, 1905.

70. E. A. Ross, "The Future Human Race," n.d., Ross Papers.

71. "Dr. Ross Coined 'Race Suicide,'" *Seattle Times*, July 4, 1906. See Newspaper Clipping File, Ross Papers.

72. Theodore Roosevelt to Edward Ross, April 6, 1907, Ross Papers.

73. Sprague, "Education and Race Suicide." Sprague's ideal replacement figure foreshadows the implementation of the 3.5 children birthrate during the 1950s. Indeed, as I will suggest in a later chapter, there is a direct relationship between the targeted goal of getting native-born, educated women to bear the number of children presented and the implementation of programs that would allow the birthrate to increase, at least among those Americans targeted as the beneficiaries of this vision (see Chapter 6).

74. Sprague, "Education and Race Suicide," 161.

75. "Coeducation and Marriage"; "Stanford's Marriage Rate." For an overview of these and other studies see Goodsell, *The Education of Women*.

76. Banker, "Coeducation and Eugenics."

77. Hamilton, "Putting Over Eugenics."

78. Ibid., 281.

79. Leta Hollingworth, who began graduate school at Columbia in 1911, met her husband at the University of Nebraska in 1906, when Ross was still a professor there. When New York laws prohibited her from teaching because she was married, she began to study psychology. Her husband's advisor had been James Cattell, who warned of the detrimental effects of women's educa-

tion in 1909. Challenging physiological theories of sex difference, Hollingworth studied the effects of menses on motor skills and mental abilities. Finding no effect, she broadened her research to the claim that men were more variable than women. After a study of 20,000 infants, Hollingworth reported that she found no greater anatomical variability in male infants than in female infants. The lack of physical variability called into question the claim of greater mental variability and so of more male geniuses. Rather, the lack of a physical foundation for differences in women's achievement turned Hollingworth to exploring the social conditions of women that denied them the opportunity to excel in areas recognized as indicators of imminence. Hollingworth, "Variability as Related to Sex Differences."

80. Hollingworth, "Social Devices."

81. Ibid., 27.

82. Popenoe, *The Conservation of the Family.*

83. For more on Popenoe see Kline, *Building a Better Race*; Ladd-Taylor, "Eugenics, Sterilization and Modern Marriage."

84. "America on the Eve of a Great Moral Revival," Newspaper Clipping Collection, Ross Papers; McMahon, *Social Control and Public Intellect.*

85. Weinberg, Hinkle, and Hinkle, "Introduction."

86. Ross, *Principles of Sociology*, 34.

87. Veblen, *Theory of the Leisure Class*, 68.

88. Ibid., 35.

89. "Upholds Race Suicide," *New York Daily People*, August 6, 1905.

90. Ross, *Principles of Sociology*, 36.

91. Ibid., 423, 433.

92. Ibid., 386.

93. Ibid., 390–91.

94. Ibid., 26.

95. Ross, *The Social Trend*, 46.

96. Ross, *Principles of Sociology*, 428.

97. Ross, *The Social Trend*, 49–51.

98. While rural sociology received much of its impetus from the national recognition of the need to improve country life, rural sociologists also continued to idealize the rural family and hold up its stability and vitality as a negative appraisal of the effects of urbanization. Howard, *A Social History*, 74–75; Sorokin and Zimmerman, *Principles of Rural-Urban Sociology.*

99. Ross, *Principles of Sociology*, 392–93.

100. Ibid., 388.

101. See Dyer, *Theodore Roosevelt*; Gordon, *Woman's Body, Woman's Right*; Reed, *From Private Vice*; Weinberg, *Edward Alsworth Ross*.

102. Gilman (and Ross) consider the power of writing and language to be part of these governing institutions. Gilman, however, extends her analysis beyond language to art and sports as well. Her analysis of language particularly evinces the way in which she sees social institutions constructed. For example, she notes that "effeminate" means too female, while there is no such counterpart for too masculine and, in fact, "emasculate" means not masculine enough. Lane, *To Herland and Beyond*, 280.

103. Ross, *Principles of Sociology*, 677–78. While Ross learned from Gilman's feminism, it is important to note that Gilman's views on race and immigration were similar to Ross's and endorsed a biological understanding of racial hierarchy. See Newman, *White Women's Rights*.

104. Edward A. Ross, "How Much Truth Is There in Malthus?" Written for the *Christian Century*, 1947. Typescript in Ross Papers.

CHAPTER FIVE

1. Indeed, Gifford Pinchot's mother was the head of the DAR committee on conservation, although she did not speak at the congress.

2. Foster, "The Conservation of Child Life," 92. See Brechin, "Conserving the Race."

3. Pringle, *Theodore Roosevelt*.

4. Dyer, *Theodore Roosevelt*, 6–7; Gossett, *Race*.

5. Dyer argues that Roosevelt himself did not refer to the "Anglo-Saxon race." However, he did celebrate the white population of the United States even if he was careful enough not to assume that everyone in that population had Anglo-Saxon ancestry.

6. Dyer, *Theodore Roosevelt*, 1, 3; Slotkin, *Gunfighter Nation*, 29–62.

7. Dyer, *Theodore Roosevelt*, 24–25; Roosevelt, "The Winning of the West," 421.

8. Dyer, *Theodore Roosevelt*, 41–43.

9. Ibid., 36–37.

10. Bederman, *Manliness and Civilization*, 187–96.

11. Roosevelt, *California Addresses*, 22–23.

12. Roosevelt, "Seventh Annual Address," 441.

13. Roosevelt, "The Man Who Works," 133.

14. Ibid., 134.

15. The rural family was not necessarily the nineteenth-century patriarchal family. The separation of spheres essential to the patriarchal family was not as strong a feature of rural families, who tended to act as a productive unit to a greater extent than their urban counterparts.

16. Roosevelt, "The Man Who Works," 143.

17. Roosevelt's stance on women's duty to reproduce on behalf of the state was discussed in detail in Chapter 4 within the context of the debate over race suicide.

18. Bowers, *The Country Life Movement*, 16–17. For more on Pinchot and conservation see Miller, *Gifford Pinchot*. For more on Plunkett see West, *Horace Plunkett*. For a review of the historiography on the Country Life Commission see Peters and Morgan, "The Country Life Commission."

19. Plunkett, "Conservation and Rural Life," 262.

20. Roosevelt, "Rural Life."

21. Plunkett, "Conservation and Rural Life," 262. My emphasis.

22. Pinchot, *The Fight for Conservation*, 22–23.

23. Plunkett, *Ireland in the New Century*, 186. Also Plunkett, "Conservation and Rural Life," 261.

24. Despite arguable parallels between the Irish Land League and the critique by the People's Party of the 1890s of land tenancy and the producer ethic, Plunkett ascribed the federal Department of Agriculture's appropriation for agricultural colleges, some railway legislation, and other boons to such political organization but noted that the American farmers fell "under the enervating influence of a little temporary prosperity." Plunkett, *The Rural Life Problem*, 111.

25. Toward this end, Plunkett met with the staff of the Hampton Institute, but I have not been able to determine the consequences of that meeting. Ibid., 94.

26. Cutright, *Theodore Roosevelt*, 229.

27. Bowers, *The Country Life Movement*, 25; Danbom, *The Resisted Revolution*, 43.

28. Bowers, *The Country Life Movement*, 26.

29. Ibid., 29.

30. Plunkett, "The Neglected Farmer," 301.

31. Ibid., 299. This was not race suicide per se, but a related phenomenon that Ross called "folk depletion." Ross, *The Social Trend*, 34–51.

32. Danbom, *The Resisted Revolution*, 44.

33. Ibid., 66.

34. Bowers, *The Country Life Movement*, 70.

35. Ibid., 70–71; Rossiter, "The Decrease in Rural Population," 80.

36. Danbom, *The Resisted Revolution*, 62.

37. Gill and Pinchot, *The Country Church*, 3–5.

38. Bowers, *The Country Life Movement*, 87–88.

39. Gill and Pinchot, *The Country Church*, ix.

40. Ibid., 19.

41. Ibid., 33–36.

42. Ibid., 39.

43. Plunkett, "Better Farming."

44. Knapp quoted in Danbom, *The Resisted Revolution*, 72.

45. T. M. Campbell, "Succinct Report on Negro Extension Work for the Year Ending December 31st, 1923 (Not for Publication)," box 1, file labeled "1923," Thomas Monroe Campbell Collection, Tuskegee Institute Archives, Tuskegee, Ala. Campbell, *The Movable School*.

46. Thomas M. Campbell, "The Story of a Boy," ms., box 1, untitled file, Thomas Monroe Campbell Collection, Tuskegee Institute Archives, Tuskegee, Ala.

47. For more on racial uplift and African American attitudes toward race suicide see Gaines, *Uplifting the Race*; Mitchell, *Righteous Propagation*.

48. Danbom, *The Resisted Revolution*, 53.

49. Plunkett, "Better Farming," 499.

50. *Cornell Nature Study Leaflets*.

51. Bailey, "A Children's Garden," 23.

52. Plunkett, "The Neglected Farmer," 299.

53. Mark Haller also draws connections between conservation and eugenics, as well as country life and eugenics, but does not discuss the connections between conservation and country life or the racialized agrarian ideal that informed both. Haller, *Eugenics*, 191–201.

54. Hays, *Conservation*, 132.

55. Ibid., 138.

56. Ibid., 141.

57. Ibid., 143.

58. Pinchot, *The Fight for Conservation*, 102. Also *Addresses and Proceedings*.

59. Hays, *Conservation*, 177–78.

60. For more on Fisher's interests in health see Hirschbein, "Masculinity."

61. Fisher, *National Vitality*.

62. *Addresses and Proceedings*; Hays, *Conservation*, 176.

63. Merchant, "Women and Conservation."

64. Ibid.

65. *Addresses and Proceedings*, 275–76. Also see Brechin, "Conserving the Race," 238.

66. Hays, *Conservation*, 143.

67. Handwritten note by Leon Whitney, dated March 12, 1973, AES Papers.

68. Isabelle Kendig, "One Massachusetts Family," unpublished ms., n.d., 1, AES Papers.

69. Rafter, *White Trash*.

70. Isabelle Kendig, "One Massachusetts Family," unpublished ms., n.d., 2, AES Papers.

71. Ibid., 4.

72. Ibid., 9.

73. Leon Whitney to Alexander E. Cance, February 16, 1928, AES Papers.

74. Ross, *The Social Trend*, 26.

75. Leon Whitney, "Cellarholes: The Story of the Rise and Fall of a New England Village," unpublished ms., n.d., AES Papers.

76. Leon Whitney to John T. Pratt, November 20, 1928, AES Papers.

77. Leon Whitney, "Cellarholes: The Story of the Rise and Fall of a New England Village," unpublished ms., n.d., AES Papers.

78. Leon Whitney, "Leon Fradley Whitney, 1894–1973," (Autobiographical Extract), 196–97. AES Papers.

79. Clark, *Quabbin Reservoir*, 74.

80. Middlekauff, *The Glorious Cause*, 600–601.

81. Bowden, "The Invention of American Tradition"; Wood and Steinitz, "A World We Have Gained"; Wood, " 'Build, Therefore, Your Own World.' "

82. The Quabbin Reservoir was created in 1936 as a water source for Boston. Four towns in the Swift River valley were flooded in the process.

83. Gallagher, *Breeding Better Vermonters*, 121.

84. Quoted in Dann, "From Degeneration to Regeneration," 25–26.

85. Ibid., 17. For an excellent account of eugenics and the country life movement in Vermont, see Gallagher, *Breeding Better Vermonters*.

86. Hays, *Conservation*, 269.

1. Kansas Bureau of Child Research, "Fitter Families," 1.

2. Ibid., 1–2; Mary T. Watts to Charles Davenport, June 17, 1922, Davenport Papers. Watts notes the date of Davenport's second letter as September 13, 1913.

3. Sherbon, "Popular Education," 36.

4. Kansas Bureau of Child Research, "Fitter Families."

5. Meckel, *Save the Babies*, 102–3.

6. Pernick, "Eugenics and Public Health"; Shah, *Contagious Divides*; Stern, "Making Better Babies."

7. On this sense of modernism see Berman, *All That Is Solid*, 1–36; Cotkin, *Reluctant Modernism*; Ross, "Modernism Reconsidered"; Scott, *Seeing Like a State*.

8. For a discussion of the political organization and maneuverings of the Children's Bureau under Julia Lathrop as part of Progressive women's reform networks and settlement work see Ladd-Taylor, *Raising a Baby*, and *Mother-Work*; Lindenmeyer, "A Right To Childhood"; Muncy, *Creating a Female Dominion*.

9. Klaus, *Every Child a Lion*, 227–40; Ladd-Taylor, *Mother-Work*, 76; Muncy, *Creating a Female Dominion*, 39.

10. The popularity of the child crop story elides the more complicated political origins of the Children's Bureau. See Ladd-Taylor, *Raising a Baby*, and *Mother-Work*; Lindenmeyer, "A Right To Childhood."

11. Ladd-Taylor, *Mother-Work*, 76–81.

12. Meckel, *Save the Babies*, 102–3; Muncy, *Creating a Female Dominion*, 47.

13. *Baby Week Campaigns*, 7.

14. The Sheppard-Towner Act allocated $7 million from the federal government to states for "pioneer" grants-in-aid programs to promote infant and maternal health. It was allowed to expire in 1929 because of intense opposition from the medical profession, according to Zelizer, and opposition from the insurance industry, according to Muncy. Leach, *Land of Desire*, 180–81; Muncy, *Creating a Female Dominion*; Zelizer, *Pricing the Priceless Child*.

15. Paradise, *Maternity Care*; U.S. Children's Bureau, *Infant Mortality Man-chester*, *Infant Mortality Johnstown*, *Infant Mortality Waterbury*, *Infant Mortality Akron*, and *Causal Factors in Infant Mortality*.

16. Grace Meigs, "Memorandum for Heads of Divisions," January 1916, 1, Children's Bureau Papers (4-11-0). At the same time another female physician, Dr. Bradley, was hired to conduct Children's Health Conferences in North Carolina.

17. "Victoria Sanitarium."

18. Horace S. Hollingsworth to Florence Sherbon, March 12, 1916, Florence Sherbon Papers, Personal Papers 97 1916, Kenneth Spencer Research Library, University of Kansas, Lawrence, Kans.

19. Sherbon and her husband divorced.

20. Dorey, *Better Baby Contests*.

21. Comparisons between animal and human care and breeding abound during this time period. For more examples see ibid., 25–26; Pernick, *The Black Stork*.

22. Dorey, *Better Baby Contests*, 25–27.

23. Quoted in ibid., 30.

24. For the use of Better Babies in magazine advertising see ibid., 192–96; DuPuis, *Nature's Perfect Food*.

25. Dorey, *Better Baby Contests*, 36.

26. Florence Sherbon to Julia Lathrop, June 22, 1916, 3, Children's Bureau Papers (4-12-4).

27. "Maud Brown," Florence Sherbon Papers, Kenneth Spencer Research Library, University of Kansas, Lawrence, Kans.

28. Quoted in Meigs, "Rural Obstetrics," 65.

29. Klaus, *Every Child a Lion*, 231–43.

30. Florence Sherbon to Julia Lathrop, June 22, 1916, Children's Bureau Papers (4-12-4); Florence Sherbon to Viola Paradise, July 4, 1916, Children's Bureau Papers (4-11-3-5).

31. Holt, *Linoleum, Better Babies*, 105–8.

32. Lydia DeVilbiss to Julia Lathrop, November 23, 1915, Children's Bureau Papers (4-15-2-1-8).

33. Florence Sherbon to Grace Meigs, January 27, 1916, Children's Bureau Papers (4-11-1-5).

34. Klaus, *Every Child a Lion*, 227–40; Ladd-Taylor, *Mother-Work*.

35. Sherbon to Lathrop, June 22, 1916, 2–3, Children's Bureau Papers (4-12-4).

36. Thomen, "Doctor Sherbon Named." On Kansas public health and Dr. Crumbine see Holt, Linoleum, Better Babies.

37. Kansas University Catalogue 1917, University Archives, University of Kansas, Lawrence, Kans.

38. Her child care course from 1920 was described as covering "practical facts regarding maternity and child care; prenatal and infant mortality, cause and prevention; prenatal care; maternal mortality; development, hygiene, morbidity and mortality of children by age groups; health of the mother as a factor in family living; modern health movements directed toward the improvement of health standards in the home." Board of Administration, The University of Kansas, Lawrence General Information.

39. Kansas Bureau of Child Research, "Fitter Families," 1–2.

40. Paul, Controlling Human Heredity, 10.

41. Kevles, In the Name of Eugenics.

42. Ibid., 54.

43. Paul, Controlling Human Heredity, 120.

44. It was first called the Ad Interim Committee of the United States of America, which became the Eugenics Committee of the USA, then the Eugenics Society of America, and, in 1925, the AES. Selden, Inheriting Shame, 22.

45. Hirschbein, "Masculinity, Work."

46. This is not to say that all eugenicists neglected the role of the environment before the AES. For the role of environmental reform in early eugenics see Cooke, "The Limits of Heredity," and "Duty or Dream?"

47. Letterhead for AES, June 5, 1935, Subject File American Eugenics Society Group 1, series IV, box 31, folder 319, Huntington Papers.

48. Charles Davenport to Ellsworth Huntington, April 3, 1937, Subject File American Eugenics Society Group 1, series IV, box 28, folder 284, Huntington Papers.

49. Pernick, The Black Stork, 44, and "Eugenics and Public Health."

50. "Annual Report," (1927) American Eugenics Association, AES Papers. Also see Rosen, Preaching Eugenics.

51. Mary Watts to Charles Davenport, June 17, 1922, Davenport Papers.

52. Charles Davenport to Mary Watts, June 26, 1922, Davenport Papers.

53. Charles Davenport to Mary Watts, August 19, 1922, Davenport Papers.

One of the prerequisites for eugenic action in Nazi Germany was the creation of a national health registry.

54. Mary Watts to Charles Davenport, December 31, 1924. Also Florence Sherbon to Charles Davenport, November 13, 1924, Davenport Papers.

55. Florence Sherbon to Irving Fisher (copied to Charles Davenport), December 9, 1924, Davenport Papers.

56. Florence Sherbon to Irving Fisher (copied to Charles Davenport), December 9, 1924, Davenport Papers.

57. Mary Watts to Charles Davenport, April 18, 1925, Davenport Papers.

58. Charles Davenport to Mary Watts, June 6, 1925, Davenport Papers.

59. Florence Sherbon to E. H. Lindley, April 2, 1929, Appendix II, Lindley Papers.

60. It is important to note that these categories were the same ones used for most of the publications by the Children's Bureau in their work on maternal, infant, and children's health concerns. While the demonstration clearly equates ethnic and racial traits with literacy, many eugenicists during this period embraced the idea of racial hierarchies with regard to almost every trait. Indeed these supposedly biologically based racial scales were used to justify immigration restriction culminating in the 1924 system of racially and ethnically based immigration quotas. See Kevles, *In the Name of Eugenics*; Paul, *Controlling Human Heredity*.

61. Quoted in Rydell, *World of Fairs*, 40–50.

62. A sample fitter family contest form is reprinted in West, "Practical Application of Eugenic Principles."

63. Sherbon attributed her innovative and collaborative use of experts with inspiring the Yale Institute for Human Relations. While I've not found direct evidence of this influence in print, it does speak to her vision of the contests' impact. For more on the history of the fitter families medal see Cogdell, *Eugenic Design*, 56–58.

64. Florence Sherbon to Charles Davenport, January 28, 1925, Davenport Papers.

65. Cal, "The Influence of Animal Breeding," 720; Derry, *Bred for Perfection*.

66. "Eugenics at State Fairs."

67. Brown, *Teaching Health in Fargo*, and "Fargo and the Health Habits."

68. Shawn Smith locates these ideas on bodily and eugenic norms in

practices of measurement and photography advocated by eugenics' founder Francis Galton; see Smith, *American Archives.* Charles Colbert's analysis of the impact of phrenology on popular perceptions of the body, as exemplified in Hiram Power's sculpture *The Greek Slave,* draws a clear connection between science and cultural norms. Christina Cogdell extends this argument connecting eugenicists' idealization of efficiency and form with the emergence of streamlined design in the 1930s. See Cogdell, *Eugenic Design.*

69. Wiggam, "New Styles in Ancestors," 144.

70. "Eugenics at State Fairs"; "The 'Fitter Family Contest.'" Rydell reports that eugenics workers selected the families eligible to participate and that at least one hundred had been selected within the first four years of the Kansas contests (1920–24). Rydell, *World of Fairs,* 51.

71. Quoted in "Report of the President of the American Eugenics Society," 27–29.

72. Lewis, *Arrowsmith.*

73. West, "Practical Application of Eugenic Principles," 94.

74. Sherbon, "A Unique Experience."

75. West, "Practical Application of Eugenic Principles," 106.

76. Ibid., 110–11.

77. Florence Sherbon to E. H. Lindley, April 2, 1929, Appendix II, Lindley Papers.

78. "Report of the President of the American Eugenics Society," 14. This perspective on rural life was put into action in Vermont. See Gallagher, *Breeding Better Vermonters.*

79. Whitney, "Fitter Families Again."

80. Mary Watts to Charles Davenport, July 6, 1922, Davenport Papers.

81. Sherbon, "Popular Education."

82. "Large Families are Few."

83. Anderson, *The Department of Home Economics,* 23. Similar shifts were occurring nationwide. See Grant, "Modernizing Mothers."

84. Sherbon's program of research is laid out in reports for the Bureau of Child Research at the University of Kansas in "Child Research," Lindley Papers.

85. Dr. Florence Sherbon to Prof. Irving Fisher, November 9, 1924. Copy sent to Charles Davenport, Davenport Papers.

86. Child Research 1928/1929, Lindley, Florence Sherbon Papers, Kenneth Spencer Research Library, University of Kansas, Lawrence, Kans.

87. Collier, "Some Findings."

88. Sherbon, *Health of the Family*.

89. Sherbon, *The Child*.

90. Ibid., frontispiece.

91. Ibid., 11.

92. Ibid., 17.

93. Ibid., 88–89.

94. Sherbon, *Family in Health and Illness*, 22–23.

95. Ibid., 163–64.

96. This type of approach was initially labeled euthenics by nutritional chemist Ellen Swallow Richards. Cooke, "The Limits of Heredity," 270.

97. On the transition in the AES see, Mazumdar, " 'Reform' Eugenics"; Selden, *Inheriting Shame*; and Kline, *Building a Better Race*.

98. Kevles, *In the Name of Eugenics*. For disputes over this shift see Mazumdar, " 'Reform' Eugenics"; Selden, *Inheriting Shame*.

99. In *Building a Better Race*, Kline explains positive eugenics as a response to the Great Depression (p. 96). The Fitter Family and other popular eugenics campaigns clearly demonstrate that the shift to positive eugenics occurred earlier than Kline suggests.

100. "Report of the President of the American Eugenics Society," June 26, 1926, 14. AES Papers.

101. Martin, *Ellsworth Huntington*.

102. Ellsworth Huntington, "Tentative Suggestions as to Future Policies of the American Eugenics Society," December 1934, Classified Subject File, group 1, series IV, box 29, folder no. 293, Huntington Papers.

103. Frederick Osborn, "Notes for Eugenic Program," November 7, 1934, Classified Subject File, group 1, series IV, box 73, folder no. 2815, Huntington Papers.

104. Ibid. See also Cogdell, *Eugenic Design*, 168–69.

105. Huntington also claimed that "cooperative measures have proved wonderfully successful among people like the farmers of Denmark and the fruit growers of California. They are growing in favor along many lines. In the present instance the best method may not be to leave the care of the children

entirely to the volunteer efforts of the mothers." Ellsworth Huntington, "Tentative Suggestions as to Future Policies of the American Eugenics Society," December 1934, Classified Subject File, group 1, series IV, box 29, folder no. 293, Huntington Papers.

106. Ibid.

107. Conkin, *Tomorrow a New World.*

108. Ellsworth Huntington, "Tentative Suggestions as to Future Policies of the American Eugenics Society," December 1934, Classified Subject File, group 1, series IV, box 29, folder no. 293, Huntington Papers.

109. Miles Colean to Irving Fisher, March 29, 1935, Classified Subject File, group 1, series IV, box 34, folder no. 358, Huntington Papers.

110. Ellsworth Huntington, "A Family Community," Classified Subject File, group 1, series IV, box 27, folder no. 277, Huntington Papers. Huntington, *Tomorrow's Children.* Also see Cogdell, *Eugenic Design,* 168–69.

111. Conference on Eugenics Aspects of Housing, April 1, 1938, Classified Subject File, group 1, S *Recent Trends in American Housing* series IV, box 27, folder no. 280, Huntington Papers.

112. Ibid.

113. Wood, *Recent Trends in American Housing,* 296.

114. Hayden, *Building Suburbia,* 125–26.

115. Jackson, *Crabgrass Frontier.*

116. Conference on Eugenics Aspects of Housing, April 1, 1938, Classified Subject File, group 1, S *Recent Trends in American Housing* series IV, box 27, folder no. 280, Huntington Papers.

117. Wood, " 'One Third of a Nation.' "

118. Haller, *Eugenics,* 175.

119. Pernick, "Taking Better Baby Contests Seriously," 707.

CHAPTER SEVEN

1. "American Mirror."

2. Rydell, *World of Fairs.*

3. Ibid.; Susman, *Culture as History.*

4. "Builders Approve Fair Home Plan," *New York Times,* October 3, 1937, 193; Post, "East Meets West."

5. Post, "East Meets West."

6. *The City*.

7. The New York World's Fair also ran a typical American boy contest. Susman, *Culture as History*.

8. Klaus, *Every Child a Lion*; Kline, *Building a Better Race*.

9. Coontz, *The Way We Never Were*; May, *Barren in the Promised Land*; Weiss, *To Have and to Hold*.

10. Peck and Senderowitz, *Pronatalism*.

BIBLIOGRAPHY

ARCHIVAL SOURCES

Cambridge, Mass.

    Massachusetts Institute of Technology Archives

        Class Records

    Widener Library, Harvard University

        Theodore Roosevelt Collection

College Park, Md.

    National Archives II

        U.S. Children's Bureau Papers

Denver, Colo.

    National Archives

        Reclamation Bureau Papers

Lawrence, Kans.

    University Archives, Kenneth Spencer Research Library, University of
        Kansas

        E. H. Lindley Papers

        Florence Sherbon Papers

Madison, Wis.

    State Historical Society of Wisconsin

        Edward A. Ross Papers (microfilm)

New Haven, Conn.

    Mudd Library, Yale University

        Clippings on Marriage, Family, Intercourse, and Prostitution

    Yale University Library

        Ellsworth Huntington Papers

New York, N.Y.

    Labor Archives, New York University

Philadelphia, Pa.

    American Philosophical Society Archives

        American Eugenics Society Papers

        Charles Davenport Papers

Phoenix, Ariz.

    Arizona State Archives

        George H. Maxwell Papers

Topeka, Kans.

    Kansas State Historical Society

        Mary Elizabeth Lease Clippings File

Tuskegee, Ala.

    Tuskegee Institute Archives

        Thomas Monroe Campbell Collection

NEWSPAPERS AND PERIODICALS

Canton (Ohio) Repository	*New York World*
Charleston News	*Richmond Dispatch*
Christian Science Monitor	*Sacramento Bee*
Farmer's Wife	*San Francisco Call*
Kansas City Star	*Seattle Times*
Kansas Farmer	*Topeka Advocate*
Maxwell's Talisman	*Topeka Capital*
National Irrigation	*Union Signal*
New York Daily People	*Washington (D.C.) National*
New York Telegram	*Wellington (Kans.) Monitor*
New York Times	*Wichita Independent*

PUBLISHED SOURCES AND DISSERTATIONS

Abramovitz, Mimi. *Regulating the Lives of Women*. Boston: South End Press, 1988.

Addams, Jane. *Twenty Years at Hull House*. New York: Signet Classics, 1910.

Addresses and Proceedings of the First National Conservation Congress. Washington, D.C.: Executive Committee of the National Conservation Congress, 1909.

"Advice to Raise 'Less Corn and More Hell' Still Good, Says Mary Ellen Lease at 78." *Kansas City Star*, March 29, 1931.

"American Mirror: Most Typical American." *Christian Science Monitor*, October 18, 1940, 6.

Anderson, Henry S. "The Little Landers' Colonies: A Unique Agricultural Experiment in California." *Agricultural History* 5 (1931): 145–49.

Anderson, Viola. *The Department of Home Economics: The First 50 Years, 1910–1960.* Lawrence: University Press of Kansas, 1963.

Annals of Kansas 1 (November 1894): 45

Anthony, Susan B., and Ida Husted Harper. *The History of Woman Suffrage.* Vol. 4. New York: Hollenbeck Press, 1902.

Argesinger, Peter H. *Populism and Politics: William Alfred Peffer and the People's Party.* Lexington: University Press of Kentucky, 1974.

———. *The Limits of Agrarian Radicalism: Western Populism and American Politics.* Lawrence: University Press of Kansas, 1995.

Armitage, Susan. "Through Women's Eyes: A New View of the West." In *The Women's West,* edited by Susan Armitage and Elizabeth Jameson, 9–18. Norman: University of Oklahoma Press, 1987.

Autobee, Robert. "Every Child a Garden: George H. Maxwell and the American Homecroft Society." *Prologue* 28 (1996): 195–206.

Baby Week Campaigns: Suggestions for Communities of Various Sizes. Misc. Series, no. 5, Children's Bureau publ. no. 15. Washington, D.C.: Government Printing Office, 1915.

Bailey, Liberty Hyde. "A Children's Garden." In *Cornell Nature Study Leaflets,* 23–25. Albany, N.Y.: J. B. Lyon, 1904.

Banker, Howard. "Coeducation and Eugenics." *Journal of Heredity* 8 (1917): 208–14.

Banta, Martha. *Taylored Lives: Narrative Productions in the Ages of Taylor, Veblen, and Ford.* Chicago: University of Chicago Press, 1993.

Bederman, Gail. *Manliness and Civilization: A Cultural History of Gender and Race in the United States, 1880–1917.* Chicago: University of Chicago Press, 1995.

Bellamy, Edward. *Looking Backward, 2000–1887.* Boston: Houghton Mifflin, 1915.

Berg, Allison. *Mothering the Race: Women's Narratives on Reproduction, 1890–1930.* Urbana: University of Illinois Press, 2001.

Berman, Marshall. *All That Is Solid Melts into Air: The Experience of Modernity.* New York: Penguin Books, 1982.

Blake, Judith. "Coercive Pronatalism and American Population Policy." In *Pronatalism: The Myth of Mom and Apple Pie,* edited by Ellen Peck and Judith Senderowitz, 29–67. New York: Thomas Y. Crowell, 1974.

Blumberg, Dorothy Rose. "Mary Elizabeth Lease, Populist Orator: A Profile." *Kansas History* 1, no. 1 (1978): 3–15.

Board of Administration. *The University of Kansas, Lawrence General Information, Catalogues.* Topeka: Kansas State Printing Plant, 1920

Bordin, Ruth. *Women and Temperance: The Quest for Power and Liberty, 1873–1900.* Philadelphia: Temple University Press, 1981.

Boris, Eileen. *Art and Labor: Ruskin, Morris, and the Craftsman Ideal in America.* Philadelphia: Temple University Press, 1986.

Boris, Eileen, and Peter Bardaglio. "The Transformation of Patriarchy: The Historic Role of the State." In *Families, Politics, and Public Policy,* edited by Irene Diamond, 70–93. New York: Longman, 1993.

Bowden, M. J. "The Invention of American Tradition." *Journal of Historical Geography* 18 (1992): 3–26.

Bowers, William J. *The Country Life Movement in America, 1900–1920.* Port Washington, N.Y.: Kennikat Press, 1974.

Boyd, Julian P., ed. *The Papers of Thomas Jefferson, Vol. 7: March 1784 to February 1785.* Princeton: Princeton University Press, 1953.

Bradley, Karen. "Cultivating the Terrain: Public Image and Politics of California Farming from the Depression to the Postwar Years." Ph.D. diss., University of California, 1995.

Brady, Marilyn Dell. "Populism and Feminism in a Newspaper by and for Women of the Kansas Alliance." *Kansas History* 7 (1984–5): 280–90.

Brady, Nancy. *The Book of the Roycrofters.* Aurora, N.Y.: House of Hubbard, 1919.

Brechin, Gray. "Conserving the Race: Natural Aristocracies, Eugenics, and the U.S. Conservation Movement." *Antipode* 28 (1996): 229–45.

Brigham, Sarah M. "Waverland: A Tale of Our Coming Landlords." *Labette Statesman,* 1890.

Brown, Maud Anna. "Fargo and the Health Habits: A Chapter from a Community Adventure." *Hygeia,* June 1928, 267–69.

———. *Teaching Health in Fargo.* New York: Commonwealth Fund Division of Publications, 1929.

Brownell, Blaine A. "The Agrarian and Urban Ideals: Environmental Images in Modern America." *Journal of Popular Culture* 5 (1971): 576–87.

Bryan, William Jennings. "Cross of Gold." In *Three Centuries of American Rhetorical Discourse,* edited by Ronald F. Reid, 601–6. Prospect Heights, Ill.: Waveland Press, 1988.

Burns, Edward McNall. *David Starr Jordan: Prophet of Freedom*. Palo Alto, Calif.: Stanford University Press, 1953.

Burns, Sarah. *Pastoral Inventions: Rural Life in Nineteenth-Century American Art and Culture*. Philadelphia: Temple University Press, 1989.

Bush, Corlann Gee. "The Way We Weren't: Images of Women and Men in Cowboy Art." In *The Women's West*, edited by Susan Armitage and Elizabeth Jameson, 19–34. Norman: University of Oklahoma Press, 1987.

Cahn, Susan K. *Coming on Strong: Gender and Sexuality in Twentieth-Century Women's Sport*. New York: Free Press, 1994.

Cal, Enrique Ucelay da. "The Influence of Animal Breeding on Political Racism." *History of European Ideas* 15 (1992): 717–25.

Calhoun, Arthur. *A Social History of the American Family from Colonial Times to the Present*. 3 vols. Cleveland: Arthur H. Clark, 1917–19.

Camiscioli, T. C. "Producing Citizens, Reproducing the 'French Race': Immigration, Demography, and Pronatalism in Early Twentieth-Century France." *Gender and History* 13 (2001): 593–621.

Campbell, Thomas M. *The Movable School Goes to the Negro Farmer*. Tuskegee, Ala.: Tuskegee Institute Press, 1936.

Carstensen, Vernon, ed. *The Public Lands: Studies in the History of the Public Domain*. Madison: University of Wisconsin Press, 1963.

Christensen, Carol A. *The American Garden City and New Towns Movement*. 1978. Reprint, Ann Arbor, Mich.: UMI Research Press, 1986.

The City. Film directed by Ralph Steiner and Willard von Dyke, 1939.

Clanton, O. Gene. "Intolerant Populist?: The Disaffection of Mary Elizabeth Lease." *Kansas Historical Quarterly* 34 (1968): 189–200.

———. *Kansas Populism: Ideas and Men*. Lawrence: University of Kansas Press, 1969.

Clark, Clifford Edward, Jr. *The American Family Home, 1800–1960*. Chapel Hill: University of North Carolina Press, 1986.

Clark, Walter E. *Quabbin Reservoir*. New York: Hobson Book Press, 1946.

Clarke, Edward H. *Sex in Education: A Fair Chance for the Girls*. Boston: James R. Osgood, 1873.

Clinton, Katherine. "What Did You Say, Mrs. Lease?" *Kansas Quarterly* 2 (1969): 52–59.

"Coeducation and Marriage." *Journal of Heredity* 8 (1917): 43–45.

Cogdell, Christina. *Eugenic Design: Streamlining America in the 1930s*. Philadelphia: University of Pennsylvania Press, 2004.

Collier, Edith Clark. "Some Findings in the 'Fitter Families' Examinations Held at the Kansas Free Fair." Master's thesis, Kansas University, 1928.

Commander, Lydia. "The Home Without a Child." *Delineator* 71 (1907): 720–23, 730.

Conkin, Paul. *Tomorrow a New World: The New Deal Community Program*. Ithaca: Cornell University Press, 1959.

Cooke, Kathy J. "The Limits of Heredity: Nature and Nurture in American Eugenics Before 1915." *Journal of the History of Biology* 31 (1998): 263–78.

——. "Duty or Dream? Edwin G. Conklin's Critique of Eugenics and Support for American Individualism." *Journal of the History of Biology* 35 (2002): 365–84.

Coontz, Stephanie. *The Way We Never Were: American Families and the Nostalgia Trap*. New York: Basic Books, 1992.

Cornell Nature Study Leaflets. Albany, N.Y.: J. B. Lyon, 1904.

Cotkin, George. *Reluctant Modernism: American Thought and Culture, 1880–1900*. New York: Twayne Publishers, 1992.

Cott, Nancy F. *The Bonds of Womanhood: "Woman's Sphere" in New England, 1780–1830*. New Haven: Yale University Press, 1977.

——. *The Grounding of Modern Feminism*. New Haven: Yale University Press, 1987.

Cronon, William. *Nature's Metropolis: Chicago and the Great West*. New York: W. W. Norton, 1991.

Crunden, Robert. *Ministers of Reform: The Progressives' Achievement in American Civilization, 1889–1920*. Champaign: University of Illinois Press, 1985.

Curry, Lynne. *Modern Mothers in the Heartland: Gender, Health and Progress in Illinois, 1900–1930*. Columbus: Ohio State University Press, 1999.

Cutright, Paul. *Theodore Roosevelt: The Making of a Conservationist*. Chicago: University of Illinois Press, 1985.

Danbom, David. *The Resisted Revolution: Urban America and the Industrialization of Agriculture, 1900–1930*. Ames: Iowa State University Press, 1979.

Dann, Kevin. "From Degeneration to Regeneration: The Eugenics Survey of Vermont, 1925–1936." *Vermont History* 59 (1991): 5–29.

Davies, Margery. *Woman's Place Is at the Typewriter: Office Work and Office Workers, 1870–1930*. Philadelphia: Temple University Press, 1982.

Davison, Roland. *The Leadership of the Reclamation Movement, 1875–1902*. New York: Arno Press, 1979.

Deegan, Mary Jo. *Jane Addams and the Men of the Chicago School, 1892–1918*. New Brunswick, N.J.: Transaction Books, 1988.

Delegard, Kirsten. "Women's Movements, 1880s–1920s." In *A Companion to American Women's History*, edited by Nancy A. Hewitt, 328–47. New Brunswick: Rutgers University Press, 2002.

Derry, Margaret. *Bred for Perfection: Shorthorn Cattle, Collies, and Arabian Horses Since 1800*. Baltimore: Johns Hopkins University Press, 2003.

Dorey, Annette K. Vance. *Better Baby Contests: The Scientific Quest for Perfect Childhood Health in the Early Twentieth Century*. Jefferson, N.C.: McFarland, 1999.

Duffy, John. *The Sanitarians: A History of American Public Health*. Urbana: University of Illinois Press, 1990.

DuPuis, Melanie. *Nature's Perfect Food: How Milk Became America's Drink*. New York: New York University Press, 2002.

Durkheim, Emile. *Suicide: A Study in Sociology*. Translated by John A. Spaulding and George Simpson. London, U.K. · Routledge and K. Paul, 1952.

Dyer, Thomas. *Theodore Roosevelt and the Idea of Race*. Baton Rouge: Louisiana State University Press, 1980.

Edwards, Rebecca. *Angels in the Machinery*. New York: Oxford University Press, 1997.

Esper, Michael. "Letter to the Editor." *Delineator*, January 1907, 6.

Esping-Andersen, Gøsta. *The Three Worlds of Welfare Capitalism*. Cambridge, U.K.: Polity Press, 1990.

Ethington, Philip. *The Public City: The Political Construction of Urban Life in San Francisco, 1850–1900*. Cambridge, U.K.: Cambridge University Press, 1994.

"Eugenics at State Fairs." *Eugenical News* 10 (1925): 130.

Fisher, Irving. *National Vitality, Its Wastes, and Conservation*. 1910. Reprint, New York: Arno Press, 1976.

"The 'Fitter Family Contest.'" *Eugenical News* 8 (1923): 88.

Forman-Brunell, Miriam. *Made to Play House: Dolls and the Commercialization of American Girlhood, 1830–1930*. Baltimore: Johns Hopkins University Press, 1998.

Foster, Ellen. "The Conservation of Child Life." In *Addresses and Proceedings of the First National Conservation Congress*, 90–96. Washington, D.C.: Executive Committee of the National Conservation Congress, 1909.

Gaines, Kevin. *Uplifting the Race: Black Leadership, Politics and Culture in the Twentieth Century*. Chapel Hill: University of North Carolina Press, 1996.

Gallagher, Nancy. *Breeding Better Vermonters: The Eugenics Project in the Green Mountain State.* Hanover: University Press of New England, 1999.

Gardner, Martha M. "Working on White Womanhood: White Working Women in the San Francisco Anti-Chinese Movement, 1877–1890." *Journal of Social History* 33 (1999): 73–95.

Gill, Charles, and Gifford Pinchot. *The Country Church.* New York: MacMillan, 1913.

Gilman, Charlotte Perkins. *Herland.* 1909–16. Reprint, New York: Pantheon Books, 1979.

——. "What Diantha Did." *The Forerunner* 1 (1909–11): 14.

——. *What Diantha Did.* New York: Charlton, 1910.

——. "The Devout Farmer." *The Forerunner* 3 (1919): 20–21.

Goldberg, Michael. *An Army of Women: Gender and Politics in Gilded Age Kansas.* Baltimore: Johns Hopkins University Press, 1997.

Goodsell, Willystine. *The Education of Women: Its Social Background and Its Problems.* New York: Macmillan, 1923.

Goodwyn, Lawrence. *The Populist Moment.* New York: Oxford University Press, 1978.

Gordon, Linda. *Woman's Body, Woman's Right.* New York: Grossman Publishers, 1976.

——. *Pitied But Not Entitled.* New York: Free Press, 1994.

——. "Putting Children First: Women, Maternalism, and Welfare in the Early Twentieth Century." In *U.S. History as Women's History*, edited by Linda Kerber, Alice Kessler-Harris, and Kathryn Kish Sklar, 63–86. Chapel Hill: University of North Carolina Press, 1995.

Gordon, Linda, and Theda Skocpol. "Gender, State, and Society: A Debate." *Contention* 2 (1993): 139–89.

Gossett, Thomas. *Race: The History of an Idea.* New York: Oxford University Press, 1997.

Grant, Julia. "Modernizing Mothers: Home Economics and the Parent Education Movement, 1920–1945." In *Rethinking Home Economics*, edited by Sarah Stage and Virginia Vincenti, 55–76. Ithaca: Cornell University Press, 1997.

Gundlach, James, and Steven Stack. "The Impact of Hyper Media Coverage on Suicide: New York City, 1910–1920." *Social Science Quarterly* 71 (1990): 619–27.

Hahn, Stephen. *The Roots of Southern Populism*. New York: Oxford University Press, 1983.

Haller, Mark. *Eugenics: Hereditarian Attitudes in American Thought*. New Brunswick, N.J.: Rutgers University Press, 1963.

Hamilton, A. E. "Putting Over Eugenics: Making It a Living Force Depends on Sound Application of Psychology and Sociology—Camp Fire Girls an Organization Which Will Create Eugenic Ideals in Women in an Indirect but Effective Way." *Journal of Heredity* 6 (1915): 281–88.

Hamilton, Charles F. *As Bees in Honey Drown: Elbert Hubbard and the Roycrofters*. South Brunswick, N.J.: A. S. Barnes, 1973.

Handlin, David P. *The American Home: Architecture and Society, 1815–1915*. Boston: Little, Brown, 1979.

Hayden, Dolores. *Building Suburbia: Green Fields and Urban Growth, 1820–2000*. New York: Pantheon Books, 2003.

Hays, Samuel. *Conservation and the Gospel of Efficiency: The Progressive Conservation Movement, 1890–1920*. Cambridge: Harvard University Press, 1959.

Heitlinger, Alena. *Women's Equality, Demography, and Public Policies: A Comparative Perspective*. New York: St. Martin's Press, 1993.

Henry, Robert S. "The Railroad Land Grant Legend in American History Texts." *Mississippi Valley Historical Review* 32 (1945): 171–94.

Heston, J. W. "The American Farmer's Future: Irrigation Will Be an Important Factor." *National Homemaker* 7, no. 2 (1902): 1.

Hibbard, Benjamin Horace. *History of the Public Land Policies*. New York: MacMillan, 1924.

Hicks, John D. *Populist Revolt*. Minneapolis: University of Minnesota Press, 1931.

Higham, John. *Strangers in the Land: Patterns in American Nativism, 1860–1925*. New York: Atheneum, 1974.

Hirschbein, Laura Davidow. "Masculinity, Work, and the Fountain of Youth: Irving Fisher and the Life Extension Institute, 1914–31." *Canadian Bulletin of Medical History / Bulletin canadien d'histoire de la médecine* 16 (1999): 89–124.

Hodgson, Dennis. "The Ideological Origins of the Population Association of America." *Population and Development Review* 17 (1991): 1–34.

Hofstadter, Richard. *The Age of Reform*. New York: Vintage Books, 1955.

Hofstadter, Richard, and Richard P. Metzger. *The Development of Academic Freedom in the United States*. New York: Columbia University Press, 1955.

Hollinger, David. "The Knower and the Artificer." *American Quarterly* 39 (1987): 37–55.

Hollingworth, Leta. "Variability as Related to Sex Differences in Achievement: A Critique." *American Journal of Sociology* 19 (1913–14): 510–30.

———. "Social Devices for Impelling Women to Bear and Rear Children." *American Journal of Sociology* 22 (1916): 19–29.

Holt, Marilyn. *Linoleum, Better Babies, and the Modern Farm Woman.* Albuquerque: University of New Mexico Press, 1995.

Horowitz, Helen Lefkowitz. *Alma Mater: Design and Experience in the Women's Colleges from Their Nineteenth-Century Beginnings to the 1930s.* New York: Alfred A. Knopf, 1984.

Howard, Ronald. *A Social History of American Family Sociology, 1865–1940.* Westport, Conn.: Greenwood Press, 1981.

Hoy, Suellen. *Chasing Dirt: The American Pursuit of Cleanliness.* New York: Oxford University Press, 1995.

Hubbard, Elbert. "Agriculture Montana's Great Resource." *Homemaker* (June 1903): 108.

Hudanick, Andrew. "George Hebard Maxwell: Reclamation's Militant Evangelist." *Journal of the West* 14 (1975): 108–19.

Huntington, Ellsworth. *Tomorrow's Children: The Goal of Eugenics.* New York: John Wiley, 1935.

"In Ernest Now." *Topeka Capital*, January 22, 1901.

Inness, Sherrie. " 'It Is Pluck But Is It Sense?': Athletic Student Culture in Progressive Era Girls' College Fiction." *Journal of Popular Culture* 27, no. 1 (1993): 99–123.

Iyenaga, T., and Kenoske Sato. *Japan and the California Problem.* New York: G. P. Putnam, 1921.

Jackson, Kenneth. *Crabgrass Frontier.* New York: Oxford University Press, 1985.

Jeffery, Julie Roy. "Women in the Southern Farmer's Alliance: A Reconsideration of the Role and Status of Women in the Late Nineteenth Century South." *Feminist Studies* 3 (1975): 72–91.

Jellison, Katherine. *Entitled to Power: Farm Women and Technology, 1913–1963.* Chapel Hill: University of North Carolina Press, 1993.

Kammen, Michael. *Mystic Chords of Memory: The Transformation of Tradition in American Culture.* New York: Alfred A. Knopf, 1991.

Kansas Bureau of Child Research. "Fitter Families for Future Firesides: A
Report of the Eugenics Department of the Kansas Free Fair, 1920–1924."
In *American Eugenics Society Papers, American Philosophical Society Archives*, 1–
39. Philadelphia, 1924.

Kaplan, Amy. "Manifest Domesticity." *American Literature* 70 (1998): 583–606.

Kazin, Michael. *The Populist Persuasion*. New York: Basic Books, 1995.

Kevles, Daniel. *In the Name of Eugenics: Genetics and the Uses of Human Heredity*.
New York: Alfred A. Knopf, 1985.

King, Leslie. " 'France Needs Children': Pronatalism, Nationalism and
Women's Equity." *Sociological Quarterly* 39 (1998): 33–52.

———. "From Pronatalism to Social Welfare? Extending Family Allowances to
Minority Populations in France and Israel." *European Journal of Population* 17
(2001): 305–22.

———. "Demographic Trends, Pronatalism, and Nationalist Ideologies in the
Late Twentieth Century." *Ethnic and Racial Studies* 25 (2002): 367–89.

Klaus, Alisa. *Every Child a Lion: The Origins of Maternal and Infant Health Policy in
the United States and France, 1890–1920*. Ithaca: Cornell University Press,
1993.

Kline, Wendy. *Building a Better Race*. Berkeley: University of California Press,
2001.

Kolodny, Annette. *The Lay of the Land: Metaphor as Experience and History in
American Life and Letters*. Chapel Hill: University of North Carolina Press,
1975.

Koonz, Claudia. *Mothers in the Fatherland: Women, the Family and Nazi Politics*.
New York: St. Martin's Press, 1988.

Koven, Seth, and Sonya Michel, eds. *Mothers of a New World*. New Brunswick,
N.J.: Rutgers University Press, 1993.

Kuhl, Stefan. *The Nazi Connection: Eugenics, American Racism, and German National
Socialism*. New York: Oxford University Press, 1994.

Ladd-Taylor, Molly. *Raising a Baby the Government Way: Mothers' Letters to the
Children's Bureau, 1915–1932*. New Brunswick, N.J.: Rutgers University
Press, 1986.

———. *Mother-Work: Women, Child Welfare, and the State, 1890–1930*. Urbana:
University of Illinois Press, 1994.

———. "Eugenics, Sterilization and Modern Marriage in the USA: The Strange
Career of Paul Popenoe." *Gender and History* 13 (2001): 298–327.

LaFeber, Walter. *The New Empire: An Interpretation of American Expansion, 1863–1898*. Ithaca: Cornell University Press, 1963.

Lane, Ann J. *To Herland and Beyond: The Life and Work of Charlotte Perkins Gilman*. New York: Pantheon Books, 1990.

"Large Families are Few." *New York Times*, October 2, 1927, 6.

Lawson, Laura J. *City Bountiful: A Century of Community Gardening in America*. Berkeley: University of California Press, 2005.

Leach, William. *Land of Desire: Merchants, Power, and the Rise of a New American Culture*. New York: Pantheon Books, 1993.

Lears, T. J. Jackson. *No Place of Grace: Antimodernism and the Transformation of American Culture, 1880–1920*. Chicago: University of Chicago Press, 1981.

Lease, Mary Elizabeth. "Editorial Department." *Wichita Independent*, November 17, 1888, 1.

———. "Do Kansas Women Want the Right to Vote?" *Agora Quarterly: A Kansas Magazine* 2 (January 1893): 196–99.

———. "Address on the Legal Disabilities of Women." *Kansas Sunflower* 1 (February 1894): 2, 7–8.

———. *The Problem of Civilization Solved*. Chicago: Laird and Lee Publishers, 1895.

———. "Address." In *Verbatim Report of the Speeches Delivered at the Banquet of the Eastern Commercial Teacher's Association*, 31–40. New York: E. N. Miner, 1905.

Lee, Lawrence. "The Little Landers of San Ysidro." *Journal of San Diego History* 21 (1975): 36.

Leonard, Thomas C. " 'More Merciful and Not Less Effective': Eugenics and American Economics in the Progressive Era." *History of Political Economy* 35 (2003): 687–711.

Levenstein, Harvey. *Revolution at the Table: The Transformation of the American Diet*. Berkeley: University of California Press, 2003.

Levine, Lawrence. *The Unpredictable Past*. New York: Oxford University Press, 1993.

Lewis, Jane. "Gender and the Development of Welfare Regimes." *Journal of European Social Policy* 2 (1992): 159–73.

———. "Gender and Welfare Regimes: Further Thoughts." *Social Politics* 4 (1997): 160–77.

Lewis, Sinclair. *Arrowsmith*. New York: Harcourt Brace, 1925.

Lilley, William, III, and Lewis Gould. "The Western Irrigation Movement,

1878–1902." In *American West: A Reorientation*, edited by Gene M. Gressley, 57–77. Cheyenne: University of Wyoming Publications, 1966.

Limerick, Patricia. *The Legacy of Conquest: The Unbroken Past of the American West*. New York: W. W. Norton, 1987.

Lindenmeyer, Kriste. *"A Right to Childhood": The U.S. Children's Bureau and Child Welfare, 1912–1936*. Urbana: University of Illinois Press, 1997.

Love, Eric. *Race Over Empire: Racism and U.S. Imperialism, 1865–1900*. Chapel Hill: University of North Carolina Press, 2004.

Lovett, Laura L. "The *Popeye* Principle: Selling Child Health in the First Nutrition Crisis." *Journal of Health Politics, Policy, and the Law* 30 (2005): 803–38.

Malone, Michael P. *James J. Hill: Emprire Builder of the Northwest*. Norman: University of Oklahoma Press, 1996.

Malthus, Thomas. *An Essay on the Principle of Population*. 1798. Reprint, New York: Oxford University Press, 1993

Marsh, B. C. "City Planning in Justice to the Working Population," *Charities* 19 (1908): 15–16

Martin, Albro. *James J. Hill and the Opening of the Northwest*. New York: Oxford University Press, 1976.

Martin, Geoffrey. *Ellsworth Huntington: His Life and Thought*. Hamden, Conn.: Archon Books, 1973.

Maxwell, George H. "A Problem for the Statesman." *Homemaker* (1903): 138–40.

———. "Makes Homes of Desert Wastes." *Homemaker* (1903): 167–69.

———. *The First Book of the Homecrofters*. Watertown, Mass.: National Homecroft Association, 1906.

———. *Our Nation's Defense*. New Orleans: Rural Settlements Association, 1917.

May, Elaine Tyler. *Barren in the Promised Land: Childless Americans and the Pursuit of Happiness*. New York: Basic Books, 1995.

Mazumdar, Pauline. " 'Reform' Eugenics and the Decline of Mendelism." *Trends in Genetics* 18 (2002): 48–52.

McMahon, Sean. *Social Control and Public Intellect: The Legacy of Edward A. Ross*. New Brunswick, N.J.: Transaction Publishers, 1999.

Mead, Elwood. *Helping Men Own Farms*. New York: Macmillan, 1920.

Meckel, Richard A. *Save the Babies: American Public Health Reform and the*

Prevention of Infant Mortality, 1850–1929. Ann Arbor: University of Michigan Press, 1998.

Meigs, Grace. "Rural Obstetrics." *Transactions of the American Association for the Study of Infant Mortality* 7 (1916): 65.

Merchant, Carolyn. "Women and Conservation." In *Major Problems in American Environmental History*, edited by Carolyn Merchant, 373–82. Lexington, Mass.: D. C. Heath, 1993.

Middlekauff, Robert. *The Glorious Cause: The American Revolution, 1763–1789*. New York: Oxford University Press, 1982.

Miller, Char. *Gifford Pinchot and the Making of Modern Environmentalism*. Washington, D.C.: Shearwater Books, 2001.

Mink, Gwendolyn. "The Lady and the Tramp." In *Women, the State, and Welfare*, edited by Linda Gordon, 92–122. Madison: University of Wisconsin Press, 1990.

Mintz, Steven, and Susan Kellogg. *Domestic Revolutions: A Social History of American Family Life*. New York: Free Press, 1988.

Misra, Joya, and Frances Akins. "The Welfare State and Women: Structure, Agency, and Diversity." *Social Politics* 5 (1998): 259–85.

Mitchell, Michele. *Righteous Propagation: African Americans and the Poltics of Racial Destiny after Reconstruction*. Chapel Hill: University of North Carolina Press, 2004.

Montmarquet, James. *The Idea of Agrarianism: From Hunter-Gatherer to Agrarian Radical in Western Culture*. Moscow: University of Idaho Press, 1989.

Morgan, W. Scott. "Over-production—The Law of Supply and Demand." In *The Populist Reader: Selections from the Works of American Populist Leaders*, edited by George Tindall, 11–17. New York: Harper and Row, 1966.

"Mr. Roosevelt's Views on Race Suicide." *Ladies' Home Journal*, February 1906, 21.

"Mrs. Lease Beards the Red Dragon of Wall Street." *Kansas City Star*, October 25, 1914.

"Mrs. Lease, 'Who Pursues Man—Not Woman—All Women Know This.' " *Topeka Capital*, 1906.

"Mrs. Lease's Debts." *Topeka Capital*, May 31, 1901.

Muncy, Robyn. *Creating a Female Dominion in American Reform*. New York: Oxford University Press, 1990.

Neth, Mary. *Preserving the Farm Family: Women, Community, and the Foundations of*

Agribusiness in the Midwest, 1900–1940. Baltimore: Johns Hopkins University Press, 1995.

Newman, Louise. *White Women's Rights: The Racial Origins of Feminism in the United States.* New York: Oxford University Press, 1999.

Nugent, Walter. *The Tolerant Populists: Kansas Populism and Nativism.* Chicago: University of Chicago Press, 1963.

O'Callaghan, Jerry. "The War Veteran and the Public Lands." In *The Public Lands*, edited by Vernon Carstensen, 109–20. Madison: University of Wisconsin Press, 1963.

Odem, Mary. *Delinquent Daughters: Protecting and Policing Adolescent Female Sexuality in the United States, 1885–1920.* Chapel Hill: University of North Carolina Press, 1995.

Orloff, Ann Shola. "Gender and the Social Rights of Citizenship: The Comparative Analysis of Gender Relations and Welfare States." *American Sociological Review* 58 (1993): 303–328.

Orr, Brooke Speer. "Mary Elizabeth Lease: Nineteenth-Century Populist and Twentieth-Century Progressive." Ph.D. diss., George Washington University, 2002.

Ostler, Jeffrey. "The Rhetoric of Conspiracy and the Formation of Kansas Populism." *Agricultural History* 69 (1995): 1–27.

Paradise, Viola. *Maternity Care and the Welfare of Young Children in a Homesteading County in Montana.* Rural Child Welfare Series, no. 3, Children's Bureau publ. no. 34. Washington, D.C.: Government Printing Office, 1917.

Paul, Diane. *Controlling Human Heredity: 1865 to the Present.* Atlantic Highlands, N.J.: Humanities International Press, 1995.

Peck, Ellen, and Judith Senderowitz, eds. *Pronatalism: The Myth of Mom and Apple Pie.* New York: Thomas Y. Crowell, 1974.

Peffer, William. "Editorial." *Kansas Farmer,* November 2, 1888.

Pernick, Martin. *The Black Stork: Eugenics and the Death of "Defective" Babies in American Medicine and Motion Pictures Since 1915.* New York: Oxford University Press, 1996.

——. "Eugenics and Public Health in American History." *American Journal of Public Health* 87 (1997): 1767–72.

——. "Taking Better Baby Contests Seriously." *American Journal of Public Health* 92 (2002): 707–8.

Peters, Scott J., and Paul A. Morgan. "The Country Life Commission:

Reconsidering a Milestone in American Agricultural History." *Agricultural History* 78 (2004): 289–316.

Pinchot, Gifford. *The Fight for Conservation*. 1910. Reprint, Seattle: University of Washington Press, 1967.

——. *Breaking New Ground*. New York: Harcourt Brace, 1947.

Pisani, Donald J. "Reclamation and Social Engineering in the Progressive Era." *Agricultural History* 57 (1983): 46–63.

——, ed. *From the Family Farm to Agribusiness: The Irrigation Crusade in California, 1850–1931*. Berkeley: University of California Press, 1984.

——. *Water and American Government: The Reclamation Bureau, National Water Policy, and the West, 1902–1935*. Berkeley: University of California Press, 2002.

Pivar, David. *Purity Crusade: Sexual Morality and Social Control, 1868–1900*. Westport, Conn.: Greenwod Press, 1973.

Plunkett, Horace. *Ireland in the New Century*. 1904. Port Washington, N.Y.: Kennikat Press, 1970.

——. "Better Farming, Better Business, Better Living: Two Practical Suggestions." *The Outlook* (1910): 497–502.

——. "Conservation and Rural Life: An Irish View of Two Roosevelt Policies." *The Outlook* (1910): 260–64.

——. "The Neglected Farmer." *The Outlook* (1910): 298–302.

——. *The Rural Life Problem of the United States*. New York: Macmillan, 1912.

Popenoe, Paul. *The Conservation of the Family*. Baltimore: Williams and Wilkins, 1926.

Post, Pamela. "East Meets West: The Model Homes Exhibits at the 1939–1940 New York and San Francisco World's Fairs." Ph.D. diss., University of California Santa Barbara, 2000.

Pringle, Henry F. *Theodore Roosevelt:*. 1931. Reprint, New York: Smithmark, 1995.

Proceedings of the First National Conservation Congress. Washington, D.C.: Executive Committee of the National Conservation Congress, 1911.

Rafter, Nicole. *White Trash: The Eugenic Family Studies, 1877–1919*. Boston: Northeastern University Press, 1988.

Reed, James. *From Private Vice to Public Virtue: The Birth Control Movement and American Society Since 1830*. New York: Basic Books, 1978.

Reisner, Marc. *Cadillac Desert: The American West and Its Disappearing Water*. New York: Penguin Books, 1993.

"Report of the President of the American Eugenics Society." New Haven, Conn.: American Eugenics Society, 1926.

Reynolds, Ray. *Cat'spaw Utopia*. El Cajon, Calif.: Bordeaux Printers, 1972.

Richards, Ellen. "The True Cause of Race Suicide." *Good Health* 46 (1911): 258.

Robertson, Stephen. "Age of Consent Law and the Making of Modern Childhood in New York City, 1886–1921." *Journal of Social History* 35, no. 4 (2002): 781–98.

Rodgers, Daniel. *Atlantic Crossings: Social Politics in a Progressive Age*. Cambridge: Belknap Press of Harvard University Press, 1998.

Roosevelt, Theodore. "First Annual Message." In vol. 15 of *The Works of Theodore Roosevelt*, 81–138. 1901. Reprint, New York: Charles Scribner's Sons, 1926.

———. *California Addresses*. San Francisco: California Promotion Committee, 1903.

———. "Sixth Annual Address to Congress." In vol. 15 of *The Works of Theodore Roosevelt*, 342–409. 1906. Reprint, New York: Charles Scribner's Sons, 1926.

———. "Seventh Annual Address." In vol. 15 of *The Works of Theodore Roosevelt*, 410–88. 1907. Reprint, New York: Charles Scribner's Sons, 1926.

———. "The Successful Mother." *Ladies' Home Journal* 25 (1908): 10.

———. "Rural Life." *Outlook* 95 (1910): 919–22.

———. *Realizable Ideals*. San Francisco: Whitaker and Ray-Wiggin, 1912.

———. "The Man Who Works With His Hands." In vol. 16 of *The Works of Theodore Roosevelt*, 133–44. New York: Charles Scribner's Sons, 1926.

———. "The Winning of the West." In vol. 11 of *The Works of Theodore Roosevelt*. New York: Charles Scribner's Sons, 1926.

Rosen, Christine. *Preaching Eugenics: Religious Leaders and the American Eugenics Movement*. New York: Oxford University Press, 2004.

Rosenberg, Rosalind. *Beyond Separate Spheres: The Intellectual Roots of Modern Feminism*. New Haven: Yale University Press, 1982.

Ross, Dorothy. *The Origins of American Social Science*. New York: Cambridge University Press, 1991.

———. "Modernism Reconsidered." In *Modernist Impulses in the Human Sciences, 1870–1930*, 1–25. Baltimore: Johns Hopkins University Press, 1994.

———. "Modernist Social Science in the Land of the New/Old." In *Modernist Impulses in the Human Sciences, 1870–1930*, 171–89. Baltimore: Johns Hopkins University Press, 1994.

Ross, Edward A. "The Causes of Race Superiority." *Annals of the Institute for Political Science* 18 (1901): 67–89.

———. *Social Control: A Survey of the Foundations of Order*. New York: Macmillan, 1901.

———. *Foundations of Sociology*. New York: Macmillan, 1905.

———. *Principles of Sociology*. New York: Century, 1920.

———. *The Social Trend*. New York: Century, 1922.

———. *Seventy Years of It*. New York: Appleton-Century, 1936.

Rossiter, Wiliam. "The Decrease in Rural Population." *Review of Reviews* 24 (1906): 74–80.

Ryan, Mary P. *Civic Wars: Democracy and Public Life in the American City during the Nineteenth Century*. Berkeley: University of California Press, 1997.

Rydell, Robert. *World of Fairs*. Chicago: University of Chicago Press, 1993.

Schmitt, Peter J. *Back to Nature: The Arcadian Myth in Urban America*. New York: Oxford University Press, 1969.

Schwendinger, Herman, and Julia Schwendinger. *The Sociologists of the Chair, 1883–1922*. New York: Basic Books, 1974.

Scott, James C. *Seeing Like a State: How Certain Schemes to Improve the Human Condition Have Failed*. New Haven: Yale University Press, 1998.

Scott, Mel. *American City Planning Since 1890*. Berkeley: University of California Press, 1969.

Seaton, Beverly. "Making the Best of Circumstances: The American Woman's Back Yard Garden." In *Making the American Home: Domestic Material Culture, 1840–1940*, edited by Marilyn Ferris Motz and Pat Browne, 90–104. Bowling Green, Ky.: Bowling Green State University Popular Press, 1988.

Selden, Steven. *Inheriting Shame: The Story of Eugenics and Racism in America*. New York: Teacher's College Press, 1999.

Shah, Nayan. *Contagious Divides: Epidemics and Race in San Francisco's Chinatown*. Berkeley: University of California Press, 2001.

Shapiro, Laura. *Perfection Salad: Women and Cooking at the Turn of the Century*. New York: Modern Library, 2001.

Sherbon, Florence. *Health of the Family: A Program for the Study of Personal, Home,*

and *Community Health Problems*. Washington, D.C.: Federal Board of
   Vocational Education, 1923.

——. "Popular Education: The Agriculturalist." *Eugenics* 2 (1928): 36.

——. "A Unique Experience." In *Proceedings of the Third Race Betterment
   Conference*, 120–21. Battle Creek, Mich.: Race Betterment Foundation, 1928.

——. "Popular Education: Fitter Family Winners." *Eugenics* 2 (1929): 36.

——. *The Child: His Origin, Development, and Care*. 1934. 2nd ed., New York:
   McGraw-Hill, 1941.

——. *The Family in Health and Illness*. New York: McGraw-Hill, 1937.

Shi, David. *The Simple Life: Plain Living and High Thinking in American Culture*.
   New York: Oxford University Press, 1985.

Shinn, Millicent. "Marriage Rate of College Women." *The Century* (1895): 252.

Singal, Donald. "Toward a Definition of American Modernism." *American
   Quarterly* 39 (1987): 7–26.

Skocpol, Theda. *Protecting Mothers and Soldiers*. Cambridge: Harvard University
   Press, 1992.

——. *Protecting Soldiers and Mothers: The Political Origins of Social Policy in the
   United States*. Cambridge: Belknap Press of Harvard University Press, 1992.

Slotkin, Richard. "Nostalgia and Progress: Theodore Roosevelt's Myth of the
   Frontier." *American Quarterly* 33 (1981): 608–37.

——. *Gunfighter Nation: The Myth of the Frontier in Twentieth Century America*. New
   York: Harper Collins, 1992.

Smith, Henry Nash. *Virgin Land: The American West as Symbol and Myth*.
   Cambridge: Harvard University Press, 1950.

Smith, Shawn. *American Archives: Gender, Race, and Class in Visual Culture*.
   Princeton: Princeton University Press, 1999.

Smythe, William. *The Conquest of Arid America*. Seattle: University of
   Washington Press, 1899.

Solomon, Barbara. *Ancestors and Immigrants: A Changing New England Tradition*.
   Cambridge: Harvard University Press, 1956.

Solomon, Barbara Miller. *In the Company of Educated Women: A History of Women
   and Higher Education in America*. New Haven: Yale University Press, 1985.

"Sore on Reporters." *Wichita Eagle*, May 2, 1901.

Sorokin, Pitrim, and Carle Zimmerman. *Principles of Rural-Urban Sociology*. New
   York: Henry Holt, 1929.

Sprague, Robert J. "Education and Race Suicide: Women's Colleges Have Heavy Responsibility for Disappearance of Old Americans Stock in the United States—Reforms That Are Needed." *Journal of Heredity* 6 (1915): 158–62.

"Stanford's Marriage Rate." *Journal of Heredity* 8 (1917): 170–73.

Stern, Alexandra M. "Making Better Babies: Public Health and Race Betterment in Indiana, 1920–1935." *American Journal of Public Health* (2002): 742–52.

Stiller, Richard. *Queen of the Populists: The Story of Mary Elizabeth Lease.* New York: Dell Publishing, 1970.

Stoll, Steven. *The Fruits of Natural Advantage: Making the Industrial Countryside in California.* Berkeley: University of California Press, 1998.

Susman, Warren. *Culture as History: The Transformation of American Society in the Twentieth Century.* New York: Pantheon, 1984.

Takaki, Ronald. *Strangers from a Different Shore: A History of Asian Americans.* New York: Penguin Books, 1989.

——. *Iron Cages: Race and Culture in 19th-Century America.* New York: Oxford University Press, 1990.

Tamony, Peter. "The Teddy Bear: Continuum in a Security Blanket." *Western Folklore* 33 (1974): 231–38.

Taylor, George, ed. *The Turner Thesis: Concerning the Role of the Frontier in American History.* 3rd ed. Lexington, Mass.: D. C. Heath, 1972.

Thomen, Kate. "Doctor Sherbon Named." *Topeka Capital,* June 6, 1919.

Tomes, Nancy. *The Gospel of Germs: Men, Women and the Microbe in American Life.* Cambridge: Harvard University Press, 1998.

Trattner, Walter I. *From Poor Law to Welfare State: A History of Social Welfare in America.* 3rd ed. New York: Free Press, 1984.

Turner, Frederick J. "The Significance of the Frontier in American History." In *Annual Report of the American Historical Association for the Year 1893,* 199–227. Washington, D.C.: American Historical Association, 1894.

Ullman, Sharon. *Sex Seen: The Emergence of Modern Sexuality in the America.* Berkeley: University of California Press, 1997.

U.S. Children's Bureau. *Infant Mortality: Results of a Field Study in Manchester, NH., Based On Births in One Year.* Publ. no. 20. Washington, D.C.: Government Printing Office, 1917.

———. *Infant Mortality: Results of a Field Study in Johnstown, PA., Based on Births in One Year.* Publ. no. 9. Washington, D.C.: Government Printing Office, 1918.

———. *Infant Mortality: Results of a Field Study in Waterbury, CT., Based on Births in One Year.* Publ. no. 29. Washington, D.C.: Government Printing Office, 1918.

———. *Infant Mortality: Results of a Field Study in Akron, Ohio, Based on Births in One Year 1920.* Publ. no. 72. Washington, D.C.: Government Printing Office, 1920.

———. *Causal Factors in Infant Mortality: A Statistical Study Based on Investigations in Eight Cities.* Publ. no. 142. Washington, D.C.: Government Printing Office, 1925.

Veblen, Thorstein. *The Theory of the Leisure Class: An Economic Study of Institutions.* New York: Macmillan, 1902.

Verbrugge, Martha. "Recreating the Body: Women's Physical Education and the Science of Sex Differences in America, 1900–1940." *Bulletin of the History of Medicine* 71, no. 2 (1997): 273–304.

Via, Marie, and Marjorie B. Searle, eds. *Head, Heart and Hand: Elbert Hubbard and the Roycrofters.* Rochester, N.Y.: University of Rochester Press, 1994.

"Victoria Sanitarium." In *Past and Present of Jaspar County, Iowa,* 681–83. Indianapolis: B. F. Bowden, 1912.

Wagner, Mary Jo. "Farms, Families, and Reform: Women in the Farmer's Alliance and Populist Party." Ph.D. diss., University of Oregon, 1986.

Walker, Francis A. "Immigration and Degradation." *The Forum* 11 (1891): 634–43.

Weinberg, Julius, Gisela J. Hinkle, and Roscoe C. Hinkle. "Introduction." In *Social Control: A Survey of the Foundations of Order,* i–ix. Cleveland: Press of Case Western Reserve University, 1969.

———. *Edward Alsworth Ross and the Sociology of Progressivism.* Madison, Wis.: State Historical Society Press, 1972.

Weiner, Lynn. "Maternalism as a Paradigm: Defining the Issues." *Journal of Women's History* 5 (1993): 96–98.

Weiss, Jessica. *To Have and to Hold: Marriage, the Baby Boom, and Social Change.* Chicago: University of Chicago Press, 2000.

West, Luther S. "The Practical Application of Eugenic Principles." In *Proceedings of the Third Race Betterment Conference,* 91–117. Battle Creek, Mich.: Race Betterment Foundation, 1928.

West, Trevor. *Horace Plunkett: Co-Operation and Politics, an Irish Biography.* Washington, D.C.: Catholic University of America Press, 1986.

White, Richard. *"It's Your Misfortune and None of My Own": A History of the American West.* Norman: University of Oklahoma Press, 1991.

White, W. Thomas. "Main Street on the Irrigation Frontier: Sub-Urban Community Building in the Yakima Valley, 1900–1910." *Pacific Northwest Quarterly* 77 (1986): 94–103.

White, William Allen. *The Autobiography of William Allen White.* New York: Macmillan, 1946.

Whitney, Leon. "Fitter Families Again." *Journal of Heredity* 17 (1926): 68–69.

Wiggam, A. E. "New Styles in Ancestors: Science Asks, 'Are You Fit to Be a Forefather?'" *World's Work* 55 (1927): 142–50.

Wilder, D. W. *The Annals of Kansas.* Vol. 1. New York: Arno Press, 1975.

Willard, Francis. "Tenth Annual Address, 1889." In *"Do Everything Reform": The Oratory of Francis E. Willard,* edited by Richard W. Leeman, 145–59. New York: Greenwood Press, 1992.

Wood, Edith E. *Recent Trends in American Housing.* New York: MacMillan, 1931.

——. "That 'One Third of a Nation.'" *Survey Graphic* 29 (1940): 83.

Wood, J. S., and M. Steinitz. "A World We Have Gained: House, Common, and Village in New England." *Journal of Historical Geography* 18 (1992): 105–20.

Wood, Joseph S. "'Build, Therefore, Your Own World': The New England Village as Settlement Ideal." *Annals of the Association of American Geographers* 81 (1991): 32–50.

Worster, Donald. *Rivers of Empire: Aridity and the Growth of the American West.* New York: Pantheon Books, 1985.

Wright, Gwendolyn. *Building the Dream: A Social History of Housing in America.* New York: Pantheon Books, 1981.

Yeo, Eileen J. *The Contest for Social Science: Relations and Representation of Gender and Class.* London: Rivers Oram Press, 1996.

Zelizer, Viviana. *Pricing the Priceless Child: The Changing Social Value of Children.* New York: Basic Books, 1985.

INDEX

Children's Bureau. *See* United States Children's Bureau

Chinese Exclusion Act (1882), 82–83

Church, country, 118–20

Cities, green, 165, 170

City beautiful movement, 61

Civilian Conservation Corps, 73

Clarke, Edward, 92

Colean, Miles, 157

Colonization, tropical, 38–40

Columbian Exposition, 61, 65

Commander, Lydia, 97

Commonwealth Fund, 146

Conservation, 2, 15, 110, 114–22, 123–24, 130, 168; race, 110, 113, 122, 168. *See also* Roosevelt, Theodore

Coolidge, Dane, 84

Coolidge, Mary Roberts Smith, 84, 85

Copland, Aaron, 165

Country life, 2, 15, 75, 110, 120–21, 124, 168

Country Life Commission, 114–17, 118, 121, 125, 127; and home demonstration and extension systems, 120

Coxey, Jacob, 57

Crumbine, Samuel, 139

Daughters of the American Revolution (DAR), 12, 110, 123–24

Davenport, Charles, 132, 140, 141, 142–43

Debs, Eugene V., 82

Democrats: Populist fusion with, 34, 37. *See also* Populism

Development, suburban, 3, 157

DeVilbiss, Lydia, 137, 139

Diggs, Annie, 19, 29

Downing, Andrew Jackson, 57

Duluth, Minn., 72

Durkheim, Emile, 79, 87, 89

Duty: patriotic, 42; women's, 91

Elections: 1890, 28; 1894, 37

Esper, Reverend, 95

Ethic: industrial family, 6, 74, 75–76; producer, 13, 30; producer family, 73–76

"Eugenic Family," 149

Eugenics, 2, 15, 22, 39, 87, 102, 123, 129–30, 132, 136, 140–46, 153, 155, 161; "positive" defined, 9, 152–56, 161, 169; "negative" defined, 9, 169; and family studies, 125–27; and fitter family contests, 151; "mainline," 154; "reform," 154; and insurance, 156–57; and housing, 156–60; and New Deal spending, 157; and housing loans, 160

Eugenics Record Office, 125, 132, 140, 142, 160

Euthenics, 154

Family: rural, 4, 120–22, 168; ideal of rural, 8, 30, 151; egalitarian political, 18; patriarchal farm, 18; producer, 43; ideal of "dysgenic," 156; ideal of four-child, 156; ideal of suburban, 161; "most typical American," 165

Maxwell, Ruth, 62

Maxwell's Talisman, 59, 64, 66. *See also* Maxwell, George

McGee, W. J., 116

Mead, Elwood, 72

Menninger, Karl, 146

Migration: country to city, 90, 105, 113, 117, 125, 151

Modernism, 10–12, 174 (n. 29)

Morris, William, 62–63

Mortality, infant, 132

Mortality rates, 98, 103, 123; of mothers, 101

Mother's Day, 98

Movable Schools, 120

Mt. Holyoke College, 94, 99

Mumford, Lewis, 165

Naismith, James, 146

National Child Labor Committee, 134

National Conference on City Planning and the Problems of Congestion (1909), 62

National Conservation Commission, 114–17, 122

National Conservation Congress, 110, 124

National Homecroft Bill (1909), 69–70

National Homemaker, 53, 56

National Housing Act (1934), 160

National Irrigation, 51, 53, 54

National Irrigation Association, 13, 52, 53, 56. *See also* Irrigation

Nazi Germany, 8, 169

Newell, F. H., 52

Newlands, Francis G., 50, 57

Newlands Act, 50, 56

New women, 42, 92

New York World, 41

New York World's Fair, 164

Nostalgia, 10, 56; and idealization of motherhood, 3; and modernism, 11–12, 132, 175 (n. 42); for farm family, 132; for rural family, 161

Olmsted, Frederick Law, 61

Osborn, Frederick, 141, 156

Overproduction, 29–30

Owen, Alfred K., 40

Page, Walter Hines, 116

Page Law, 84

Parks and playgrounds movement, 62

Parvin, Theophilus, 93

Peffer, William A., 25

Pelham, Mass., 125, 127, 128

People's Party, 176 (n. 2)

Perkins, Henry, 129–30

Pinchot, Gifford, 115–16, 118–19, 121, 122–24

Pisani, Donald, 50, 70, 183 (n. 15)

Plunkett, Horace, 115–16, 117, 120, 196 (n. 24)

Popenoe, Paul, 10, 102

Populism, 12, 13, 166, 178 (n. 36); Populist Party, 18–19, 28, 30, 40–43; and suffrage plank, 37; and producer family ethic, 75; and reform, 166

Powell, John Wesley, 57
Pratt family. *See* Huck family study
Prescott, Mass., 125, 127
Pressey, Edward Pearson, 65–66
Price, Overton, 116
Pronatalism, 54–55, 167, 169;
    French, 2; German, 2; American,
    2, 165–66, 171; programs pro-
    moting, 3; ideology of, 3–4;
    eugenic, 169–70; agrarian, 170
Public health, 123

Quabbin Reservoir, 129

Race, "American," 111, 113
Race Betterment Conference, Third,
    150
Race Betterment Foundation, 143,
    150, 153
Race degeneracy, 123–30
Race suicide, 7, 9, 14, 78–80, 82, 86,
    89, 91, 93, 94, 103, 107, 160, 167,
    168; as problem of urbanization,
    87; as antifeminist backlash, 92;
    and large family photographs,
    95; Roosevelt campaign against,
    113
Racism, scientific, 3, 169
Radburn, N.J., 159, 165
Reclamation, land, 2, 4, 47, 49–51,
    52–53, 54, 56–57, 60, 70, 73, 74,
    100, 108
Reclamation Act, 49, 50, 56, 73, 122
Reform, country life, 116–18
Regional Planning Association of
    America, 159, 165

Reproduction, 2, 8, 93, 102–3, 168;
    indirect promotion of, 3; regula-
    tion of, 7, 103, 107, 166
Resettlement Administration, 159
Richards, Ellen Swallow, 78
Roche, Paul, 165
Roosevelt, Theodore, 4, 7, 14, 50, 53–
    54, 70, 115, 118–22, 130, 168; and
    "gentleman's agreement" with
    Japan, 84; views on race suicide,
    91–92, 120; and women's educa-
    tion, 94–95; and photographs of
    large families, 95; and Teddy
    bears, 96–97, 193 (n. 64); and
    family size, 98; and race conserva-
    tion, 110; and "strenuous life,"
    111, 113; *The Winning of the West*,
    112; and "white man's burden,"
    113; and support of farmers, 113–
    14; and conservation, 115, 122–
    23; and race degeneracy, 123; and
    White House Conference on the
    Care of Dependent Children, 134
Ross, Edward A., 4, 14, 79, 81, 90,
    92, 167–69; *Social Control*, 79, 85,
    103, 168; advocacy of immigra-
    tion restriction, 82, 103; and Japa-
    nese immigration, 82–84, 108;
    resignation from Stanford, 85;
    views on race suicide, 86–87; and
    "American type," 89; and
    "patent-leather life," 97–98;
    ideas of family size, 98, 104, 108;
    and eugenics, 102; and social
    control, 103–5; and folk deple-
    tion, 105; and social selection,